The Way and the Water

Finally, this fine, precise and concise overview of the Baptist tradition is now available in English. Now the book can reach the readership it deserves, but can also widely be used for teaching and research. The author is an academic expert and knows how to present his expertise in a very accessible style, perfectly combining theology and history.

Herman Selderhuis
Theological University Apeldoorn

Bakker's Dutch point of orientation provides an especially helpful and fresh way of thinking about Baptists, Anabaptists and their tangled and complex history. The excurses on issues such as baptism, government, church discipline and the Sermon on the Mount, are creative and very helpful. The concluding reflection on the relevance of (Ana)baptist witness today is original and thoughtful. I believe this book offers important contributions to the discussion of Baptist and Anabaptist Christianity for the English-speaking world.

David P. Gushee
Distinguished University Professor of Christian Ethics, Mercer University; Chair in Christian Social Ethics, Vrije Universiteit Amsterdam

The origins of Baptist churches in Europe cannot be understood adequately without an awareness of the existing Anabaptist movement that commenced nearly a century earlier. Prof. Bakker has written a helpful study contextualizing the social and religious context in the Netherlands in which the churches associated with John Smyth and Thomas Helwys were formed. It provides greater detail than previous studies on the interactions between these early Baptists and contemporary Anabaptists. Its publication in English prior to the 500th anniversary celebrations of the formation of the Anabaptist movement in 1525 is timely as it can introduce the witness of these courageous Christians of a former generation to present day followers of Jesus and to others interested in their story in the twenty-first century. It is warmly commended.

Brian Talbot
Senior Research Fellow, International Baptist Theological Seminary, Amsterdam

The earliest Baptist church was formed at the opening of the seventeenth century by John Smyth in the Netherlands. *The Way and the Water* is a fresh perspective on Baptist origins from a Dutch viewpoint. The book provides valuable illumination not just on Smyth's English Puritanism but also on the Dutch context—socio-economic, political and especially theological—and on the Anabaptists who already practiced believer's baptism.

David Bebbington
Emeritus Professor of History, University of Stirling

That the Baptist movement emerged in seventeenth century England out of the context of radical Puritanism is historically uncontestable. The influence of Dutch Anabaptists on the English Separatist exiles who established the first Baptist church in the Netherlands is likewise indisputable. The matter in question is whether the Baptists who returned to England brought Anabaptist ideas with them that continued to shape the next generation of Baptists. Favouring a radically reformed influence on English Baptists, as Ernest Payne once observed, was the fact that "ideas had legs in the sixteenth and seventeenth centuries, as they have today." In this book, Henk Bakker exposes some of the legs that brought Dutch ideas to England, suggesting a vital Anabaptist influence on the Baptists. Anyone interested in this question will benefit greatly from this book.

Curtis W. Freeman
Research Professor of Theology and Director of the Baptist House of Studies, Duke University Divinity School

The study of Baptist origins has long been quite an industry. This volume quickly justifies its place within this field of study by the author, richly informed on seventeenth-century Dutch culture, placing the searches of English migrant believers within the context of debates already occurring within the reformed churches in Holland, and the challenge of emerging Anabaptist congregations there. It helpfully leads to a wider discussion of the emergence of Anabaptist congregations across Europe and how they came into conflict with both civic authorities and the leaders of the magisterial reformation.

John Briggs
Emeritus Professor of History, University of Keele

The Way and the Water

Exploring Baptistic Roots

Henk Bakker

Translated by Aize Smit

HERITAGE SEMINARY PRESS

Heritage Seminary Press, Cambridge, Ontario
An imprint of H&E Publishing, West Lorne, Ontario, Canada

heritageseminarypress.com

© 2025 Henk Bakker. All rights reserved. This book may not be reproduced, in whole or in part, without written permission from the publishers.

First published in Dutch as: *De Weg van het Wassende Water*
(Zoetermeer: Boekencentrum, 2008)

Cover & book design and editing by Janice Van Eck

Unless otherwise indicated, Scripture quotations are from the ESV® Bible (The Holy Bible, English Standard Version®), © 2001 by Crossway, a publishing ministry of Good News Publishers. Used by permission. All rights reserved.

The Way and the Water: Exploring Baptistic Roots
By Henk Bakker
Translated by Aize Smit

ISBN 978-1-77484-171-6 (paperback)
ISBN 978-1-77484-172-3 (eBook)

To my wife, Jenny,
who was the first to introduce me to a Baptist church
and to Baptist life in the late seventies.

The restoration of the church must certainly come through a new kind of monastic life, which only corresponds to the old one in maintaining—without compromise—the life in accordance with the Sermon on the Mount, in the imitation of Christ. I believe that today is the time to gather people for this purpose.[1]

Dietrich Bonhoeffer
January 14, 1935, in a letter to his brother Karl-Friedrich

---

[1] From the German: "Die Restauration der Kirche kommt gewiß aus einer Art neuen Mönchtums, das mit dem alten nur die Konpromißlosigkeit eines Lebens nach der Bergpredigt in der Nachfolge Christi gemeinsam ist. Ich glaube, es ist an der Zeit, hierfür die Menschan zu sammeln" in *Dietrich Bonhoeffer Werke*, ed. Hans Goedeking, Martin Heimbucher, Hans-Walter Schleicher, Vol. 13 (Band: London, 1933–35; Gütersloh: Chr. Kaiser Verlag, 1994) 273.

Contents

Foreword by Michael A.G. Azad Haykin — xi
Acknowledgements — xiii
Introduction — xv

1. **The first Baptist congregation** — 1
   1.1 The Golden Age — 2
   1.2 The national dispute — 5
   1.3 Joost van den Vondel — 13
   1.4 England — 18
   1.5 Summary — 48

2. **Anabaptists** — 53
   2.1 Münster — 54
   2.2 Peaceful Anabaptists persecuted — 60
   2.3 A brief history of Anabaptist origins — 65
   2.4 Excursus 1: Believer's baptism — 91
   2.5 Balthasar Hubmaier — 102
   2.6 Schleitheim — 124
   2.7 Excursus 2: The Sermon on the Mount — 138
   2.8 Anabaptists and the Ottoman Muslims — 145

3. **The character of the early Baptist church** — 149
   3.1 Menno Simons — 149
   3.2 Excursus 3: Church discipline — 154
   3.3 The confessions of Smyth and the Waterlanders — 161
   3.4 "Propositions and Conclusions" — 170
   3.5 The confession of Helwys — 176
   3.6 Anabaptism and openness — 182
   3.7 Excursus 4: The Overtons — 184
   3.8 Excursus 5: Margret Hottinger — 188
   3.9 General Baptists — 190
   3.10 Particular Baptists — 195

4 Church and government — 201
- 4.1 Luther and the state — 201
- 4.2 Calvin and the state — 204
- 4.3 Michael Servetus — 207
- 4.4 Calvin and the Anabaptists — 212
- 4.5 "Radical Christian materialism" — 214

5 Congregation, baptism and freedom — 221
- 5.1 Relevance of Baptist and Anabaptist history today — 222
- 5.2 The church's service to the government — 233

Appendices: The early church and non-violence — 241
- Appendix 1: Peace-loving and tolerant — 241
- Appendix 2: No military service — 247
- Appendix 3: Martin of Tours — 253
- Appendix 4: A Constantinian turn of events? — 255
- Appendix 5: Lactantius — 261
- Appendix 6: Chiliasm and the lack of royal ideology — 263

Select bibliography — 271

Foreword

In recent days, the significant contribution of the Anabaptists to the life and witness of the Church catholic has been overshadowed to some degree. The recovery and resurgence of Reformed thinking in the Anglophone world especially in the past fifty years or so—admittedly to the mind of this author, a good thing—has nonetheless had the unfortunate consequence of marginalizing the amazing and fortitudinous testimony of whose whom we call Anabaptists. They rightly saw that central to the problematic nature of medieval Christendom was not only matters of superstitious and idolatrous worship and a misunderstanding of the nature of salvation—which the magisterial Reformers also recognized—but also the issue of state-enforced orthodoxy, which had been bequeathed to the Western Church by the Constantinian revolution.

This new study of the Anabaptists and its links to the fledgling Baptist movement in the Netherlands, namely the congregation of John Smyth and Thomas Helwys, by Professor Bakker is therefore most welcome. It not only provides a masterful and deft overview of the world and thought of the evangelical Anabaptists but it also draws helpful connections between that world and the fountainhead of Anglophone Baptist witness. This English translation of Professor Bakker's work by Aize Smit comes at a timely juncture. 2025 will witness the celebration of the 500th anniversary of the first Anabaptist baptism, that of Jörg vom Haus Jacob, otherwise known as George Blaurock, by Conrad Grebel in Zürich. Moreover, among some Western evangelical circles there is afoot a wistful longing for a revival of Christendom. It is deeply disturbing to this historian that the long struggle of the Anabaptist and Baptist movements for religious freedom is being dismissed cavalierly as part and parcel of the political failure of western liberalism.

May this work, then, not only inform our minds about the importance of the witness of the Anabaptists and their influence on the English Baptists but also encourage to steadfast adherence to their theological insights in our chaotic age.

Michael A.G. Azad Haykin
Dundas, Ontario
July 2023

Acknowledgements

With much pleasure I started in 2023 revising and updating the first edition of this book, published in 2008 in the Dutch language, on the historic roots of Baptist churches. The initial intention was to provide a brief overview of the most important events in the history of Baptist churches, but over time it became clear that a broad introduction would be desirable. Now, the reader has here a book with a lot of information, which is certainly not redundant in light of the shortage of Dutch literature on the history of Baptist churches.

Special words of appreciation go to Aize Smit, who translated the book from Dutch into English, and who took time and effort to also meticulously check on historical details, figures and maps, and made suggestions for adding new information where necessary. As a born Friesian he knows Holland, its culture and history. I am also grateful for the warm interest of Dr. Michael Haykin in the content of the book, for his involvement in publishing this English version and for the foreword he has written.

A book like this cannot come about without the input of others. I have appreciated the availability of many existing resources, which are listed at the end of this book. I am also indebted to some critical reviewers, who have helped to shape this book with their comments on the draft. I have incorporated many suggestions and recommendations for improvement, although sometimes I have gone my own way. Naturally, I am responsible for the choices made and for the final product.

I am thankful for Michael Gorsira's (1960–2024) heartfelt involvement and for all his suggestions for improved clarity and additions. Also, I want to thank my colleagues at the Baptist Seminary for their encouragement and moral support. I was especially helped by our former director, Teun van der Leer, and our late professor of special appointment, Olof de Vries (1941–2014). Just as valuable were the comments and critique of Stefan Paas, Marjan Blok, Wim Verboom, and Piet Visser.

My greatest thanks are for my wife, Jenny. She was my first (and most wonderful) introduction to a Baptist church in Haarlem, some forty-seven years ago.

Henk Bakker
Liberation Day, May 5, 2008[1]
Spring 2024

---

[1] In the Netherlands, May 5 is a national holiday, remembering the liberation from Nazi-German occupation in 1945, where the Canadian army played a key role.

Introduction

World-wide, Baptist churches may well be the second largest group of churches. Nevertheless, many Baptists will not know how this came about, as they are not familiar with their own history.[1] Until this book by Henk Bakker, there was no book in the Dutch language describing this history. This is all the more surprising since the roots of the Baptist churches are to be found not only in England but also in the Netherlands. This book was written to fill this gap.

In the rapidly changing Europe of the seventeenth century, the young Baptist church spread fairly rapidly in the world of that

---

[1] One year after this book was originally published in Dutch, Olof de Vries published his own book, also in Dutch, opening with the rise of Baptist churches within the English historical context, then within the American context, and finally (the greater part) within the Dutch context, see Olof H. de Vries, *Gelovig gedoopt – 400 jaar baptisme, 150 jaar in Nederland* (Kampen: Kok, 2009).

time. From the outset, it has been characterized by a strong missionary focus. Other features of special attention include:

1. The Great Commission, given by Jesus.
2. The following or imitation of Christ.
3. Freedom of faith and conscience.
4. The independence of local congregations.
5. Faithfulness to the Word of God.
6. Exercising the communion of saints.

The decision to follow Christ was always expressed in the believer's baptism, whether or not by full immersion. This "sign" of Christ became, for Anabaptists and Baptists alike, their primary distinctive. In a way, this is unfortunate as it distracts from other distinguishing characteristics. Baptists were always careful to be visibly Christocentric (as followers of Christ in all areas of life), observing few formalities and treasuring a sense of community and mutual responsibility. We cannot understand the Baptists without their baptism (the name *Baptist* is derived from the Greek word *baptidzein*, which refers to *immersion* or *dipping*), nor if we fail to see them as a community of Christian believers, which is their "household of faith." When people enter a Baptist congregation, they can experience a "communal turn"—a real reversal from thinking in terms of "me" to thinking in terms of "us." Communal thinking is for Baptists a vital element of the Christian life.

In this book, we will focus on the roots of Baptist churches in Europe, not just the start of the typical Dutch Baptist church, whose roots are predominantly found in the nineteenth century (with Elias Feisser, 1805–1865).[2] We take the reader to the start of the Dutch Golden Age,[3] to the Amsterdam of poet and playwright Joost van den Vondel, as well as the England of John Smyth, Thomas Helwys and King James I. Next, we will focus on some

---

[2] On the rise of Dutch Baptist churches, see de Vries, *Gelovig gedoopt*, 77–330.
[3] The Dutch Golden Age was a period in the history of the Netherlands, roughly spanning the era from 1588 (the birth of the Dutch Republic) to 1672 (the "Disaster Year"), in which Dutch trade, science, art and the Dutch military were among the most acclaimed in the world (Wikipedia).

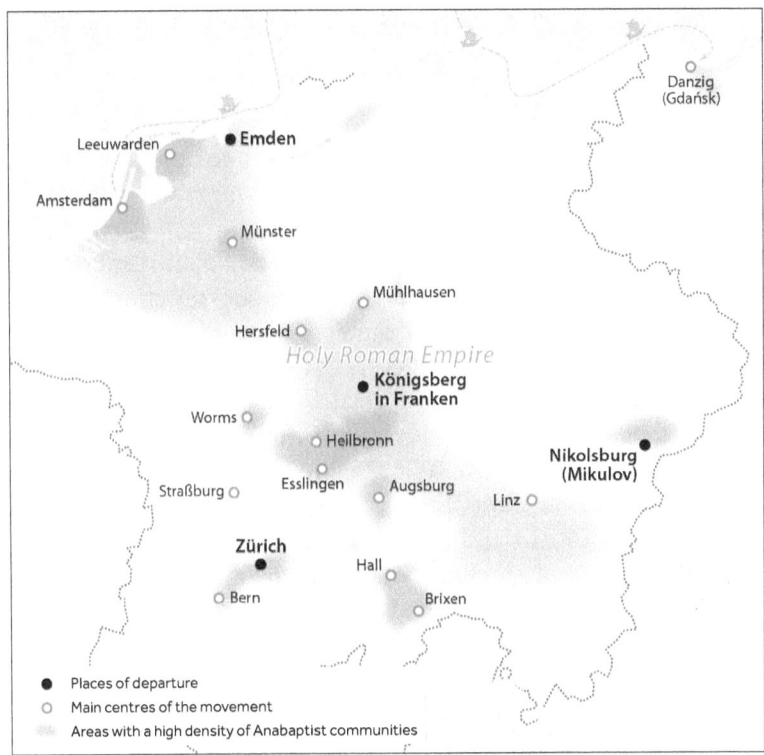

The spread of Anabaptists in the Holy Roman Empire
1525–1550

English Separatist churches in the Netherlands and the development of Anabaptism in Switzerland and Germany. The reader will appreciate the diversity of the Baptist movement, with occasionally even some violent anomalies. The tradition the Anabaptist stream, shaped in the Netherlands by Menno Simons, taught an ethical life of non-violence, and this is the tradition that to a certain extent shaped the "fathers of the Baptist church."

Therefore, we cannot speak of just one great history of the Baptist movement, but rather of various historical lines of development that at times (sometimes only briefly) make contact. We see the history of the Baptist movement more as a braided river, with various smaller streams and rivulets that sometimes meet and then separate again.

This book on the earliest roots of the Baptist churches is, therefore, not a smooth, chronological story. This was a deliberate choice.

We open, in the first chapter, with a historical exposé of the time and circumstances in which the English Separatists (Smyth and Helwys) lived; they can be called the founders of the Baptist movement. They landed in Amsterdam where they came in contact with the Anabaptists.

In the second chapter, we describe the Anabaptist movement with special attention to their pacifism—the rejection of "the sword" and violence. In this chapter we included two excurses (detailed explanations): on believers' baptism and on the Sermon on the Mount. These give the reader an opportunity to delve deeper, exegetically and theologically, into the themes of baptism and the ethics of the Sermon on the Mount.

Next, in chapter three, the reader is informed about the positions of John Calvin and Martin Luther on the relationship of church and state, after which (in chapter four) the confessions of the English Separatists and the Dutch Anabaptists are compared. What did the early Baptists adopt from the Puritans and Anabaptists in their views on faith, congregation, the church-government relationships and non-violence? We will try to provide answers to these questions. By comparing the confessions, it becomes clear that in many respects the early European Baptist congregations (in England later known as the *General Baptists*) showed quite a unique character. A few years later, another Baptist branch developed and these *Particular Baptists* were more Calvinistic in nature. This development is briefly explained in this book, without going into great detail.

Chapter four contains some excurses. Church discipline was a central doctrine for Baptists and Anabaptists. Therefore, in the third excursus, we will study Matthew 18. In the last two excurses, we consider two women of the faith: Mrs. Overton and Margret Hottinger. These women are good exemplars for the Anabaptist and early Baptist sentiments in the sixteenth and seventeenth centuries.

The final chapter concludes with what the Baptists confess in practical terms. Emphasis will be on the church's proper role as *peacemaker* in society.

The appendix demonstrates how the early church was generally in agreement on the Sermon on the Mount: Christians do

Introduction xix

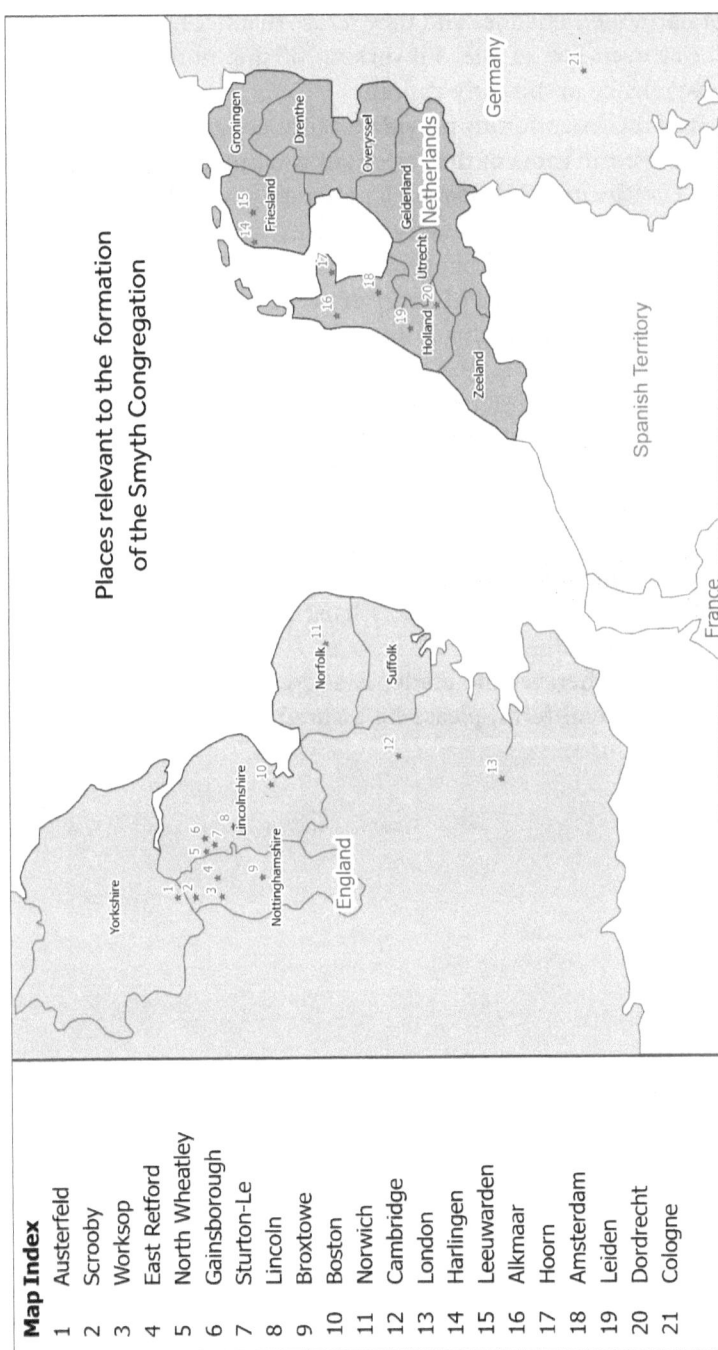

not harm their enemies and they refuse to kill. The reader receives a brief overview of the outworking of this notion of Christian non-violence in the early church.

It is the intention to provide a fairly comprehensive overview of the historic roots of the early Baptist church. The words in the title *The Way and the Water* are an attempt to put the reader on the right track. We follow the way of Christians, who had themselves *washed* in the *Water* of baptism, in the desire to follow the *Way* of Christ by the guidance of the river of life.

I hope and expect this historical and theological overview will fascinate the reader, providing moments of surprising insight. This book is not just for *specialists*. In writing this book, I especially aimed at the interested laity and freshmen. Meanwhile, we travel these roads of history in the hope to meet people of different persuasion, so that we may shake hands in the name of God. For Jesus said, "Blessed are the peacemakers."

Using timelines, maps and a complete bibliography should facilitate the use of this book. I trust the reader will profit from the use of these.

Finally, wherever the reader is addressed as *he*, or where *he* is used as general term, please be assured that it could just as well have read *she*.

Introduction   xxi

The Low Countries in the seventeenth century

1

The first Baptist congregation

To find the first Baptist church, we must not look in America, Eastern Europe or England. The first Baptist congregation was formed in continental Europe, in Amsterdam in 1609. At that time, the Netherlands was at war with Spain. The country was in religious terms already quite pluralistic, but Spain was trying to impose Spanish rule and the Roman Catholic faith. England was also at war with Spain at that time.

Flemish and English people who refused to bow to Roman Catholic or Anglican authority[1] fled to the Low Lands at the

---

[1] The Anglican Church may not have been Roman Catholic, but under the reigns of Elizabeth I (r. 1558–1603), James I (r. 1603–1625) and Charles I (r. 1625–1649), it forced the English people to conform to the reforms set by the crown. For many Puritan Christians, the English reforms did not go far enough. Thousands fled to the mainland during the Puritan century (1560–1660), especially to the northern Netherlands. See Henk Bakker, *Draads en tegendraads. Leren van de puriteinen* (CHE Reeks; Zoetermeer: Boekencentrum, 2006).

2 The Way and the Water: Exploring Baptistic Roots

Sea.[2] Many refugees found shelter there, including writers, painters, scientists and inventors. Nevertheless, they did not arrive in an altogether peaceful place, for in the first decade of the seventeenth century, it was the stage of a doctrinal battle.

In this chapter, we first want to pay attention to this conflict, since it shaped the political and spiritual landscape at the time and impacted the incoming refugees, especially English Christians, as they were mostly Calvinists.

We realize this means the reader is thrown into the deep end, as it were, but this explantion is required to understand the interests that were at stake in the formation of the Baptist faith. It also provides a brief impression of the social and cultural progress in those years, and we will briefly explore the poet Joost van den Vondel (1587–1679) to understand the church-political scene.

1.1 The Golden Age

The seventeenth century or, more accurately, the period from 1588 to 1672,[3] is rightfully called the Golden Age of Holland. It was a period of prosperity and great activity in the fields of architecture, visual arts, literature and science. It was also the period of the Republic of the Seven United Netherlands.

We may safely claim this was when important foundations were established for the Netherlands;[4] today's Dutch citizens still reap the rewards of these today. One of these foundations is the right of freedom of religion and conscience.

At the beginning of the seventeenth century, the land and people of The Netherlands at the North Sea were experiencing turbulent times. The coastline was then quite different from the situation today. Few dikes were built and few lakes were drained prior to the seventeenth century, which was to become the age of land reclamation. The area north of Amsterdam was a vast lake

---

[2] The northern provinces, united at the Union of Utrecht in 1579, declared their independence from Spain in the Act of Abjuration in 1581.

[3] The Republic of the Seven United Netherlands (Latin: *Belgica Foederata*) was the name of the republic proclaimed in 1588 during the Eighty Years' War in the territory of what is now roughly the Netherlands.

[4] Herman J. Selderhuis, ed., *Handboek Nederlandse Kerkgeschiedenis* (Kampen: Kok, 2006), 363.

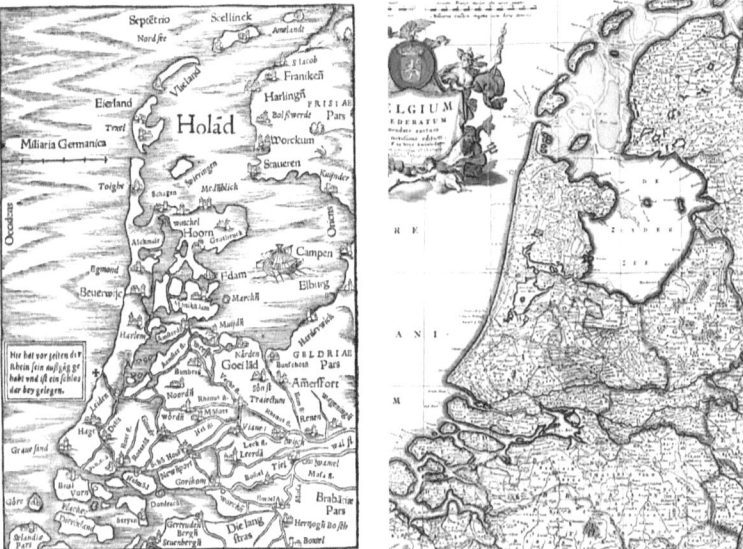

North-West Holland before and after the Golden Age

district with an archipelago of islands. The many lakes contained either fresh or salt water, as many were interconnected and open to the sea. In 1607, a number of entrepreneurs in Amsterdam took the initiative to drain the first of these lakes. A 38 km long dike was first built around (lake) De Beemster, surrounded by a canal. Jan Adriaenszoon Leeghwater (1575–1650) managed to drain the lake using forty-three windmills. In about five years, the Dutch had added a section of land.

Later in the seventeenth century, more lakes and wetlands were drained, so that the total territory of the Netherlands was significantly increased. In the northern provinces, land was also reclaimed along the coast.

During the Golden Age, the Dutch population also showed strong growth. Within seventy-five years (from 1600 to 1675), the Dutch population of about 1.5 million people grew by more than 30 per cent, so that by the year 1700 the population was over 2 million.

Economic growth was an important factor in this population growth. A great leap forward came with the establishment of the

VOC, the United East-India Company, commonly known as the Dutch East India Company (highly controversial nowadays because of its colonial aspirations). Trade with the East Indies was a golden opportunity for Holland, and it contributed to a prosperous period. Business flourished, which stimulated construction and architecture. Artistic expressions also flourished, as wealthy citizens in the cities could now afford beautiful monuments, dwellings, paintings and gardens. After the fall of Antwerp in 1585, cities like Rotterdam and Amsterdam became significant transit ports for European shipping. Holland, the coastal region along the North Sea coast, experienced growing prosperity and increasing urbanization.

In addition, the Battle at Nieuwpoort in 1600, a strategic victory for prince Maurice van Nassau, son of William of Orange and Anna van Saksen,[5] gave an important boost to Dutch morale and self-confidence. The Northern Netherlands managed to escape the stranglehold of foreign rulers in Spain and Rome.[6]

All kinds of scientific discoveries demonstrate how the Dutch spirit in the Golden Age was dominated by exploration, freedom and progress.[7] Christiaan Huygens (1629–1695), for instance, was one of the greatest scholars of the time. This brilliant son of the well-known Constantijn Huygens made great discoveries in mathematics, optics and astronomy. He was able to prove many ideas from scholars such as Copernicus and Galilei, such as the fact that the earth orbits around the sun.

In literature, too, we discern a certain spirit of openness and freedom. After the fall of Antwerp, the centre of arts and culture

---

[5] See A. Algra, H. Algra, *Dispereert niet. Twintig eeuwen historie van de Nederlanden*, deel 2 (Franeker: T. Wever, 1987), 137–140. William of Orange had been assassinated on July 10, 1584.

[6] After his death, a search was made for a substitute monarch (French king, English queen), but none was found. Eventually, William of Orange's country lawyer and advisor Johan van Oldenbarnevelt arranged for Prince Maurice, who was already *stadholder* of Holland and Zeeland, to also be recognized as *stadholder* of Overijssel, Utrecht and Gelderland. Maurice was a successful general and stabilized the Republic as an independent state.

[7] Holland's influence on cultural developments in England was also significant during the seventeenth century, see Lisa Jardine, *Going Dutch: How England Plundered Holland's Glory* (2009), translated: *Gedeelde weelde. Hoe de zeventiende-eeuwse cultuur van de Lage Landen Engeland veroverde en veranderde* (Amsterdam: De Arbeiderspers, 2008), 214.

shifted from the Southern to the Northern Netherlands. Artists and scientists who had left the country, ordinary people and notables, were often only too happy to settle in the cultural capital of Holland, the colourful city of Amsterdam. The master-poet Joost van den Vondel was one of those, who came from the Southern Netherlands. His parents were Anabaptists, who for religious reasons had left the city of Antwerp. So, from 1597 on, the van den Vondel family lived in Amsterdam. For most of his youth Joost lived there, and he developed into one of the most impressive and prolific authors of his time. His *oeuvre* demonstrates how he was very much involved with the political and religious discussions of his time. Especially in his famous satires, he spared neither the political nor the ecclesiastical establishment, especially if, in his opinion, some injustice had been done.

1.2 The national dispute

Van den Vondel was annoyed with the religious disputes among the Protestants in the first decade of the seventeenth century, and he closely followed the fiery discussions on predestination. This debate focused on the persons of Jacobus Arminius (1560–1609) and Franciscus Gomarus (1563–1641).[8] In 1603, Arminius became professor in the faculty of theology at the University of Leiden. Educated in Reformed circles, he gradually distanced himself from the traditional doctrine of double predestination.[9] In 1604, during a debate on this doctrine where a student defended some theses, Arminius clarified that only believers had been predestined (by God, to faith and life everlasting). According to the professor, God had not predestined anyone to unbelief

---

[8] For the dispute between Arminius and Gomarus and the origins of the Canons of Dort, see especially W. Verboom, *De belijdenis van een gebroken kerk. De Dordtse Leerregels—voorgeschiedenis en theologie* (Zoetermeer: Boekencentrum, 2005), and Richard A. Muller, *God, Creation, and Providence in the Thought of Jacob Arminius: Sources and Direction of Scholastic Protestantism in the Era of Early Orthodoxy* (Grand Rapids: Baker, 1990).

[9] See Willem Jan Otten, *Waarom komt u ons hinderen* (Amsterdam: Van Oorschot, 2006) 91–97. The word *predestination* literally means "prior determination of one's destiny." The doctrine of "double predestination" holds that before the creation of the world, God decided to choose a certain number of people for salvation and to grant faith for it and to reject the rest of humanity and to determine judgement for them.

and eternal perdition. The eternal God had foreseen which sinners would accept Christ, and therefore those would have been the ones God then "predestined."[10]

This was the basis for God's election, so that humans had total personal freedom to choose (their destiny). With this conviction, he placed himself in opposition to his colleague Gomarus. Soon a conflict ensued that proved to be more than merely a discussion among professors, as it even engaged the mind of the layman in the street.

The trustees of the university urged that the dispute be settled by calling a national synod. The government first responded positively, but later they decided against it. They feared major discord if this would lead to a revision of the creeds (the Belgic Confession and the Heidelberg Catechism), and an official revision of the confession would prove to be polarizing and stir up conflicts in the church.

Arminius then addressed the provincial government of Holland, where he was allowed to explain his views; Gomarus was also invited to attend. When this failed to resolve the issue, Arminius decided to give a statement (*de Verclaringhe*), in which he rejected three Reformed variants on the doctrine of predestination.[11]

According to the "heaviest" Reformed view, *supralapsarianism*, God elected people to salvation and perdition even before he had decided to create human beings.[12] Somewhat less heavy-sounding was the *infralapsarian* view that God elected people to salvation after he had decided to create human beings and to let them fall into sin.[13] Arminius bypassed these views and approached the

---

[10] For a biography on Arminius, see Carl Bangs, *Arminius: A Study in the Dutch Reformation* (Grand Rapids: Asbury Press, 1985).

[11] Verboom, *De belijdenis van een gebroken kerk*, 39–40. Also see Eef Dekker, *Rijker dan Midas. Vrijheid, genade en predestinatie in de theologie van Jacobus Arminius (1559–1609)* (Zoetermeer: Boekencentrum, 1993), 232–250.

[12] See: G.J. Hoenderdaal, *Verklaring van Jacobus Arminius, afgelegd in de Vergadering van de Staten van Holland op 30 oktober 1608* (Lochem: De Tijdstroom, 1960). See also W. Stephen Gunter, *Arminius and His Declaration of Sentiments: An Annotated Translation with Introduction and Theological Commentary* (Waco: Baylor University Press, 2012). This so-called "falling above" or "before the Fall" theory claims that God decided to choose people for salvation and damnation even before he decided to make them and make them fall into sin. The supralapsarians were in the minority by far.

[13] Infralapsarianism claims God decided to elect people to salvation and damnation after he decided to make them and make them fall into sin ("under or after the Fall").

Jacobus Arminius (1560–1609)

Franciscus Gomarus (1563–1641)

doctrine of election from a totally different perspective. His key question to Gomarus remained: *How could God's grace be forced upon humans without affecting their freedom?*[14]

If God granted faith, did he not at least require the consent of humans themselves? In his view, Arminius distinguished between *sufficient grace* (*gratia sufficens*) and *effective grace* (*gracia efficax*).[15] It was through *effective grace* that a person would put their faith in Christ, accept the gospel and be saved. This was, so to speak, saving and redeeming grace, which is distinguished from the grace that preceded it, namely *sufficient grace*. It was through this *sufficient grace* that a person received the capacity that enabled them to believe. Human approval was required to turn this form of grace into saving, *effective* grace.

Van den Vondel went along with this to the extent that, according to him, the plan of the incarnation (of humanity and Christ) preceded the plan of redemption, see his *Lucifer*.
14 Selderhuis, *Handboek*, 418.
15 See Eef Dekker, *Rijker dan Midas*, 158.

In other words, Arminius believed a person by themself was incapable of faith. Every human is captive to sin; God's liberating, *sufficient grace* had to provide the freedom to start believing. Yet, this freedom implied the possibility to reject salvation. Freedom obtained by God's *sufficient grace* implied real freedom, so God could not force a person to a certain decision.

For Arminius, this concept of grace meant it would not be automatically effective and saving. Even though someone was enabled to respond to God's *sufficient grace* in faith, there was no certainty this would be the case.[16] Anybody could choose to remain indifferent to God's *sufficient grace* and reject it. While God, in his love and by his Spirit, was trying to bend the human will, he had at least enough freedom to turn down Christ's invitation.

Arminius posited that God had first decided in eternity to choose Christ as Saviour, and then to save all those he could foresee would come to faith (by their own free choice). God's election, for Arminius, was based on his foreknowledge.[17] Again, unbelievers would go to perdition, not because of God's decree but because of their chosen unbelief.

Unfortunately, Arminius would not live to see the further course of the debate and the prelude to the Synod of Dordt. Less than a year after his *Verclaringhe*, he died on October 19, 1609. Subsequently, Arminius' supporters presented a Remonstrance (discourse of protest) to the provincial legislatures of Holland and West Friesland in which they defended their views under five headings. They suggested that, if necessary, a government ought to have the authority to interfere in church affairs and discussions.

This is the content of their five points:

---

[16] Arminus' thoughts in this regard resemble what John Wesley would call "prevenient grace" 130 years later. *Prevenient grace* is also called *enabling grace, empowering grace* or *responsible grace*. Man by nature has no free will according to Wesley, but is enabled by God's prior grace to make choices. He can therefore also refuse salvation. On this topic, see: M.B. Wynkoop, *A Theology of Love: The Dynamic of Wesleyanism* (Kansas City: Beacon Hill Press, 1972), 98–99, Randy L. Maddox, *Responsible Grace: John Wesley's Practical Theology* (Nashville: Kingswood Books, 1994), 159–161. Yet, by his own admission, Wesley was only "a hair's breadth from Calvinism" removed. See H.R. Dunning, *Reflecting the Divine Image: Christian Ethics in Wesleyan Perspective* (Downers Grove: IVP, 1998) 57, and S. Kisker, "John Wesley's Puritan and Pietist Heritage Reexamined," *Wesleyan Theological Journal* 34 (1999): 278.

[17] For an overview of the differences between Arminius and Gomarus, see Verboom, *De belijdenis van een gebroken kerk*, 61–62.

1. Prior to the creation of the world, God had decided to save in Christ all who—through the grace of the Holy Spirit—would believe in God's Son, Jesus, and would persevere in this faith. Also, God decided to condemn all those who would remain unrepentant and unbelieving.
2. The Saviour, Jesus Christ, died for each human being, working forgiveness and reconciliation for all people, even though only believers will enjoy these blessings. People are lost by their own unbelief.
3. Nobody has faith in Christ or can acquire faith by his own power or will. The spiritual rebirth is required to enable people to comprehend faith.
4. Without the grace of God, nobody is capable of doing any saving good. People require the prevenient, cooperating grace of God to will and work that which is good. All human good deeds are to be ascribed to the grace of God, but this grace can be resisted.
5. Anyone who shares in God's grace and Holy Spirit can resist the Evil One, the sinful world and their own sinful lusts to be victorious in the power of God.

According to the Remonstrants, further research was required to see whether those who leave the path of grace and fall back into sin and worldliness could actually lose their salvation.[18]

It should be clear that the Counter-Remonstrants argued for the opposite with respect to these five points.

1. All humans are—by the Fall—corrupted in all facets of their nature.
2. God decided to elect part of all humanity unto salvation, leaving the others in their state of condemnation. God set no conditions for those whom he elected to live, for how could he require this if they were spiritually dead? Whoever has been elected will be found and shall certainly come to faith in Christ.

---

[18] For an overview of the differences between Arminius and Gomarus see Verboom, *De belijdenis van een gebroken kerk*, 111–116.

3. Although Christ died for all humanity, yet the resulting salvation will only be applied to those whom God has so elected.
4. God's saving grace for the elect is irresistible. Those, who are not elected will not receive this irresistible grace. Even if they would seek to believe, they would be unable to do so.
5. (True) believers cannot fall from (this) grace, no matter how grave their sins would be, for this faith cannot be extinguished.[19]

Even after 400 years, this debate in the Christian faith has not waned. So we cannot say Arminius and Gomarus were merely splitting hairs, involved with useless, irrelevant theological arguments. Rather, we are time and again confronted with the question of how God's sovereignty relates to human freedom. A great emphasis on the one truth always seems to diminish the other. If humans get the real freedom of choice, it appears that God's supremacy and sovereignty are being challenged. When God's total sovereignty and freedom is invoked, little freedom seems to be left for humankind. In Arminius' reasoning, the mutuality of our engagement with God receives more emphasis.[20]

One of the advocates of the Remonstrance was Johan van Oldenbarnevelt (1517–1619), chancellor to Maurice, Prince of Orange. He was not truly convinced by their arguments, but he sought to establish mutual understanding and appreciation for both ecclesiastical parties.

Personally, he was also trying to achieve greater influence in the national government. He argued that the Remonstrants ought to be heard, especially since the prince became increasingly supportive of the Counter-Remonstrants, and it was clear the prince had significant power. The disagreement between Maurice and van Oldenbarnevelt developed into an irreconcilable rift.

A year earlier (in April 1609), van Oldenbarnevelt had secretly managed to establish a truce with Spain, but Maurice and his

---

[19] See Verboom, *De belijdenis van een gebroken kerk*, 137–139. I have not mentioned all the Counter Remonstrant points and arguments, just the main ones. See the Canons of Dort for a complete overview.

[20] See C. Graafland, *Van Calvijn tot Comrie. Oorsprong en ontwikkeling van de leer van het verbond in het Gereformeerd Protestantisme*, deel 5 & 6 (Zoetermeer: Boekencentrum, 1996), 186–210.

The Synod of Dordt (Dordrecht)

followers viewed this milestone as a capitulation to the much-hated Spain and Rome. So, when the same advisor also tried to compromise in a doctrinal battle, it resulted in a serious power struggle. In the end, van Oldenbarnevelt was arrested and condemned as traitor.[21] His execution on May 13, 1619, can justifiably be viewed as a black page in the turbulent national history, and it underscores the severity and complexity of the political conflict.

It would, however, be wrong to view van Oldenbarnevelt as a dramatic hero and martyr for freedom in faith and political opinion. His efforts for religious freedom and tolerance received insufficient public support and approval; he was aware of that. He played with fire and when he got burned, this did not happen by accident.[22] When he was publicly executed by beheading in

---

21 Officially, the word *treason* is not mentioned in the verdict. He was charged with "overthrowing the existing order."
22 Andrew Pettegree, "Preachers versus City Administrators: The Politics of Tolerance in the Free Netherlands," in *Vrijheid in verdeeldheid. Geschiedenis en actualiteit van religieuze tolerantie* (*Freedom in Division: History and Actuality of Religious Tolerance*), ed. Stephan van Erp (Nijmegen: Valkhof Pers, 2008), 81.

Johan van Oldenbarnevelt (1517–1619) was publicly beheaded on May 13, 1619, in The Hague

front of the *Ridderzaal* in The Hague (the thirteenth-century Hall of the Knights, which is still the ceremonial centre of the Dutch government), the Synod of Dordt had almost concluded.[23]

The death of this *éminence grise* still casts a certain blemish on the decisions that were made there. Although the synod was an international affair, and the execution of van Oldenbarnevelt was a national event, we cannot see the political turmoil in the Northern Netherlands apart from this ecclesiastical battle. At the time, church and world were not experienced as separate spheres of life.

In the synodical discussions, it was the Counter-Remonstrants (Calvinists), who stood out as the moral "winners." The task had been to test the new theological ideas of Arminius and his followers against the Reformed confessional Scriptures. In hindsight, we may wonder if there had been enough dialogue, prior to the meetings, for progress at the synod was arduous. Among those present were 23 foreign theologians (from England, Scotland, Heidelberg, Hessen, Geneva, Bremen and others), 56 delegates

---

[23] The synod lasted from November 13, 1618, to May 6, 1619. On May 6, the established declaration of the synod was proclaimed in the Great Church of Dordt. One week later, van Oldenbarnevelt was beheaded.

(pastors and elders) from Dutch churches and 18 high commissioners from the political world.

Thirteen Remonstrants were summoned. One of them was Professor Episcopius, who protested the summons. The Remonstrants did not show up until more than three weeks after the opening procedures. From the start of the meetings they were treated as the accused,[24] giving the impression of ecclesiastic court proceedings, rather than communal theological deliberations. Perhaps it was both of these. Tensions ran so high that Johannes Bogerman (1576–1637), president of the synod—two months into the deliberations—expelled the Remonstrants, keeping their delegation indefinitely on standby in the city.[25]

1.3 Joost van den Vondel

We can well imagine that someone like Joost van den Vondel, who experienced the turmoil in Amsterdam church circles closely, loved to use his pen to criticize the so-called victors of the "spiritual war." The theologizing on predestination certainly did not bypass the minds of the people. In the circumstances of daily life, they understood all too well some of the implications. For van den Vondel, for instance, it implied—among other things—that the Lord would send little children (sometimes even before birth) to hell, unless of course he had elected them to go to heaven. The Synod of Dordrecht had claimed that children of believers, unless they had given evidence of rejecting the faith, should be considered as elect.[26]

The seventeenth century was a time of high infant mortality and death was much more part of daily life than for us today. In the midst of the Golden Age, the mortality rate was actually higher than the national birthrate. In a village like Broek in Waterland,

---

[24] See J.N. Bakhuizen van den Brink, *Handboek der kerkgeschiedenis*, part 3 (Leeuwarden: De Tille, 1980), 278.
[25] Bogerman used the words, "We will send you away, go away, go away!" (*dimittimini, ite, ite!*). See Pettegree, "Preachers versus City Administrators," 81.
[26] "Since we are to judge of the will of God from his Word, which testifies that the children of believers are holy, not by nature, but in virtue of the covenant of grace, in which they, together with the parents, are comprehended, godly parents have no reason to doubt of the election and salvation of their children, whom it pleaseth God to call out of this life in their infancy." *Canons of Dordt* I.17. https://www.prca.org.

Joost van den Vondel
(1587–1679)

for instance, 374 of 1,000 infants died in their first year.[27] The issue of predestination, therefore, touched upon essential pastoral questions, such as: Where is my deceased child now? With God in heaven or in hell?

Van den Vondel was also faced with this question. In 1632, he lost a son in infancy: *Constantijntje* (Li'l Constantine). Van den Vondel wrote a gripping poem about this. Remarkably, he portrays the infant boy as a little angel with God in heaven. He does not wonder about his blessed destiny; he supposes this to be self-evident. The familiar opening phrases of the poem are:

> Little Constantine, blessed child of mine
> Little Cherubim, in the sky
> beholds the vanities below
> mockingly with dreamy eye.
> Mom, he says, why shouldst thou cry?
> Why doest thou weep on my remains?
> It's high up, here, that I now flutter,
> Little angel in the sky.

When, a year later, also his eight-year-old daughter dies, van den Vondel expresses his bitter pain:

> The cruel death, she hates our joy,
> The older folk, she does avoid,
> And yet, her deadly spear she hurls

---

[27] Selderhuis, *Handboek*, 419.

At innocent and playful girls,
And then she mocks when in the parting,
Sad mothers—she beholds—are smarting,
She spotted one, who darting, dancing free,
The joy of the neighborhood was she,
Quickly sprang into the skipping rope,
Singing songs of joy and hope, ...
And then, alas, the sobbing group,
With tears around the casket stood,
To cry on their beloved playmate,
Wishing now to share her fate,
And to be with her up there,
Dead, like their beloved Sarah.

Van den Vondel obviously loved his daughter; in his poetry he was able to beautifully sketch her at play outside with her friends. Therefore, we will not be surprised that the master of satirical poetry lunges with sarcasm at the—in his eyes, godless—decree of predestination. A few verses of his *Decretum horribile* (horrible decree) will serve to demonstrate his provocative, challenging expression:

God tears the innocence from mother's breast away,
plunging her into the lake of fire to dismay![28]...
Where am I now? Under the great theologians' glow?
Or under Lucifer, amidst dark vapors, the inferno?...
Who sprinkles flesh with blood, what use for me is God's good deal,
if my lass serves now as Devil's ghastly meal?...
That's right, Gomaar, just burn the foul remains,
it stinks, just like the theology your mouth ordains!...
that smears God's face with chimney soot,
as on the Moorman, as origin of all that's good.

---

[28] The Canons of Dort, in their conclusion, strongly reject this idea: "...that many children of the faithful are torn, guiltless, from their mothers' breasts, and tyrannically plunged into hell; so that, neither baptism, nor the prayers of the Church at their baptism, can at all profit by them; and many other things of the same kind, which the Reformed Churches not only do not acknowledge, but even detest with their whole soul." Note that van den Vondel, in his first lines, actually uses this very language.

Gomarus gets quite a whipping from van den Vondel. For Arminius, he has great sympathy:

> This is the face of Armin', who in writing and in speaking,
> Gave Calvin's reprobation such a beating,
> That Lucifer still shudders at the fierceness of his lectures,
> While the abyss slaves and sweats to fix the fractures.
> He said: Be still, you midwife, you may depart in peace,
> For God will not cast an infant into the fiery abyss.

By 1625, van den Vondel even studied Greek, so he could write his famous *Palamedes*. The occasion for this was the controversy between van Oldenbarnevelt and Prince Maurice, and naturally the execution of the former. In Palamedes, the story is told of the Greek *Palamédes*, who—at the city wall of Troy—is unjustly accused of treason and sentenced to death. Behind the person of Agamemnon, the reader clearly recognizes Prince Maurice who, while he realizes the accusations are false, still decides to enforce the execution.

After the publication of Palamedes, van den Vondel had to go into hiding for a while. There were groups in The Hague who demanded he be judged in that city, but the nobility and rulers of Amsterdam refused to cooperate with this. In the end, van den Vondel got away with paying a hefty fine of 300 guilders. This was far too low a penalty in the eyes of the prince's supporters, especially since van den Vondel's publisher paid the fine for the writer.

In this tragedy, van den Vondel had publicly presented himself for the first time as an obstinate warrior for justice, freedom and tolerance.[29] He now refused to restrain himself, and took the risk of public participation in the debate. His weapons were satire, tragedy and drama. One could feel the tension during the performances of his political works. The audience could almost taste the injustice that was being challenged. Van den Vondel defended the freedom of religion, and he was averse to the suppression of

---

[29] See Frans-Willem Korsten, "De bereidheid tot risico. Joost van den Vondel over soevereiniteit en tolerantie," *Vrijheid in verdeeldheid* (*Freedom in Division*), ed. van Erp, 84–85, 94, and H.W.E. Moller, *Joost van den Vondel. Toneelspelen, part 1* (Amsterdam: Elsevier, 1939), 24–25.

doctrinal positions. Although he was no Remonstrant himself, he was troubled by the way the Counter-Remonstrants reasoned and seem to want to meddle with the consciences of others.

In a moving poem, he sings about the cane on which van Oldenbarnevelt leaned as he climbed the scaffold for his execution. This cane supported a *father* of Holland, who fought for the freedom of faith and conscience. This cane, therefore, represented solidarity with this national freedom, which was so necessary for the Netherlands.

The familiar opening phrases are:

May my wish protect you, not degraded,
Oh, stick and staff that not a blighter
but Holland's patriarch and freedom fighter
on cruel scaffold well has aided.

Van den Vondel lashed out particularly hard at the twenty-four judges, members of an improvised Court of Holland who sentenced Johan van Oldenbarnevelt. According to the poet, there could never be any comfort or easing of their consciences, but only eternal agony for the murder they had committed.

Be content, bring in your ministers of the Word
   from West and East:
Go, and seek them from the saints of Dort
Blessing and comfort, it's no use, the Lord comes knocking,
   with his Word
and none can stop the spilling of the blood.

Joost van den Vondel is a time-honoured writer who incorporated the questions and issues of his time into his work. In 1640, he left the Anabaptists and joined the Roman Catholic church, not for the purpose of provocation but because he felt more at home there and appreciated their liturgy and sense of mystery.[30]

---

[30] See Korsten, "De bereidheid tot risico," 84. I did not introduce van den Vondel because I agree with him in everything in a theological sense. Joost van den Vondel's work is strongly timebound and therefore lends itself perfectly to a brief and powerful ecclesiastical and political exploration of his time. The reader perceives immediately where the issues are and how fierce things were.

It is mysterious how this could override, for him, the fact that the Roman Catholic church was far from tolerant, as it still fought a bloody battle for domination throughout Europe.

Van den Vondel is just one seventeenth century example whose life and work demonstrate the turbulence of those times and the debates that occupied the population. At the same time, the Netherlands stood on the brink of civil war. The ecclesiastical battle was also a social struggle.[31] Individual cities could hire mercenaries to maintain the peace in church and state, and naturally this led to serious conflicts. In those times, a religious war could easily culminate in a civil war.

It was during these turbulent times that the world's first Baptist congregation was formed in the Northern Netherlands. And this happened in Amsterdam, the city of van den Vondel. To understand its origins, we return to the year 1604—the year of Arminius' dispute at the University of Leiden.

1.4 England

The early history of Baptist churches is uniquely intertwined with the seventeenth-century history of the Northern Netherlands as well as this history of England. Therefore, we want to briefly focus our attention on the changes on the English throne in the early seventeenth century and how the Puritans reacted to it.

James I

Just a few weeks before Arminius "threw the bat into the hen house," the illustrious Hampton Court Conference was held, in which the newly appointed king played a questionable role.[32] There, too, it was about controversial ecclesiastical matters, and tempers were running high. When James I (r. 1603–1625) ascended the English throne in 1603, Puritans had high hopes for the new king, but soon these hopes were painfully dashed. About a thousand Puritans had formulated and signed a petition, asking the king for radical reforms in the church of England.

---

[31] Selderhuis, *Handboek*, 425.
[32] The Hampton Court Conference took place on Saturday, January 14, Monday, January 16 and Wednesday, January 18, 1604, at Hampton Court Palace, then a well-known royal palace in the London Borough of Richmond upon Thames.

Ever since the reign of Henry VIII (r. 1509–1547), the Puritan reformers had fought for far-reaching changes in the national church. Many Puritans had been directly or indirectly influenced by the ideas of Martin Luther (1483–1546) and soon thereafter by John Calvin (1509–1564) and Martin Bucer (1491–1551). In 1549, Bucer fled to England, where he held a post as professor in Cambridge and solidified Puritan beliefs.

The core idea of the Reformed mindset is the absolute sovereignty of God. This implies total freedom, and can certainly be seen as a key characteristic of Protestantism. Luther saw the Roman Catholic church as having lapsed into an institution that had taken over the work of God. The straw that broke the camel's back was the trade in indulgences that Luther had to deal with in his pastoral work in Wittenberg and the surrounding area. A brisk trade had developed in church-issued certificates that could be purchased to guarantee people forgiveness of sins and provide a reduced time of punishment in purgatory. The Dominican preacher Johan Tetzel was successful in the Wittenberg area in the sale of indulgences, which essentially were "proofs of merit." The profits were used to pay off the debts of the archbishop of Mainz and to finance the construction of St. Peter's in Rome. These abuses were the reason Luther nailed his *Ninety-Five Theses* to the door of the chapel at Wittenberg on October 31, 1517. He wanted to bring about a public dispute with those who defended the trade in indulgences.[33]

God's freedom

Martin Luther believed God did not allow himself to be confined by church forms, traditions or rituals. Human beings could not capture God,[34] for ultimately God did not need anyone, not even the church to prove his grace for the world. As we have said, Luther was not the only one to stress this. God's sovereignty was, in fact, a thoroughly Reformed notion.

Even many humanists were convinced that the Roman Catholic cultural patterns were neither absolute nor universally valid.

---

[33] It is possible that Luther first sent his theses to his church superiors and only later made them public.
[34] See Mark 14:58, Acts 7:48; 17:24, Ephesians 2:11; Hebrews 9:11, 24. "The Most High does not dwell in houses made by hands" (Gr. *cheiropoiètos*).

This critique is, for instance, found in the free spirit of the humanist Desiderius Erasmus (*c*.1466–1536).[35]

During the later Middle Ages, no one was as cynical in his writings concerning the spiritual establishment as Erasmus. In 1508, he wrote his *In Praise of Folly*,[36] in which the personified foolishness brags about her essential role in all areas of life. So, she praises her own virtue, for how could the world exist without foolishness? Everyone, young and old, men and women, scientists and authors, philosophers and theologians, bishops and popes, all love to make use of her services. Folly seems to be a real blessing for humanity. According to Erasmus, Folly's pride showed up in all kinds of superstition and ecclesiastical abuses, such as the trade in indulgences and the levying of tithes. Humanity just loves to be deceived. With disregard for the common people, popes were grabbing power, wealth, horses, servants and all kinds of pleasures. Erasmus wondered how much the popes would stand to lose in benefits and luxuries if "Wisdom would make its appearance." Erasmus also noted that superstitious folk "allowed themselves to be wonderfully lulled to sleep with misleading letters of indulgence."[37] Erasmus had considerable influence on the Reformers, as well as the spirit of Anabaptism.

In Luther's view, the indulgence trade was an exponent of a pagan mentality that sought to make God dependent on human whims. Of course, a rich man could not just buy off his guilt with God; money or possessions could never accomplish that which could only happen through heartfelt sorrow and repentance. The church was not an institution that could market and sell the grace of God. For Luther, only the Holy Scriptures were the lawful authority to return the church to her proper place. The church had tried to gag its God, but God's Word cannot be muzzled. Luther let the "Living Word of God" (*viva vox Christi*) be heard again and made a thorough study of the Scriptures. Christ, in his Word is not always our companion; regularly his Word—according to Luther—functions as the church's adversary (*adversarius*

---

[35] See Anton Constandse, *Geschiedenis van het humanisme in Nederland* (*History of Humanism in the Netherlands*) (The Hague: Kruseman, 1980), 18–41.

[36] Lat. *Moriae encomium, id est laus Stultitiae*. Erasmus, *Roterodami declamatio* (1511).

[37] Erasmus, *Lof der Zotheid* (Prisma 1359; Utrecht: Het Spectrum, 1977), 127, 72.

Desiderius Erasmus (c.1466–1536)

Martin Luther (1483–1546)

noster).[38] And this is exactly the reason why the church has a tendency to turn away from the Word. Priests and prelates cast themselves as guardians of Scripture with the intention of manipulating its teachings so they may control the voice of God. For Luther, the Scriptures had a far greater authority than the church, and it was certainly not the other way around.

Naturally, the church could not accept such a challenge from a monk, and resistance was inevitable. The church authorities struck back with force, and in January 1521, Luther was banned from the church he had hoped to serve.

---

[38] D. *Martin Luther's Werke*, 3. Band, *Dictata super Psalterium* (Weimar: Herman Böhlaus Nachfolger, 1966), 574 (on Psalm 78:18): "*Quicquid audimus, quod nobis placet, suspectum esse debet. Et econtra: Quicquid audimus, quod nos offendit atque durum est, suscipiendum est. Quia sic Euangelium habet nomen et verbum dei, quod sit adversarius noster.*" See D. *Martin Luther's Werke*, 56. Band, *Epistula ad Romanos* (Weimar: Herman Böhlaus Nachfolger, 1970), 446–447 (on the first verses of Rom 12): "*Ita enim verbum Dei, quoties venit, venit in spetie contraria menti nostrae, que sibi vera sapere videtur; ideo verbum contrarium sibi mendacium Iudicat adeo, ut Christus Verbum suum appellaverit adversarium nostrum.*"

For Luther, the sovereign freedom of God also implied and qualified the freedom of the Christian.[39] For a Christian who believed in Christ and had put his trust in the redemptive work Christ had accomplished, faith was sufficient—he did not need to add good works to be justified. Also, in principle, he no longer needed the law[40] because he now acted out of gratitude, and in love and through love fulfilled the law's requirements.[41] Christians, in the eyes of the reformers, were spiritually free people who no longer needed to be guarded and patronized by the church. After all, by faith, the Christian himself now had direct access to God. He was no longer dependent on a priest to take his confession and absolve him of his sins (after confession, the priest would say the words *absolvo te*, meaning: "I absolve you" or "I declare you righteous").

Even the celebration of the Eucharist was no longer a matter of high ecclesiastical order and privilege for the reformers. The church and her offices were put into perspective and gradually became less important than the believing person himself.[42] We see in the time of the Reformation that the individual gradually became more aware of his personal role and freedom and, in doing so, leaned more heavily on his own conscience and his own reading of Scripture. With an open Bible, a deeper appreciation of one's own individuality and inner self developed. That is, the individual defined himself less and less in the light of the large church collective. Questions such as, "What does God ask of me in Scripture?" and "What do I think of it myself?" became more and more important in the course of the sixteenth century.

---

[39] See especially Luther's 1520 tract, "Von der Freiheit eines Christenmenschen," translated into Dutch by C.N. Impeta, *De vrijheid van een christenmenschen* (Kampen: De Groot-Goudriaan, 1983).

[40] "So sehen wir, daß ein Christenmensch an dem Glauben genug hat; er bedarf keines Werkes, damit er fromm sei. Bedarf er denn keines Werkes mehr, so ist er gewiß entbunden von allen Geboten und Gesetzen. Ist er entbunden, so ist er gewiß frei. Das ist die christliche Freiheit...", Karin Bornkamm, Gerhard Ebeling, *Martin Luther: Ausgewählte Schriften, I. Band: Aufbruch zur Reformation* (Frankfurt am Main: Insel Verlag, 1983), 244.

[41] See Romans 13:8–10 and Galatians 5:22–24.

[42] See C. van der Kooi, "Om de toegang tot heil en leven. Een zoektocht naar het eigene van het protestantisme," *Kerk en Theologie* 55 (4, 2004): 329–343.

No genuine reformation

From the days of Luther's spiritual reversal in the northern countries, the Reformation proceeded to thoroughly transform church and culture. In England, however, this was not the case. Here, the Reformation became an entirely different story. Henry VIII shied away from a reformation of Lutheran or Calvinist magnitude and scope. Though he broke with Rome, he took charge of the church itself while he fought those who were truly reformation minded. Henry feared that a true reformation would weaken the power of the throne. Although, he did introduce some innovations, he did not truly return the Bible and the church to the people. The reformation-minded men who continued to make themselves heard, and did not give up challenging everything that still reminded them of Roman Catholic forms and traditions, were opposed or condemned. Soon they were addressed with the curse words of *puritan* and *purifier*. The name *Puritan*, which was soon taken up as a slogan, stood for, among other things, the pursuit of a pure church with pure preaching and a pure lifestyle.

Likewise, under the long reign of Elizabeth I (r. 1558-1603),[43] the Reformation did not really gain a foothold in England. She was a very capable queen and was unreservedly devoted to the cause of her country, but she acted harshly and mercilessly against Christians and churches that did not show loyalty to the crown. Even though Elizabeth changed and stabilized the Church of England in many ways, there was no profound inner reformation. She never got around to truly renewing the clergy, for example. It regularly happened that parishioners in the countryside had to be content with only one sermon a month, which was usually just read from a script. Sometimes they had to do without services for years, because there were simply too few priests or bishops.

We can imagine the Puritans saw some light on the horizon when, after Elizabeth's death in 1603, James VI of Scotland, also became king of England and Ireland, where he was called James I. In Presbyterian Scotland, the church was no longer ruled by bishops. Church elders (*presbyters*), many of whom were

---

[43] Elizabeth was a daughter of Henry's second marriage, to his lady-in-waiting Anne Boleyn. This marriage was the main reason Henry turned his back on Rome. The pope had forbidden him a divorce from Catherine of Aragon.

laymen, exercised authority over the local congregations. Could James I pick up the Reformation in England where Henry and Elizabeth had left off? By now, about ten percent of the Anglican Church consisted of Christians who held Puritan beliefs. On the day James left Scotland for England, a petition signed by about a thousand Puritans (the Millenary Petition) was handed to him, in which they presented the new king with their wishes and ideas.[44] James realized he could not ignore the Puritan cause and therefore decided to hold a three-day meeting in January 1604 at Hampton Court Palace.

The conference ended in bitter disappointment for the Puritans. James clung frenetically to the authority over the church granted to him as king and had no intention of implementing large-scale reforms. His words, "No bishop, no king," were well known. In other words, this Anglican Church with its episcopal structure could not fall without the king falling as well. Church and king belonged together; if one fell, so did the other. The English king could only rule with the necessary ecclesiastical mandate. Without this Anglican Church there was no king, for only this Anglican Church allowed him to be both head of the country and head of the Church.

James was not willing to allow local churches even the slightest bit of freedom to select pastors and devise the liturgy for Sundays as they saw fit—and it was precisely these kinds of changes the Puritans were after. They wished, for example, to banish from their churches the prescribed *Book of Common Prayer*, the reading from apocryphal writings and the wearing of official robes. They also wanted more and better preaching.

James listened to the requests and explanations of the four-person Puritan delegation, which only served to upset him. When the king thought the four were too set in their ways, the ill-tempered king threatened them with the words: "Comply or you will be expelled from the country or worse!" So, the delegation left empty-handed.

The disappointing Hampton Court conference marked a transitional moment in the history of the English church. From that

---

[44] See John R.H. Moorman, *A History of the Church of England* (London: Adam & Charles Black, 1976), 222–224.

time on, many Puritans decided to leave England. They fled to, for example, the Netherlands or the New World (America). England had become unsafe for Puritans under the new king. The king forbade all private religious meetings and insisted that only the prescribed prayer book, the *Book of Common Prayer*, be used in church meetings. Only dissenters (non-conformists) from Roman Catholic circles were tolerated. Protestant *dissenters* who deplored the paltry output of the Hampton Court conference were hunted down and taken to task. James wanted to show tolerance only to Roman Catholic peers because he figured he could still use them, but the king found Puritans generally troublesome and far too fanatical. Within the year, some 300 Puritan ministers had been driven out of their parishes.

John Smyth

Large groups of Puritans, however, did remain within the Anglican Church. Some sat out their time silently, most prayed incessantly for God to intervene and worked hard to turn the tide from within. Puritans who grew into non-conformist *dissenters* were often tired of waiting, so here and there they started their own communities on the margins of the English church or even outside it. Over time, their dissatisfaction led to alienation and eventually to separation from the Church of England. They are therefore called *separatists* as their non-conformity had an alienating effect on their church community, and this condition frequently leads to isolation and the parting of the ways.

The effects of the failed Hampton Court conference were felt throughout England, so also at Scrooby, an insignificant small town in Nottinghamshire, about 250 kilometers north of London. In Scrooby and the surrounding area, more and more Christians had gradually become convinced of the Puritan ideal of faith. It was the progressive priest Richard Clyfton (1553–1616), head of the church at Babworth, near Scrooby, who recognized that the church needed to change, and he knew how to bring God's message of change home to the local people.[45] There, in the vicinity of Scrooby, Babworth and nearby Gainsborough, a spiritual

---

[45] See Feenie Ziner, *The Pilgrims and Plymouth Colony* (New York: Harper & Row, 1961), 30.

climate arose at the beginning of the seventeenth century in which Puritan convictions could develop into the fundamental beginnings of the Baptist movement. Here, among other things, the foundations of *congregationalism* were laid, a church form that would become characteristic of Baptist churches.[46] Within a congregationalist church structure, the church council is not accountable to a classis, synod or other supra-local body, but solely to the local congregational assembly, which consists of all believers.[47]

The man who emerges in most history books as the founder of the first Baptist church is the theologian John Smyth (c. 1554–1612). He would go on to serve at some point as a pastor in Gainsborough and the surrounding area, further shaping Congregationalist thinking there.

Smyth was from a simple background, but he was privileged to study in his younger years at the famous Christ College in Cambridge.[48] In those days, this prestigious university was a stronghold of Puritanism. Among others, Edward Dering, William Perkins and Francis Johnson taught there. Francis Johnson was Smyth's mentor and would later become pastor of an English refugee congregation in Middelburg, the Netherlands, and shortly afterward pastor of a separatist Puritan church in Amsterdam.[49]

Lincoln and Gainsborough

Initially, John Smyth was a Puritan theologian who opposed any form of separatism and had nothing to do with critical voices on the Calvinist doctrine of election and predestination. Within a

---

[46] See John Briggs, "The Origins of the People Called Baptists" (2009), 6. This article was kindly entrusted to the author.

[47] Lat. *grex* meaning *flock*. Lat. *congregare* meaning *to unite as a flock*. On the positions, see the *Savoy Declaration of Faith and Order* (1658). See B. Wentsel, *Dogmatics*, Vol. 4b (Kampen: Kok, 1998), 768–774.

[48] On John Smyth in particular, see Jason K. Lee, *The Theology of John Smyth: Puritan, Separatist, Baptist, Mennonite* (Macon: Mercer University Press, 2003), 1–95, and J. Bakker, *John Smyth: De stichter van het Baptisme* (Diss. University of Utrecht, 1964; Wageningen: Veenman & Zonen, z.j.). See *The Works of John Smyth: Fellow of Christ's College, 1594–8*, Vol. 1, ed. W.T. Whitley (Cambridge: University Press, 1915; repr. 2009), xvii–cxxii.

[49] On Francis Johnson, see B.R. White, *The English Separatist Tradition: From the Marian Martyrs to the Pilgrim Fathers*, Oxford Theological Monographs (Oxford: Oxford University Press, 1971), 91–115.

few years, however, he was really changed.⁵⁰ In his college years, Smyth met John Robinson and Henry Ainsworth among others, fellow students who would also develop as non-conformists and separatists and would play important roles in the establishment of new church forms on the Continent. It is not clear exactly where Smyth became a pastor immediately after college. What we do know is that he did not follow a number of church regulations⁵¹ and had to answer to the Cambridge ecclesiastical court as early as April 1599. There was no conviction, however, because in August of the same year Smyth was released from the Anglican ministry at his own request. The decision to no longer participate from within in the reformation of the Church of England and to ask for his resignation was not at all common at that time. Yet Smyth did not immediately remove himself from the English ecclesiastical scene. In 1600, he was elected by a narrow majority as city preacher at Lincoln, England's largest diocese.

John Smyth
(c. 1554–1612)

Smyth was a gifted speaker who thoroughly prepared for each sermon. In the pulpit, he did not hesitate to clearly express his Puritan convictions. Because of this candor, Lincoln's preacher naturally made not only friends, but also enemies who began to complain about the preacher. One of the allegations that circulated was that Smyth no longer had an official preaching license. Because of this and some other accusations, Smyth was

---

⁵⁰ See James E. Tull, *Shapers of Baptist Thought*, Reprints of Scholarly Excellence (Macon: Mercer University Press, 1972), 18.
⁵¹ At church visitation, Smyth appeared not to wear the *superplie* (the white linen choir robe). At marriage confirmations, the ring was not used, and when administering baptism, Smyth refused to make the sign of the cross on the baptized person's forehead. See Bakker, *John Smyth*, 26.

summoned by the archdeacon of Lincoln in October 1602. Although Smyth had been granted leave to preach, he still could not produce a valid license and the city preacher was removed from office on October 13, 1602.

The following year Smyth worked as a teacher and preacher in North Clifton, a village west of Lincoln. Archival records show this must have been only for a short time. By 1604, Smyth was preaching regularly in the parish church of Gainsborough where his infant daughter Chara was also baptized. Smyth was evidently now married and had children. The pastorate in these years must have been a hard task for him. Church inspections were relentless, especially after the defeat of the Puritans in the first month of 1604. It is likely the Smyth family remained in Gainsborough for a number of years.

As a Puritan, John Smyth could not initially be called an outspoken opponent of the state church. Yet, the "pastor" of Gainsborough developed into an extremely critical advocate of religious freedom.[52] He became fiercely opposed to the dominant Anglican Church. According to him, the Episcopalian system held back ecclesiastical reforms and stood in the way of the pure gospel.

In Gainsborough, one had to meet in secret to preach this gospel. In Scrooby they met, among other places, in the house of the local postal official William Brewster (1568–1644). Brewster would become one of the famous pastors of the Pilgrim Fathers a few years later. Several Puritan ministers joined the movement of Smyth and Brewster. Quite a few of them had been suspended in the English church because they would not subscribe to the Hampton Court decisions of 1604. For example, immediately after his suspension Richard Clyfton was accepted into Smyth's circle. Despite this, Smyth never deliberately sought a break with the English Church. It was the poor relations with church superiors that slowly but surely quelled hopes for a change in the national church.[53] In the process, the dissenters often knew how to find each other and as a rule maintained intensive correspondence with each other. In this way new plans arose, including the idea of leaving the English mother church.

---

[52] Tull, *Shapers of Baptist Thought*, 18.
[53] See William Estep, *The Anabaptist Story: An Introduction to Sixteenth-Century Anabaptism* (Grand Rapids: Eerdmans, 1996), 287.

Smyth and Helwys

The profound development that the small community of disaffected people of Gainsborough and Scrooby went through in a short period of time has everything to do with the special friendship that developed in these years between John Smyth and Thomas Helwys (1550–1616).[54] Helwys was a nobleman who resided at a large country retreat, Broxtowe Hall, near Basford, Nottinghamshire, central England. The spiritual centre of the Lincolnshire renewal movement would be at this rustic country retreat during the years 1605 to 1607. At Broxtowe Hall, there was much debate as to whether or not it was permissible for a community of Christians, when estranged from the mother church, to start their own church. Most Puritans did not think along these lines, although the conviction was widely shared that the validity of the Anglican office (such as that of bishop) should be questioned. Their desire was to remain faithful to their church, trying to reform the church from within.

Nevertheless, more than twenty years earlier, a small separatist congregation had formed in Norwich (150 km northeast of London, on the coast) under the leadership of Robert Browne (d. 1633) and Robert Harrison (d. 1585).[55] The members of this group of dissenters together signed a declaration, making a covenant with God and with each other. The emphasis was on the covenant with God; from this bond, each member submitted to the church's order and discipline and to the associated spiritual authority.[56]

---

54 For a detailed overview see Joe Early, *The Life and Writings of Thomas Helwys*, Early English Baptist Texts (Macon: Mercer University Press, 2009), 15–46.
55 See White, *The English Separatist Tradition*, 1–90. Browne is said to have been strongly influenced by Dutch Mennonites (on Menno Simons, see Chapter 3). By 1571, nearly 3,000 Dutch, Walloon and Flemish Protestants were living in Norwich. No doubt these included Mennonites. Norwich was in fact a popular refugee city for Anabaptist Christians from the continent. On the early English dissenters, see especially Champlin Burrage, *The Early English Dissenters in the Light of Recent Research (1550–1641)*, Vol. 1–2 (Cambridge: University Press, 1912). See Estep, *The Anabaptist Story*, 281–283. In the mid-sixteenth century, Anabaptists were persecuted on the continent (see Chapters 2 and 4). On Browne's texts, thinking and legacy, see Jan Martijn Abrahamse, *Ordained Ministry in Free Church Perspective: Retrieving Robert Browne (c. 1550–1633) for Contemporary Ecclesiology*, Studies in Reformed Theology 41 (Leiden: Brill, 2020).
56 S. Paas, *De gemeenschap der heiligen. Kerk en gezag bij Presbyteriaanse en Separatistische Engelse Puriteinen 1570–1593* (Zoetermeer: Boekencentrum, 1996), 119–128.

The Brownists' view of the church was not clerical but congregationalist. The church was first and foremost a congregation of believers,[57] which was independent and led by laymen elected from among the congregational assembly, who met the spiritual requirements set forth in Scripture. In 1581, the church of Browne and Harrison fled to the Netherlands and settled in Middelburg, Zeeland. From that time on, the name Browne was so strongly associated with the emerging separatism that many separatists were then called "Brownists."

The names Henry Barrowe (c. 1550–1593) and John Greenwood (1556–1593) are also associated with early separatism in England. A friendship developed between these two Puritan Christians in the early 1580s that would continue until their deaths. Both were members of a separatist London congregation; Greenwood was a theologian, Barrowe was a lawyer. On October 8, 1587, a team of police officers raided the congregation and Greenwood and other key leaders of the "free church" were taken in for questioning. Greenwood ended up in prison and was in fear for his life. In those days, the English government acted fiercely against any form of non-conformity. When Greenwood's friend Henry Barrowe dared to visit him on November 19 of that same year, he too was arrested.

For more than five years and almost incessantly, the two dissenters had to defend their views before an official tribunal. Interrogations ran off and on. It was precisely during these years that Barrowe entrusted many valuable things to paper. His thoughts were still in full development so it is regrettable this came to an early end. After a few reprieves, on April 6, 1593, Barrowe and Greenwood were hanged in London for sedition against the state.[58]

---

[57] See Stephen Brachlow, *The Communion of Saints: Radical Puritan and Separatist Ecclesiology 1570–1625*, Oxford Theological Monographs (Oxford: Oxford University Press, 1988), 128–130, and Tull, *Shapers of Baptist Thought*, 19–22. It was Protestant to speak of the visible and invisible church because no one can really know who is truly a Christian and who is not. The church, according to Smyth, must not be a field of good and bad seed (*corpus permixtum*). The true church consisted of visible believers, visible saints, who "adopted the experimental approach to spiritual truth used by their radical contemporaries: evidence of orthodox faith and good works."

[58] See more fully on Barrowe and Greenwood and their visions of church and government: Paas, *The Community of Saints*, 205–351.

We may assume that more than twelve years later both Smyth and Helwys were aware of the misadventures of Browne, Barrowe and Greenwood and took these names into account when deliberating on the question, "To separate or not to separate?" Smyth wrestled with this dilemma for almost a year before actually separating. Prior to Smyth's decision, a conference was held at Coventry, just east of Birmingham, for in-depth discussions with several reformation minded people about the establishment of their own free church. Well-known Puritans such as Arthur Hildersam (1563–1632) were present and tried to dissuade Smyth from his position of separation. For the latter, it had now become clear that Puritan and Anglican views on the nature of the church were definitively mutually exclusive. Church hierarchy and the Reformation's *sola fide* (faith alone) did not go together. The English Church wanted to interfere too much with the content of people's faith, Smyth said. Hopes for some change in the state church seemed to have been definitively dashed after the Hampton Court conference. It therefore proved impossible to change Smyth's mind, and after the conference most appeared convinced by his argument. Thomas Helwys, Richard Clyfton, John Robinson and several others opted for John Smyth's plans and united to lead the Puritan community of Gainsborough and Scrooby through a process of liberation and church planting.

On the one hand, it was unfortunate the Puritan ranks fell apart in this way. On the other hand, it was impossible to decide for others whether or not to remain within the state church. Smyth saw no future for himself in the Anglican Church. Form worship and empty orthodoxy, abuse of power and lies had made the church he served, in his experience, into a stronghold of self-enrichment and self-preservation, where the pure proclamation of the Word of God was no longer welcome.

Covenantal congregation

Smyth instituted the young congregation in 1607,[59] in a way that was more or less taken from the Brownists. As long as the community of believers had not made a covenant with God, there was

---

[59] Not before January 1607. See Stephan Wright, *The Early English Baptists, 1603–1649* (Woodbridge: The Boydell Press, 2006),18.

no church. Only when this covenant was made could the sacraments be administered, Smyth believed. The covenant of faith with God was the foundation on which to build further. Therefore, they spent a day together in fasting and prayer, and at Gainsborough each entered the covenant of God with the words:

> I promise before God, and before this gathering, to walk in the ways of God, ways which are known to us or will be known to us, and I promise to do this to the best of my ability, whatever the cost may be, so help me God.[60]

With this solemn declaration, the entire congregation knew itself to be a new independent church with its own ministers. Shortly after the covenant, John Robinson also joined the congregation and took on the leadership of the Scrooby district. However, Smyth was the only pastor in the congregation at this stage in the development of the "brotherhood of the covenant." Robinson functioned only as a teacher; he taught and left typical pastoral duties such as blessings and the like to Smyth.

The covenantal congregation was hunted down in England and they frequently had to go into hiding and find a different location to meet. Despite the constant threat, Smyth did pioneer work in Scrooby. As mentioned, here, among other things, the foundations for the later "free" American churches were laid. Smyth led with a steady hand during these turbulent years. The course was clear—although not for long.

In the years that followed Scrooby and Gainsborough, Smyth would regularly recant previous positions. In itself, the church leader was not bothered by this, believing the Spirit clarifies the truth of Scripture through inner illumination.[61] A truth today could be further clarified tomorrow and therefore modified or changed. Had not Jesus said that God's "Spirit of truth" would show the way to "all the truth"?[62] The paths of Smyth and other separatists would diverge over time because of this twisting and

---

[60] "I covenant with God and with one another, to walk in His ways, made known or to be made known unto us, according to our best endeavors, whatsoever it shall cost us, the Lord assisting us," Bakker, *John Smyth*, 48–49.
[61] Tull, *Shapers of Baptist Thought*, 24.
[62] John 16:13.

turning on Smyth's part. Smyth's views on the covenant idea, the relationship between church and government and his ideas on infant baptism would also begin to shift. At Gainsborough and Scrooby infants were still baptized.

Leading in all the shifts, for Smyth, was the focus on the pure character of the church. The church of Christ was to be a holy community, encouraging self-discipline as an instrument of God. As was the case in the early church, the separatist community was characterized by its penitential focus. The ancient church can be seen as a powerful penitential movement that helped converts seek the forgiveness of God. Living from forgiveness, a completely new world presented itself. The Christian therefore walked in "newness of life."[63] In the covenantal congregation of Smyth this was also the case. Serious attention was therefore given to the believers' sanctification.

Doctrinal purity was not Smyth's main concern. The covenant with God had primarily practical intentions. Three elders, a pastor, a teacher and an administrator, were to oversee the life they were living and bring abuses to the attention of all the members. The congregational assembly decided on all the spiritual interests of the congregation, not the council of elders.[64] If someone refused to repent, they could be "cut off." This did not mean the person who had been cut off was to be considered an enemy. Only spiritual contact with the marked sinner was no longer possible; business contact was not forbidden, nor was marriage.

The crossing

Covenantal congregants who were arrested for meeting illegally were usually given a prison sentence or a fine. William Brewster was imprisoned several times. Smyth managed to escape the hands of court officials on two occasions. The situation eventually proved untenable for the separatists. Therefore, a plan was conceived to move to the Netherlands, and in Amsterdam to seek a *rapprochement* with the refugee congregation of Francis Johnson (1562–1618).[65] Thus, it was decided and soon it was done.

---

[63] Romans 6:4.
[64] Bakker, *John Smyth*, 54.
[65] See James Robert Coggins, *John Smyth's Congregation: English Separatism, Mennonite Influence, and the Elect Nation*, Studies in Anabaptist and Mennonite History 32

Thomas Helwys took charge of the organization of the emigration. He was probably also the financier of the venture. Since their town had a direct connection to the sea, Smyth and Helwys with the Gainsborough congregation were the first to leave. They sold their land and property, set sail and arrived in Amsterdam without any problems. The dating of this extraordinary event is uncertain but it probably took place in the fall of 1607.[66]

More complicated was the crossing for the congregation of Scrooby. The sudden departure of the Gainsborough group had alarmed the authorities. The ports were closed, and no one could sail off in the usual way. That being said, non-conformists were still forced by the authorities to leave England, but one was not allowed to leave in secret, at a time of one's choosing and certainly not with large groups at a time![67]

Scrooby's congregation required several attempts to get to Amsterdam. In the late fall of 1607, Clyfton, Robinson, Brewster and the others undertook the journey on foot to the coastal town of Boston, about a hundred kilometres southeast of Scrooby. There a ship was waiting for them. The captain undoubtedly had to have been bribed with a large sum of money if he wanted to undertake such a venture. When the group of refugees arrived at the appointed place, the captain not only showed up much too late but also turned out to be a profiteer and a traitor.[68] Boarding

---

(Waterloo: Herald Press, 1991), 44, and Early, *The Life and Writings of Thomas Helwys*, 18–20. Francis Johnson, as a Puritan Christian, came under the influence of Barrowe and Greenwood and sympathized with separatist thought. After the death of the latter, many Separatists fled to Holland in 1593. Johnson was imprisoned at the time. The group of escaped separatists settled in Kampen, among other places, where a schism took place in 1594. Part of the English congregation declared their Anabaptist convictions. In Naarden, too, schisms took place. Groups of English Separatists went over to rebaptism in those days. In 1597, Johnson came to the Netherlands, where he took up the work in the Amsterdam refugee church (this congregation had been the work of Greenwood in London and had emigrated in 1593). So, actually, an English Anabaptist church had emerged in the Netherlands as early as 1594. See Estep, *The Anabaptist Story*, 283–285.

[66] Bakker, *John Smyth*, 59.

[67] There was a law in force that stipulated that emigrants had to have permission from the crown. The permission had to be withdrawn if the head of state decided to repatriate (eg. for tax reasons or to recruit soldiers or for employment).

[68] The history was put into words by the pilgrim father William Bradford himself in his diary, published under the title *Of Plymouth Plantation* (New York: Knopf, 1952). Bradford was governor of the Plymouth Colony for thirty-five years and completed his diary around 1650.

the waiting ship late in the evening, the unsuspecting congregation was ambushed by the local police chief and some court officials, and then searched for money and robbed as well. Even the women were treated roughly and searched with groping and fondling. The group of shocked Puritans was then led to Boston, put on display in front of the assembled crowd and put behind bars in police custody for a month. Richard Clyfton, John Robinson and William Brewster were held for longer than a month, but after some time they were also allowed to return to their homes.

Nevertheless, shortly after this tragedy, the congregation of Scrooby was again ready to travel to Holland. So, in the summer of 1608, a new covert attempt was made. This time an appointment had been made with a Dutch skipper who would wait for the group on the shore somewhere between Grimsby and Hull. The men went there on foot, while women and children, possibly about thirty in number, went down the Ryton River in a barge to the mouth at the North Sea. However, the journey was so swift that the women arrived at the appointed place a day early and searched for a cove in which to tie up the barge at low tide. When the ship from Holland appeared the next morning, the women could not yet set sail because the water was still too low. In the meantime, the skipper had caught sight of the group of men who were approaching and he hurriedly sent a sloop to pick them up. The first batch of men had not yet climbed into the ship when a distant danger was spotted. A small army of heavily armed servicemen and government officials were on their way to foil the separatists' flight to Holland. When the skipper saw them coming, he immediately cast off and set sail for open sea. The group of men who were now safely on board then had to watch from a distance as their wives and children were discovered and arrested. Of the group of men still waiting on the beach, some were able to get to safety. Only those who could support the women allowed themselves to be captured voluntarily. The situation that arose, which is easy to guess, is one of horror and grief. The Dutch skipper tried to save his life and refused to turn back.

The group of women and children, along with some of the men, were then taken from place to place to be reported, but the authorities did not really know what to do with them. The women and children could not be charged merely because they went with their husbands and fathers. What could they be charged with? Nothing, really. But neither could they send them back home. After all, houses, land and property had been sold. After a while they had no choice but to grant the women and children free passage to Holland.

Meanwhile, the ship with concerned men was on its way to Amsterdam and had to contend with heavy weather. The crossing to Holland took more than two weeks. There were times when the crew despaired of their own lives. The ship was even blown toward the coast of Norway over the course of the storm. After days of uncertainty, the weather finally improved and everyone safely reached the port of Amsterdam.

Those who stayed behind also managed to make the crossing in small groups in the summer of next year. The families were thus reunited in Amsterdam. Those who only reached the quays of the Dutch city in August 1698 included Brewster, Robinson, and Clyfton. The Amsterdam of Joost van den Vondel had by then about 240,000 inhabitants and could definitely be considered a big multicultural city at the time.[69]

In Amsterdam

At the beginning of the seventeenth century, the city of Amsterdam was, so to speak, a *sanctuary* for all kinds of people who had to flee from elsewhere. This is not to say that refugees, for example, were kindly received and had a carefree life. Anything but that. Tolerance was less part of the national spirit of the Netherlands in the sixteenth and seventeenth centuries than is generally assumed.[70]

Amsterdam did open its gates to English separatists, but they had to work hard and under harsh conditions. The working and living conditions in Amsterdam were such that hundreds of immigrants were needed every year to maintain the social and economic growth of the city.[71] As a "guest worker" one therefore had to start from the bottom. Nevertheless, there were some

---

[69] See Diarmaid Macculloch, "Het Europese huis gedeeld. Religieuze tolerantie tijdens de Reformatie," *Vrijheid in verdeeldheid (Freedom in Division)*, ed. van Erp, 43–44.
[70] Pettegree, "Predikanten versus stadsbestuurders," 62, 82.
[71] See Coggins, *John Smyth's Congregation*, 44–48.

Amsterdammers (citizens of Amsterdam) who were quite sympathetic to the English guests.

In Amsterdam, Smyth, Helwys, Robinson and their supporters received a warm welcome in a building on the Amstel (number 122). This bakehouse stretched as far as the Rembrandt Square and was kindly provided and rented to the English by the Anabaptist baker Jan Munter, probably from Spring 1610.[72] Probably the name Baker's Street (Bakker Straat)[73] still remains from this time. In the building complex, a large hall lent itself to the meetings of the expatriate English.[74] Possibly the complex also housed several English families. John Smyth made his living in those days by practicing the profession of physician. In England he had studied not only theology but also medicine.

As mentioned, Amsterdam was home to the Greenwood refugee congregation, who had been expelled in 1593.[75] Since 1597, this congregation had been under the care of the Cambridge theologian Francis Johnson, who had been a mentor to Smyth. The *Amsterdammers* called all English Christians "Brownists." As English expatriates, they were naturally associated with the congregation of Robert Browne, who had settled in Middelburg in 1581 (and popped up from there in various places in the

---

[72] In her PhD research at VU University Amsterdam, Kirsten Timmer introduces a more nuanced timeline for first contacts between Smyth/Helwys and Munter/The Waterlanders. A primary manuscript (from Amsterdam archives) states that Munter became the owner of the Bakehouse on May 18, 1610. From this document, and from letters written by Smyth himself, first contact between Smyth and The Waterlanders seems merely possible between 1609 and Spring 1610, see Kirsten Timmer, "Revisiting the Chronology of Baptist Origins (1607–1610)," a paper presented at the opening of the John Smyth Research Library, IBTSC, Baptist House Amsterdam, January 24, 2019.

[73] The Bakehouse was located on the Amstel River, behind the present-day houses of Amstel 122 and 124. Built to bake hardtack or ship biscuits to feed sailors on long voyages to Asia, from about 1595 to 1603, the *Grote Backhuys* (Great Bakehouse), as it was known, served an overseas trading venture, the Compagnie van Verre, which merged with several other companies to form the Dutch East India Company. After the company abandoned bakery operations there, the building became a (military) arsenal for several years" (www.thefreelibrary.com; The church in the Bakehouse: John Smyth's English Anabaptist congregation at Amsterdam, 1609–1660).

[74] See Manfred Bärenfänger, "Der Anfang war ein Gelübde. John Smyth und die erste Baptistengemeinde," *Die Gemeinde* 11 (1975): 6–8.

[75] There were around 1,000 English refugees in Amsterdam by then and at least four English Christian congregations. The Smyth and Helwys congregation seems to be the fifth.

The Bakehouse, 1610, Amsterdam

northern provinces). Johnson's church in Amsterdam stood on a street that came to be called Brownists' Alley (Bruinisten-steeg). The building accommodated about 300 people.

Smyth and Helwys, and the congregation of Gainsborough, had already joined the Amsterdam Ancient Brethren (Brownists) some months before the arrival of the brothers and sisters of Scrooby.[76] It was now a relief for the newcomers from Scrooby to enter a congregation that no longer reminded them of the Church of England. Sunday could now be truly experienced as a day of rest before the Lord for the full covenantal congregation from Gainsborough and Scrooby. Worship before God could finally be lived differently than it had been in England.

The Brownists had meetings twice each Sunday. The first began at eight o'clock in the morning; the second early in the afternoon. The services were sober in form and content. Kneeling was not done, nor was singing accompanied by an organ—these practices were associated with the Church of England.

---

[76] See T. Crosby, *The History of the English Baptists from the Reformation to the Beginning of the Reign of King George I*, Vol. 1 (London, 1738; 2nd reprint, Lafayette, 1979), 81–104. Crosby's material is interesting because of his affinity for the seventeenth century.

The first service began early and was opened with all standing for a prayer that could sometimes last an hour. Following that, a psalm was sung and the sermon was preached. The sermon usually lasted several hours and was concluded with a song. This was followed by the celebration of the Lord's Supper, the collection and the benediction. The congregation then went home to eat and shortly thereafter gathered for the second service. This afternoon meeting was opened with prayer and a brief reflection by the pastor. Thereafter, the men present were free to respond to the sermons and to discuss spiritual matters with one another.

It was this free Puritan form of thinking and gathering, in which mutual harmony was sought, that would stamp the New World with democratic insights. The Puritans called this free discussion a time of "prophesying," that is, a time of speaking freely about the meaning of Scripture and about what God asks of man in response.[77] Thus, the meaning and intent of Scripture were not imposed or dictated from above. Knowing what God asks of the congregation requires mutual consultation. The English dissenters therefore invariably believed in studying and discussing the biblical text together. Under Catholic and Anglo-Saxon church rule, this reading and listening and searching together was forbidden, because ordinary Christians were not considered capable of meaningful participation in important spiritual matters. How different this was on an ordinary Sunday afternoon in Brownists' Alley in Amsterdam in the autumn of 1608.

Separation

It must be said that the separatists soon became divided by differences of views among them.[78] The emerging culture of free input from all church members also easily evoked conflict. For the Scrooby and Gainsborough dissenters, joining the Ancient Church was out of the question. Even an open-minded Amsterdammer could be bewildered by the vehemence with which English disagreements were sometimes accompanied.[79]

---

[77] In the Dutch refugee congregation in London in the sixteenth century they had a time of "prophecying" on Thursday afternoons, see M. Micron, *De Christelicke Ordinancien der Nederlandtscher Ghemeinte te Londen* (1554).
[78] See W. van't Spijker, R. Bisschop, W.J. op't Hof, *Het puritanisme. Geschiedenis, theologie en invloed* (Zoetermeer: Boekencentrum, 2001), 278–282.
[79] Ziner, *The Pilgrims and Plymouth Colony*, 41.

Smyth appeared to differ from his old master Johnson in many respects.[80] Smyth felt that the church government of the Brownists was not open and (spiritually) flexible enough; he thought that too much reading was done during the services, and they would not allow strangers to contribute to the collection.

For their part, Francis Johnson and Henry Ainsworth found John Smyth to be far too spiritualistic, which in their view called into question the central authority of Scripture. Smyth, however, believed that worship should have a purely prophetic character and that at some point all books, even the Bible, should be set aside. Then everyone who wished to "prophesy" had only to listen to the message that arose from his innermost heart. For Smyth, the principle of "prophesying" meant there had to be room for free and spontaneous manifestations of the Spirit.[81] The old Brownist church was thus far too formal, too one-sided and too scholastic for Smyth. It is not exactly certain how Smyth arrived at this view so early, but it is assumed he had already become acquainted with prophetic forms of speech in England.

After a hastily arranged two-day conference, Johnson, Smyth and their followers were not able to find common ground and fellowship between the two "sister churches" was broken off. No formal union had taken place yet, so the parties were able to part company without much trouble. Smyth thereby alienated not only his former teacher and his congregation, but also his own fellow brothers and sisters. Clyfton developed reservations about him, while Robinson even tried to counter Smyth's views. In early February 1609, a group of about a hundred separatist Christians left Amsterdam for Leiden with the moderate dissenter Robinson. The town of Leiden had opened its doors to the English, provided they would keep a low profile. Among the travellers, in addition to John Robinson, were William Brewster and William Bradford.

The English refugees who settled in Leiden were, however, more open-minded than Smyth. In the English church in Leiden for example, compassionate Reformed Christians were welcomed at the Lord's Supper. Robinson did not want to rigorously avoid

---

[80] See Wright, *The Early English Baptists*, 24–32; Early, *The Life and Writings of Thomas Helwys*, 20–21; White, *The English Separatist Tradition*, 143–159; and Coggins, *John Smyth's Congregation*, 46–56.
[81] Bakker, *John Smyth*, 63–64.

dissenters and for him Calvinism and congregationalism in principle went well together.[82] This did not alter the fact that in Leiden the English and the Dutch Reformed also lived in separate worlds. The Dutch mentality was in any case too free for the English. For example, the latter were much stricter in their views on the "Sabbath rest."

For Smyth, the one view totally ruled out the other. According to him, a good congregationalist could not hold to a Calvinistic way of being church. Smyth even turned from the covenant that the congregation of Gainsborough and Scrooby had made with God. This covenant, he said, could no longer be the foundation of the church. Smyth now also openly favoured believer's baptism and took up some clearly Arminian positions. For Smyth, only this sign, baptism, properly applied for mature believers, could be the cornerstone of a true Christian community of faith.[83]

Smyth's temperament and new insights had caused the English separatist "brotherhood of the covenant" to break up quite painfully, and now the people had to regroup. Consequently, the church roll of the original Scrooby and Gainsborough congregations showed significant changes. A number of members of Smyth's congregation joined Robinson's departing group and, conversely, members of the Scrooby congregation stayed with Smyth in Amsterdam. Once John Robinson had settled in Leiden, he became a furious opponent of the man he had once been such kindred spirits with.

The English congregation at Leiden would go through an accelerated process of change over the years. Refugees from other parts of England joined the dissenters, and they began gradually to adapt to the Dutch culture. The development of the English community in Leiden could certainly be called harmonious.[84] In 1620, the congregation had increased from about 100 people to at least three times that.[85]

---

[82] For a fascinating impression of the English community in Leiden, see Joke Kardux, Eduard van de Bilt, *Newcomers In An Old City: The American Pilgrims In Leiden* (Leiden: Burgersdijk & Niermans, 2007).
[83] Estep, *The Anabaptist Story*, 288.
[84] A visit to the American Puritan Museum (Beschuitsteeg 9) and a tour of Puritan sites in Leiden (a map can be obtained from the Tourist Office) would be worthwhile.
[85] Van't Spijker e.a., *Het puritanisme*, 281-282.

Leiden was the location where the debate between Arminius and Gomarus had just erupted. While a serious church war ignited in the Netherlands, the English Puritans, who developed as non-conformists and champions of free churches, could count on understanding and sympathy from many Dutch Christians. The average Dutchman could appreciate the English Calvinist. Robinson even established relationships with various people from the theological and academic world of the time.[86]

Nevertheless, despite Dutch benevolence and openness, it was impossible for John Robinson's English community in Leiden to build their own future in Holland. They felt too dependent on the Dutch situation (and the ever-threatening war with Spain) and dreamed of developing their own Puritan civilization with their own Christian constitution far away from European uncertainties. Deep down, the English separatists wanted to design a "free" society based on the Word of God. Around 1617, therefore, the idea of travelling to the New World was being considered.

The year before, an enthusiastic travel account by a certain Captain John Smith had been published. He had travelled to New England in 1614, and had published his experiences in a book, including his report on the wild colony of Virginia.[87] No doubt such publications, supplemented by other reports, led to some of Robinson's congregation (about fifty people) wanting to sail from Delfshaven via Southampton to Virginia in 1620. Americans will think here of the *Mayflower*, but they left Holland on another ship, the *Speedwell*. The *Mayflower* came from London and sailed to Southampton, where the two ships would meet and together sail for Virginia. Nevertheless, the *Speedwell* had been leaking quite a bit on the voyage from Holland, and even after repairs it kept leaking. So, after sailing some 300 nautical miles (560 km), they had to return to England. There, they decided to leave the *Speedwell* behind and travel as one group on the *Mayflower*.[88]

---

[86] For example, there was cordial contact between Willem Teellinck and John Robinson, see Van't Spijker e.a., *Het puritanisme*, 285–287.

[87] The title of the account is *A Description of New England* (1616). Captain John Smith spent several years at Jamestown, Virginia (1607–1609), then a rather inhospitable and dangerous area, where at some point he was rescued by Pocahontas, daughter of the Indian chief Powhatan. Smith returned to England wounded and in 1614 undertook a journey to Maine and Massachusetts.

[88] See http://mayflowerhistory.com/voyage

The Pilgrim Fathers Church at Delfshaven; a commemorative window in this building.

However, they would still not arrive in Virginia—they ended up at Plymouth, Massachusetts, where the inexperienced settlers had a hard time. But, through all the misery, they managed to lay the foundations for fundamental democratic values that have now characterized the United States for centuries.

Differences

Late in 1608, John Smyth had started his own congregation in Amsterdam. The question of baptism played an essential role in this church formation. The atmosphere in the Ancient Church of Johnson and Ainsworth, and also in that of Robinson in Leiden, was in Smyth's eyes too liturgical, too Calvinistic and too hierarchical. It is therefore interesting to compare some of the confessions Smyth and the Brownists drew up in that period and get a clearer picture of the essential differences and similarities.

In 1596, the Brownists had drawn up a confession (*A True Confession*) that was strongly congregationalist and Calvinistic in colour and served for the London and Amsterdam separatist congregations to clarify their religious positions. According to some experts, this confession was drafted by Henry Ainsworth.[89] Incidentally, the members of these congregations certainly did not want to be called Brownists. We can understand why, because Browne had been falsely[90] labelled as subversive and a threat to the state.[91] The confession therefore began with the words, "A sincere profession of faith and a humble confession of the allegiance which we, subjects of Her Majesty, and wrongly called 'Brownists', have with God".[92]

In *A True Confession*, the "ancient brethren" overwhelmingly professed the doctrine of double predestination. It was held that God had decided all things, even the smallest circumstances, in his eternal will and plan. Also, before the creation of the world, God had decided—according to his good pleasure—to predestine a selection of human beings and angels for salvation and eternal life and to select another part of humanity and the angelic world for rejection and eternal judgement on the basis of their own corruption.[93] It was also assumed that every human being was born in sin. By nature, human beings were sinners under judgement, even if they were only small and newborn. God sent his Son Jesus into the world to reconcile the chosen people to himself and to

---

[89] William Lumpkin, *Baptist Confessions of Faith*, rev. ed. (Valley Forge: Judson Press, 1969), 79–97.

[90] Paas, *De gemeenschap der heiligen*, 127.

[91] After all, Robert Browne's name did not signify a recommendation from the congregation to the outside world and could only encourage suspicion. Amsterdammers, for example, called the man "trouble-church Browne." Browne's separatism had failed in England (Norwich) and his church had fled to Holland (Middelburg) in 1582, where the congregation split and disintegrated. Eventually Browne left for Scotland, where he even returned to the state church. The Amsterdam separatists are actually not descended from Browne but from John Greenwood and Henry Barrow (1593), migrated via Kampen and Naarden to the Amstel city (1596). In Amsterdam this congregation was also plagued by strife and schisms. See Van't Spijker e.a., *Het puritanisme*, 278–280.

[92] "A True Confession of the Faith, and Humble Acknowledgment oe the Alegeance, which we hir Maiesties Subjects, falsely called Brownists, doo hold towards God," Lumpkin, *Baptist Confessions of Faith*, 82. The so-called "errors" that appear to the reader of today in the English rendering of confessions in this book are original.

[93] Lumpkin, *Baptist Confessions of Faith*, 82–83: "Wee beleeue…and confes…that God hath in Christ…ordeyned som men and Angells, to eternall lyfe…. And on thother hand hath likewise…ordeined other both Angels and men, to eternall condemnation." *A True Confession*, art. 3.

gather them into his church, thus separating the true Christian congregation from the corrupt world.[94]

Yet, the Calvinist-Separatist congregation of Amsterdam departed from the well-known reformers in its mode of church government. God governed the church through officebearers (such as pastors, teachers, elders and deacons) whom he himself appointed. This implied an election and appointment, which could be done independently by the local community.[95] Lutheran and Calvinist churches possessed this independence less explicitly than congregationalist churches.

Likewise, the right to put Christians under discipline was not given to just a few, to a local elite or a supra-local board, but to the entire spiritual body of the local church.[96] In this respect, the Puritan separatists worked out more consistently the principles of Luther and Calvin concerning the priesthood of all believers. Every member of the body of Christ could and should fully assume his position and participate in deciding what happened in the church. The hierarchical structure of the Anglican Church was therefore strongly criticized in *A True Confession* and rejected as "antichristian" and "foreign to Christ."[97] While children of believers were to be baptized, only true believers could partake of the Lord's Supper.[98]

The separatist community (like the Reformational community) expected worldly authorities to root out idolatry, all human forms of religion and worship, and if necessary, to appropriate church buildings, monuments and lands, to claim these for the kingdom of God. Governments had been appointed by God to defend the true religion and to subject the land to God's rules. The church, in turn, was to pray unceasingly for the authorities. However, if the authorities did not protect the true religion, then Christians

---

94 Lumpkin, *Baptist Confessions of Faith*: "(Christ) hath fully performed and suffred all those things, by which God…might bee reconciled to his elect" (85) and "Christ hath here in earth a spirituall Kindome and ae canonicall regiment ouer his servants… seperating them from emongst unbeleevers"(87), *A True Confession*, art. 14 and 17.
95 *A True Confession*, art. 17–23.
96 Lumpkin, *Baptist Confessions of Faith*, 89: "That Christ hath given this powre to receive in order to cut off anie member, to the wholl body together of every Christian Congregation, and not to anie one member aparte." *A True Confession*, art. 24.
97 *A True Confession*, art. 29.
98 *A True Confession*, art. 35.

had to obey God rather than men. In that case, the community of the righteous was free to put the commandments of God above those of men. This did not alter the fact that the conscience had to be kept clear and Christians had to try to fulfil their civic duties always within the bounds of propriety. Again, this all sounded quite Reformed.[99]

Finally, the text of *A True Confession* shook off verbatim the accusation of heresy, as well as the allegation that separatists rejected the use of the Lord's Prayer because they were opposed to this type of form prayer and no longer wanted to use it in the meetings. *A True Confession*, however, articulated that the "Our Father" was the most perfect prayer God had given his followers and this prayer was an example to the Christian.[100] The English separatists were thus opposed to form prayers imposed hierarchically and took the liberty of praying in their own meetings as it occurred to their minds and hearts. The Lord's Prayer offered a structure and content of prayer that served as a basic example.[101]

At first John Smyth thought to join this type of church and the corresponding confession of the Ancient Brethren, but as indicated, this ended in a rift somewhere around the end of 1608 or the beginning of 1609. Smyth had come to a different understanding. He could no longer reconcile himself with the Puritan views of Francis Johnson and Henry Ainsworth. Their thinking was too formalistic and too churchy and, according to Smyth, did not go far enough where it concerned the radical principles of Christ's church. The true church could only be a holy and independent congregation, baptized on the basis of the signs of repentance and contrition. Smyth thereupon dissolved his church in the winter of 1608, and shortly hereafter founded a new one by first baptizing himself (not by immersion but by pouring water), followed by the baptism of a number of associates.[102] The

---

[99] See Calvijn, *Institutes* 4.20, and the *Nederlandse Geloofsbelijdenis*, art. 36.
[100] "Not that wee should bee tyed to the use of those very words, but that wee should according to that rule make all our requests & thanksgyving unto God, forasmuch as it is a perfect forme and patterne," *A True Confession*, art. 39-43.
[101] *A True Confession*, art. 45. Lumpkin, *Baptist Confessions of Faith*, 97.
[102] However, the factuality of this "se-baptism" (self-baptism) was doubted. See Crosby, *The History of the English Baptists*, 1:92–99. By the end of the sixteenth century, however, the practice of self-baptism was apparent. See Champlin Burrage, *The Early English Dissenters in the Light of Recent Research (1550–1641)*, Vol. 1 (Cambridge: Cambridge

ritual marked the transition from the old situation to a completely new one.

However, Smyth's self-baptism was seriously questioned and criticized by some of his fellow believers. From what did such a baptism derive its sacramental validity? Had Smyth not been too premature? How could he have changed his mind so fundamentally within the span of less than a year? To answer this last question, it is assumed he had come into contact with Anabaptist congregations in Amsterdam and the surrounding area, and had been influenced by their doctrine and life.[103] However, it seems "the logic" of Smyth's Baptist convictions was already present in the concept of "visible churchmanship" in English non-conformity.[104] Still, the question remains "a widely disputed topic," and it may be safest to assume an answer cannot be found.[105] Anyway, Smyth's perception of truth throughout his ministry made him pursue "further revelation, and accept changes in opinion."[106]

The new congregation now entered a difficult and even extremely critical phase after Smyth's unusual baptism. From within and from without, the English near-Baptist church was challenged and torn apart. To survive as a community, Smyth knocked on the door of the Waterlanders (Mennonite) congregation in Amsterdam (located at Singel 452–454) in 1609. Perhaps

---

University Press, 1912), 223–224. "And so, one baptizeth [From margin: 'I knew one such, and sundry can witnes it.'] himselfe (as Abraham first circumcised himselfe: Abraham had a commandement; they haue none, nor like cause) and then he baptizeth other" (223).

103 Estep, *The Anabaptist Story*, 289–290. "Conceivably, Smyth could have arrived at his position from his own private study of the Scriptures, apart from any outside stimulus. In the light of the historical context, this is highly unlikely" (290).

104 Brachlow, *The Communion of Saints*, 150–156; Wright, *The Early English Baptists*, 33–36. "Smyth's se-baptism offered him and his friends the only way to reach the door out of Babylon" (35). Coggins, *John Smyth's Congregation*, 61–65. "Thus, although from the perspective of later historians the switch to believers baptism was a watershed, to Smyth it was only a further step into a more purified Separatism" (63) and "the change to believers baptism was accomplished before the Smyth congregation had received any significant input from the Mennonites" (65).

105 Early, *The Life and Writings of Thomas Helwys*, 24–25. "Therefore, he may have reached believer's baptism on his own. This question may never be answered" (24).

106 Lee, *The Theology of John Smyth*, 289–291. See Whitley, *The Works of John Smyth*, 1:xvii: "Smyth showed himself ready to avow when he saw his mistake, frank to retract and to guide into a truer path. Again and again he invited discussion and declared himself ready to be convinced."

they could be joined to unite efforts. Smyth had by now become well acquainted with the community of Waterlanders and had largely agreed with their religious views.[107] Officially, therefore, the request was made to be admitted to the congregation as members. This involved thirty-one persons, certainly no small matter at the time—refugee congregations were usually not that large. In order to understand Smyth's move, it is necessary to delve into the thinking and beliefs of Anabaptism and to track down what might have appealed to the English separatist in the Anabaptist way of life and confession. In the next chapter we will begin this search.

1.5 Summary

As we near the end of this first chapter, we will briefly take stock. We have seen how much the Netherlands, at the beginning of the seventeenth century, was under the spell of the national church dispute over election. The English refugees from Gainsborough and Scrooby who fled to Holland, including John Smyth and Thomas Helwys, were all initially Puritan and Calvinistic. In the Netherlands, some became convinced of believer's baptism. The connection with the Puritan English refugees who were already present in Amsterdam failed, and Smyth's congregation subsequently sought affiliation with the Waterlander Anabaptists in Amsterdam.

The Anabaptist community believed differently about election than had been decided at the Synod of Dordt. For both the group around Smyth, who after a few years merged into the Waterlander congregation, and the group around Helwys, who would return to England and introduce the denomination of General Baptists, this meant a spiritual change of direction with historical consequences.

By now it should be obvious, from these brief facts and details, no fixed theory on Baptist origins can be constructed. The matter is too elusive, and no easy answers will suffice. Of course, there is no successionist continuity between the practice of baptism in the early church, beginning with Jesus and his disciples, and early Baptists like John Smyth, Thomas Helwys or John Spilsbury,

---

[107] For a more comprehensive treatment of the Waterlanders, see Chapter 3.

one of the first Particular Baptists. History does not allow for linear cause and effect, particularly in the field of convictions such as baptism. Doctrine needs facts and faces and should consequentially also contextually be approached with the help of constructed narrative.

Of course, neither have Baptist beginnings originated from lives and beliefs spent in mere isolation. But again, how early Baptist convictions were received and passed on, and exactly how much of it was Puritan, dissenter-Puritan, separatist-Puritan and/or continental Anabaptist, is hard to say. On a more controversial tone I would maintain, that on the question, "Were (true) early Baptists English or continental in their beliefs?" there is no simple answer.[108] On the one hand it can be shown that "the roots of all Smyth's emphases can be found in his own puritan-separatist tradition."[109] On the other hand, "in the world of ideas, national and denominational compartments leaked," and consequently historians should never "exaggerate the fixity of divisions."[110] All too often there is continuity and fluidity between mixes of the traditions people live by, and by mere difference of strategy, timing, coincidence and circumstance, they follow the leads they have by intuition and thoughtful reflection.[111]

The origins of early Baptists were dynamically interconnected, with different strands and traditions of English and continental backgrounds. For that reason, it is warranted to opt for a more dynamic, *viz.* polygenetic model of Baptist beginnings.[112] The assumption that once Smyth's church was founded, "his views shifted in a distinctly Anabaptist direction,"[113] is one-sided, just

---

[108] Coggins, *John Smyth's Congregation*, 43–65. "In reality, there is no simple answer" (57).
[109] Wright, *The Early English Baptists*, 1–11, and in particular Brachlow, *The Communion of Saints*, 4, 6, 17, and "Puritan Theology and General Baptist Origins," *Baptist Quarterly* 31/4 (1985): 9–194.
[110] Wright, *The Early English Baptists*, 9, 11. See also 12–44.
[111] Brachlow, *The Communion of Saints*, 17.
[112] Martyn J. Whittock, "Baptist Roots: The Use of Models in Tracing Baptist Origins," *The Evanglical Quarterly* 57/4 (1985): 317–326.
[113] Erik Wickman, "General Baptist Origins and Original Sin," *Baptist Quarterly* 51/2 (2020): 47–55. See also Kenneth R. Manley, "Origins of the Baptists: The Case for Development from Puritanism—Separatism,' in *Faith, Life and Witness: The Papers of the Study and Research Division of the Baptist World Alliance 1986-1990*, ed. William H. Brackney and Ruby J. Burke (Birmingham: Samford University Press, 1990), 56–69.

as the presumption that "no continuity" between English Baptists and Anabaptists existed, and if there was any contact, this "was not a very close one."[114] All of this may somehow be demonstrable and true, and yet be just one side of the story. Besides linear cause and effect thinking, historical interpretation takes into account that "what follows" always revisits "what was first."

The influence of the Mennonites and other continental radical groups on the English Baptists was profound,[115] even though Smyth and others may have moved away from predominantly Calvinistic-separatist views to predominantly Mennonite views, within the span of a couple of months.

We know ideas travel fast, and early English dissenter and separatist traditions will have reciprocally cross-fertilized continental Anabaptist thinking.[116] Therefore, the kind of Puritan-separatist legacy Smyth took with him to Amsterdam, may not have been that "pure" after all. Anyhow, his convictions and confessions evolved into theological positions close to those of the Anabaptist Hans de Ries (1553–1638). Evidently, De Ries fostered Smyth on his spiritual journey in Amsterdam,[117] and accordingly put his imprint on his legacy, which was carried over the North Sea and the English Channel.

---

[114] W.T. Whitley and A.J.D. Farrer, "Continental Anabaptists and Early English Baptists," *Baptist Quarterly* 2/1 (1925): 24–36, and White, *The English Separatist Tradition*, 116–141.

[115] Stephen Holmes, "When Did John Smith Embrace Arminianism—And Was the First Baptist Congregation "Particular"?," *Baptist Quarterly* 52/4 (2021): 146–157. "*The Mennonites had a profound effect on Baptist beginnings, being the cause of the Smyth-Helwys church abandoning its Calvinism*" (157, italics in original). See also Lee, *The Theology of John Smyth*, xi–xiv, 1.

[116] See Earnest Payne, "Contacts between Mennonites and Baptists," *Foundations* 4/1 (1961): 39–55. See also Estep, *The Anabaptist Story*, 271–303. "From the available evidence, it seems more than mere chance that the separatist movement in England bore such close resemblance to sixteenth-century Anabaptism. Apparently, some segments within English Separatism only lacked a more favorable climate in order to emerge into fully developed Anabaptist churches" (283). "The General Baptists were to reflect in both their basic tenets and practices their indebtedness to John Smyth and the Mennonites" (291). Compare also Coggins, *John Smyth's Congregation*, 23–25. "The dualistic theology also led the Smyth congregation to accept (and possibly to emphasize) many aspects of Mennonite doctrine" (122).

[117] Lee, *The Theology of John Smyth*, 292: "To say that Smyth became a disciple of Hans de Ries is extreme, yet it may be the best way to capture the relationship between Smyth and Ries [*sic*].... Through his theological legacy, Smyth continued to influence the English General Baptists for decades."

It is important not to be stuck in between Anglo-centred and American-European centred theories of Baptist beginnings.[118] My position is that of multiple belonging, which evolves from the preference for dynamic and polygenetic research. Smyth was no longer "at home" in England after he left, and later he did not feel at home in Amsterdam with his predecessor Ainsworth (and Johnson too), and finally he felt no longer at home with Helwys and others, his own colleagues and friends. So, Smyth remained the nomad he had become. His faith transformed contextually, continuously, into the flux of a mind of multiple belongings.

We now want to go back about a century and focus on the genesis of Anabaptism. Smyth, after all, had developed sympathy in Amsterdam for a variant of this peculiar Christian direction.

---

[118] See Ian Sellers, "Edwardians, Anabaptists and the Problem of Baptist Origins," *Baptist Quarterly* 29/3 (1981): 97–112.

2

Anabaptists

The so-called Waterlanders formed a *Doopsgezinde* (Anabaptist) community[1] in and around Amsterdam. At the beginning of the seventeenth century, it was under the firm leadership of Lubbert Gerritsz (1535–1612) and Reynier Wijbrandtsz (1570–1645).[2] The Anabaptist tradition in Holland goes back originally to the Frisian[3] folk preacher Menno Simons (1496–1561), who has been called the spiritual "father" of Anabaptism as far as the Netherlands is concerned.

In the second half of the sixteenth century, Anabaptism had left deep scars on the ecclesiastical landscape of the Low Countries. One hundred years later, the Republic was probably

---

[1] The *Doopsgezinde* (Lit: *Baptism-minded*) Church in the Netherlands is the Mennonite branch of Anabaptism.
[2] Except for the nobility, there were no family names in use until these were introduced by Napoleon. The second name was usually a reference to the father's name. In the name Menno Simons (or Simonsz), for instance, the second name is an abbreviated form of *Simon's Zoon*, or Simon's son. Later, his name would be written as Menno Simons.
[3] Referring to the people from Fryslân (Friesland), see the map of the Netherlands of 1609 on page xix.

home to no less than 60,000 Anabaptists, which was about 3 per cent of the population at the time. The largest concentrations were in the northern provinces, and at the end of the sixteenth century, no less than a quarter of the Frisian population was Anabaptist.[4]

Because of their quirky ideas about church, baptism, government and the end times, the Anabaptists were regularly wanted by authorities and persecuted in the course of the sixteenth century. They were perceived as a spiritual aberration and a threat by both Catholics and Protestants. As reprehensible as this intolerance may seem to us, it is nevertheless understandable why, for centuries, people viewed Anabaptists with a certain resistance, almost by default. The Anabaptist movement was strongly divided, and not infrequently, dominant splinter groups developed a militant and even warlike orientation. The classic example of this is the occupation of the city of Münster, from 1534 to 1536, by violent, mainly Dutch Anabaptists.[5]

2.1 Münster

Militant piety as a spiritual attitude may be far removed from the average Christian today, but among early Dutch Anabaptists there were groups of Christians who were deeply convinced the kingdom of God was at hand, and they felt this expectation justified an aggressive stance toward the existing authorities. Thus,

---

[4] In 1665, Friesland alone had about 20,000 Mennonites. Selderhuis, *Handboek*, 398, 299.
[5] See Barbara Rommé, *Das Königreich der Täufer. Reformation und Herrschaft der Täufer in Münster*, Band 1 (Münster: Stadtmuseum, 2000) and *Das Königreich der Täufer. Die münsterischen Täufer im Spiegel der Nachwelt*, Band 2 (Münster: Stadtmuseum, 2000); Barbara Rommé, ed., *Das Königreich der Täufer in Münster—Neue Perspektiven*, Edition Kulturregiion Münsterland (Münster: Lit Verlag, 2003). See also Karl-Heinz Kirchhoff, *Die Täufer in Münster 1534/35. Untersuchungen zum Umfang und zur Sozialstruktur der Bewegung*, Geschichtliche Arbeiten zur Westfälischen Landesforschung 12 (Münster: Aschendorffsche Verlagsbuchhandlung, 1973); Hermann von Kerssenbrock, *Narrative of the Anabaptist Madness: The Overthrow of Münster, the Famous Metropolis of Westphalia*, Studies in the History of Christian Traditions 132 (Leiden: Brill, 2007); George Huntston Williams, *The Radical Reformation*, Sixteenth Century Essays & Studies 15 (Kirksville: Sixteenth Century Journal Publishers, 1992), 553–588; and Ralf Klötzer, "The Melchiorites and Münster," in John D. Roth, James M. Stayer, ed., *A Companion to Anabaptism and Spiritualism, 1521–1700*, Brill's Companions to the Christian Tradition 6 (Leiden: Brill, 2007), 217–256.

Jan Matthijsz (d. 1534) and Jan van Leiden (1502–1535)[6] (aka. Jan Beukelsz) and others believed they should act in the name of God and take the city of Münster and make it a kingdom of God. In the 1530s, both men led a fanatical Anabaptist movement in the vicinity of Haarlem, Amsterdam and Leiden.

Initially, it was believed God would intervene in 1533 and put an end to the socially and economically miserable conditions which existed in the Netherlands in that time. Industry was at a standstill, the import of precious metals from America had caused a sharp depreciation in the value of money, taxes for ordinary citizens were high and heavy, there was internal unrest and the dreaded plague made many victims.[7] In this time of economic crisis, many vulnerable and easily influenced people were eager to hear a message of hope and intervention from God. There was little to expect from the Roman Catholic Church, which seemed mostly interested in maintaining the status quo, so the message of the Anabaptists struck a chord in various circles. After all, the end of times had arrived, the world stage would soon be turned upside down and the social roles would be reversed. The lowest would be the highest and those, who were now the first would soon be made the last.

In 1533, when the end of the world did not occur, Matthijsz and van Leiden claimed faithful believers should establish the kingdom of God themselves. Matthijsz, especially, came up with revolutionary revelations in which God assigned him the leadership over various cities. After all, that is how it was written in the Bible. At the return of Christ, the Lord would ask Jesus' followers what they had earned with the "trading" of their talents. Did they make a profit or not? Those who yielded tenfold were given control of ten cities. Those who yielded five times their original capital received five cities. Those who did not want to run an investment risk and had done nothing with their growth opportunities to serve the kingdom of God would be rejected at the Lord's return.[8]

---

[6] Rather than using their fathers' names for further identification, some people were named by their place of origin. So, Jan van Leiden was said to originate from the university town of Leiden.
[7] See Bert Pauw, "Slinkse oogmerken achter het masker van godsdienst," *Haarlems Dagblad*, 15 februari 1986.
[8] Read Luke 19:11–27.

The militant Anabaptist movement certainly dared to take risks. Jan Matthijsz was already claiming God's allocation of several cities, including Amsterdam and Münster. The city of Amsterdam actually seemed to place itself under his authority for some time.[9] At the same time, some 3,000 Anabaptist Christians from the Northern Netherlands marched on Münster.[10]

The Haarlem prophet knew how to deliver his message convincingly. At the end of 1533, Jan Matthijsz and Jan van Leiden, along with several faithful followers, went to Münster to claim the German city once and for all for God and his people. For some time already, the population had been fed up with Catholic oppression, so the opportunities for the Dutch Anabaptists were strong. Moreover, Anabaptist ideas were already fomenting in Münster. The Westphalian Bernard Rothman (c.1495–1535) had gained a great deal of influence there, and can be seen as the founder of the heretical movement in the episcopal city.[11] His closest associate was the Münster cloth merchant Bernard Knipperdolling (c. 1495–1536). Münster was to be one of the kingdom places where the faithful would serve the Lord completely and they would taste the King's powers in all their perfection. According to Bernhard Rothmann, it was a misunderstanding to think the kingdom of God would only dawn at the Last Day, at the resurrection from the dead.[12]

---

[9] An attack on the Amsterdam City Hall was repelled on May 10, 1535. Some forty Anabaptists, including several women, were executed. A shocking event had taken place as early as February. A group of ecstatic Anabaptists had run naked through the streets of Amsterdam shouting, "Woe, woe upon the world and the wicked." The group was arrested and convicted. See A.F. Mellink, *De wederdopers in de noordelijke nederlanden (1531–1544)/ The Anabaptists in the Northern Netherlands (1531–1544)* (Leeuwarden: Gerben Dykstra, 1981), 67–78, 119–149.
[10] On this history, see especially Luc Panhuysen, *De beloofde stad. Opkomst en ondergang van het koninkrijk der Wederdopers* (Amsterdam: Atlas, 2000).
[11] Mellink, *The Anabaptists in the Northern Netherlands*, 20.
[12] "Ynn summa: Gades volck, welck averblyfft, dat unbefleckt und rein in aller gehorsamicheit wesen sall, moth de erden ynnemmen unde Christo dem Könninge aver de gantze erde tho deinste staen. Dit woerdt alle by dusser tydt gescheen, unde dar up erden, darup de gerechticheit alß dan wonen sal. Dat men de schrifft will vorstaen na dem Yuengesten dage, dat de dan soll vollenbracht werden, is ein mißverstand." See Bernhard Rothmann, "Eyne Restitution edder eine Wedderstellinge rechter unnde gesunder christliker Leer, Gelovens unde Levens uth Gades Genaden durch de Gemeinte Christi tho Munster an den Dach Gegevenn (eind 1534)," in *Reformatorica: Teksten uit de geschiedenis van het Nederlandse protestantisme,* ed. C. Augustijn, F.G.M.

The Dutch Anabaptists managed to secretly enter Münster through one of the city gates. The town hall was then taken by force. Immediately afterward, Matthijsz appointed himself the prophet Enoch (an end-time prophet[13]) and the inhabitants of Münster who did not want to be rebaptized were ordered to leave the city immediately. In one night, all "unbelievers," including the sick and elderly, were expelled from the city. The possessions of those who stayed behind were strictly controlled. Only Bibles were allowed to be read. All other types of books were collected and burned. Church buildings were vandalized or destroyed, ornaments and paintings were roughly removed. Furthermore, the faithful had to donate their valuables, such as gold and silver, to the "prophet Enoch." The fearful signs of a true reign of terror presented themselves, and this was only the beginning. All kinds of so-called "apostles" were sent from Münster into the surrounding areas to proclaim the message of the kingdom. Unrest broke out in many places, and wherever possible the emissaries of Münster made good use of it.

Although the bishop of Münster did everything he could to regain control of the city, the Anabaptists were able to repel the attacks. However, Prophet Matthijsz lost his life during one of the attacks. His successor, Jan van Leiden, became the new ruler of the German Zion.[14] Supported by prophecies and dreams, he encouraged the defeated citizens and, according to tradition, he walked through the city completely naked. Then van Leiden declared that God had granted him the authority of Moses. However, this authority was not enough for him, so Jan had a public assembly convened and had the prophecy pronounced that it was "God's will" that Jan Beukelsz should be king of Zion and sit on the throne of David—after which Jan announced he would accept this calling.

The new king then had himself beautifully clothed, with a golden crown, numerous rings, a chain with a golden globe and a precious sword in a golden scabbard. New money with Jan's

---

Broeyer, P. Visser, E.G.E. van der Wall (Zoetermeer: Meinema, 1996), 57.
[13] See Revelation 11:3–6. Enoch had never died and could therefore return (Gen 5:24).
[14] Zion is a hill near the city of Jerusalem, and it has become symbolic of the City of God in Scripture. See Psalm 2:6.

Jan van Leiden
(1502–1535)

image on it were also put into circulation.¹⁵ The king could regularly be admired in full regalia in the market square, where he sat on a real throne and ruled over the city. The time of God's judgement and vengeance was at hand and therefore, according to the Münster prophets, it was lawful to use violence. All ungodliness had to be rooted out, both in Münster and wherever the prophets and apostles sent by Jan van Leiden could actively assume authority. Women and children, body and soul, were to be put at risk for this purpose:

Now dear brethren, the time of avenging has come. God has begotten and equipped the promised David¹⁶ for the vengeance and punishment of Babylon and its people.... Therefore, dear brethren, be ye prepared for battle, not only with the humble weapon of the apostles in suffering, but also with the strong armor of David, to avenge with God's aid and power all Babylonian violence, and to root out all ungodliness. Be undaunted to risk goods, woman, child and your own body.¹⁷

---

15 Many of these objects can still be seen in the Museum of Münster.
16 A "new David" is foretold in Scripture. See Isaiah 11:1, 10 and Jeremiah 30:9; 33:15, 17.
17 "Nu leven breeder, de tyt der Wrake ys an uns gelanget, Godt hefft den belaveden David verwecket, gerustet thor wrake unde straffe aver Babylon mit sinem Volcke... Hirumme, leven breeder, rustet yw thom stryde, nicht alleine mit oethmoedigen wapen der Apostel thom liden, Sunder ock mit dem herliken Harnische David tho avenge, mit Gades Krafte unde Hulpe al de Babilonissche gewalt unde al dat Godlose weszen uththoradden, Weszet unvortzaget, gudt wyff, kyndt und lyff yn de schantze tho flahen." See "Eyn gantz troestlick bericht van de Wrake unde straffe des Babilonischen gruwels, an alle ware Israeliten und Bundtgenoten Christi, hir unde dar verstroyet, durch de gemeinte Christi tho Munster (1534)" in *Documenta Reformatoria: Texts from the History of Church and Theology in the Netherlands since the Reformation*, part 1, ed.

A misjudgement became more or less fatal to the Dutch "king" when he declared one day that God had given him and other believers the privilege of having more than one wife. Immediately, a commission was set up to investigate the number of marriageable young daughters in the city. All marriageable women were summoned to enter into matrimony as soon as possible.

Naturally, this measure aroused resistance and opposition among the men of Münster. Their loyalty was severely tested. Jan van Leiden immediately took three wives. His harem would, in the course of time, grow to as many as sixteen women. After all, only by marrying often and fathering many children could the number of Münster believers quickly grow to 140,000—exactly this biblical number was necessary, according to Jan, to achieve perfect salvation.[18] He was certainly not alone in thinking up such speculative end-time scenarios. End-time thinking was in the air in the first half of the sixteenth century.

When an attempt on King Jan's life was foiled, he proved to be a ruthless despot. For the slightest transgressions, the citizens were cruelly put to death. Meanwhile, one orgy after another took place in the city. After fifteen months of tyranny, Münster was again besieged by episcopal troops in the spring of 1535. In the city, the consequences of the encirclement were soon felt. The morale of the population was undermined by hunger and disease, adding to the fact that many no longer supported the king because of his delusions of grandeur and polygamy. The misery within the city walls reached such proportions that here and there people even resorted to cannibalism. Yet, the fall of Jan van Leiden's kingdom did not come through hunger, but by treachery. Some defectors pointed out a weak spot in the fortress to the besiegers and, in the night of June 24–25, 1535, the city gate was breached and episcopal troops could enter the city. Despite fierce resistance, Jan's men were defeated that day. The twenty-six-year-old Jan van Leiden himself was terribly tortured, and killed on January 22, 1536. Then, together with other leaders of the Münster kingdom, their bodies were hoisted in iron cages on the

---

J.N. Bakhuizen van den Brink, W.F. Dankbaar, W.J. Kooiman, D. Nauta, N. van der Zijpp (Kampen: Kok, 1960), 44–45.
[18] See Revelation 7:4 and 14:1.

spire of St. Lambert Church. Those who visit Münster today can still see the three cages hanging from this tower.

2.2 Peaceful Anabaptists persecuted

We can imagine that the drama of Münster was earth-shattering news in those days. Now, every Anabaptist was seen as a fantasist, a dreamer—and a possible danger. On March 9, 1535, when the power of Jan van Leiden was at its height, the Holy Roman Emperor Charles V (1500–1558) issued an imperial edict against the Anabaptists. The decree was intended "to eradicate and destroy this accursed sect of Anabaptists…which…is daily waxing and more and more proliferating."[19] No wonder peace-loving Anabaptists felt the need to distance themselves from the club of Jan van Leiden, and to clearly distinguish their own community from the Münster group.

One of the most famous Anabaptist opponents of van Leiden was Menno Simons. Menno had nothing to do with the aggressive "gospel" that was being preached in Münster. As a Christian, he renounced the sword and taught that there was only one true King, Jesus Christ. No man could sit on the chair of King Jesus. Christians ought to always obey, and certainly not to overthrow the authorities who did not forbid obedience to the Word of God:

> This we say unto you in Christ Jesus, that in a spiritual sense we teach, know, or allow no King David but the unseen King Christ Jesus, who hath all power in heaven and on earth, and who alone is Lord of lords and King of kings.… As for life on earth, we urge people to obey kings, lords, and all governments with regard to earthly matters, if they do not command us to go against God's Word, for so God has commanded it.… We teach, know and allow no other sword than the sword of the Spirit, namely God's Word.… Anyone who reaches for another sword asks to be killed by it.[20]

---

[19] A.F. Mellink, ed., *Documenta Anabaptistica Neerlandica, Part 1: Friesland and Groningen (1530–1550)*, Kerkhistorische Bijdragen VI/I (Leiden: Brill, 1975), 25.
[20] From Menno Simons, *Dat Fundament des Christelycken Leers* (1539/40) in ed. Augustijn, et al, *Reformatorica*, 63.

From their beginnings, Mennonite Anabaptism seemed to characterize itself as a kind of Christian peace movement. Obbe Philipsz (c. 1500–1588) and Dirk Philipsz (1504–1568), names of two brothers from Leeuwarden[21] proverbially associated with early Dutch Anabaptist movement, also rejected the revolutionary ideas of Matthijsz and van Leiden. Even though they were quite alone in their peace protests at the beginning of the wave of insurrection, after 1536 they and Menno Simons together laid the foundation for a form of Anabaptism that developed rapidly and could boast a continuing history.

Around 1545, fanatical and aggressive Anabaptism had all but disappeared from the scene.[22] However, the presence of peaceful Mennonites did not take away from the fact that Anabaptists still had to be on their guard. From the early Reformation until 1600, about 2,000 people were executed for their beliefs in the Northern Netherlands. The majority of this group were Anabaptists by faith. For example, on October 21, 1536, a certain Zijbrand Obbezoon was sentenced to death by the court of Friesland.[23]

Menno Simons
(1496–1561)

---

[21] The capital city of Friesland.
[22] See Mellink, *De wederdopers in de noordelijke nederlanden*, 416–420. See Nigel Wright, *Free Church, Free State: The Positive Baptist Vision* (Carlisle: Paternoster Press, 2005), 33. The Batenburgers did still constitute an aggressive continuation of the Münsterian ideal, see Piet Visser, "Mennonites and Baptists in the Netherlands, 1535-1700," in *A Companion to Anabaptism and Spiritualism, 1521-1700*, Brill's Companions to the Christian Tradition 6, ed. John D. Roth, James M. Stayer (Leiden: Brill, 2007), 301–302.
[23] On Friesland during the time of the Reformation, see Jan Juliaan Woltjer, *Friesland in Hervormingstijd* (Leiden: Universitaire Pers, 1962).

Zijbrand had been rebaptized and then pardoned, because he had done penance and recanted his baptism. When some time later he became involved in rebaptism again, he was arrested again and handed over to the executioner.

> Because the court of Friesland has found out by confession and otherwise that Zijbrand Obbezoon, who was present here, had himself rebaptized in the winter of 1534, after which, having received his punishment and having renounced the baptism, he was granted freedom, and despite this rejection and agreement he committed perjury and still joined the sect of the Anabaptists again and was found in the Oldeklooster with these rebellious and deceitful people.... therefore this Court demands...and decides that Zijbrand Obbezoon shall be put to death by the executioner with the sword, that his body shall be put on a wheel and his head on a stake. Also, all his possessions shall be confiscated. So done and declared on October 21, 1536.[24]

In 1549, Anabaptists in Friesland were still being arrested and sentenced to death. On May 27 of that year, Lysbet Dircxdochter[25] was sentenced to death, and was presumed to teach Anabaptist beliefs.[26]

She was also, probably unjustly, thought to be the wife of Menno Simons. Menno Simons had been a priest in Pingjum and Witmarsum in Friesland since 1524, but came to new insights by his careful study of the Bible. At that time, the Scriptures were sometimes still a closed book, even for clergy. In April 1535, the spiritually hungry Menno Simons came to a living faith in Jesus Christ. After a fierce inner struggle over his own impurity and hypocrisy, he came to surrender to God and truly learned the grace and forgiveness of Christ.[27] From those moments on, following Jesus coincided with carrying a cross, and Simons went among the Anabaptists in the northern provinces, to encourage and edify them.

---

[24] Mellink, *Documenta Anabaptistica Neerlandica*, Vol. 1, 49–50.
[25] The daughter of Dircx.
[26] Mellink, *Documenta Anabaptistica Neerlandica*, Vol. 1, 85.
[27] Estep, *The Anabaptist Story*, 163–165.

Early in 1536, Menno Simons was baptized and in the following year the pastor was confirmed as an elder in the Anabaptist community in Groningen by Obbe Philipsz. Miraculously, the Anabaptist reformer travelled up and down Northern Germany and the Northern Netherlands for years without ever being imprisoned. The government had even put a hefty sum of money on the head of this remarkable Dutchman. Menno Simons died in 1561, at Bad Oldesloe, at the age of sixty-five.

How humane and peaceful the Anabaptists were shortly after Menno's death is illustrated by the story of a certain Dirk Willems in 1569. Dirk Willems (d. 1569) was born in Asperen, on the Linge, near Leerdam. As a young man he had already been baptized. After some time, young people were baptized in his house as well. When the established church and the authorities got wind of this, Dirk Willems was convicted of rebaptism, searched and put behind bars.

When the Anabaptist Christian saw an opportunity to flee, he did not let it pass. He tied a rope from rags and clothing and lowered himself from the window of the prison. When he got down to the ground, he ran. He had to, because his escape had been discovered and the chase had begun. One of the pursuers was almost on Dirk's heels. The escape route led both men over the thin ice of the Hondegat. For Dirk, this was no problem.

He was not heavy; his time in prison had also made him lose a few more kilograms. Nevertheless, he was seriously weakened, so his pursuer could easily overtake him. The ice, however, was not strong enough to support the heavier man who was chasing Dirk, so under his weight, the ice broke and the man sank into the cold water. Dirk heard the ice break and looked back. His pursuer disappeared into the water, surfaced and tried to hold on to the ice, but the ice broke off. It was clear the man was in mortal danger and would drown. What was Dirk Willems to do? He was a free man and could run on—finally freed from shackles and pursuers. Or he could save the man and take a big risk. It was clear for Dirk what to do. He quickly ran up to the man and reached out to him. Only when the latter was pulled onto the ice did he realize it was the fugitive who had saved him. Then came the curious moment when the shivering man had to arrest

Dirk Willems rescues his pursuer

Dirk and take him back to prison. He wanted to give his rescuer his freedom, but his superiors demanded Dirk Willems be held in prison.

Weeks of confinement passed, until it was proclaimed in the courtroom that

> since Dirk Willems, born at Asperen, has confessed that at the age of fifteen he was rebaptized at Rotterdam and that in his house at Asperen he has repeatedly had people rebaptized, the aforementioned judges sentence Dirk Willems to be put to death by fire.[28]

---

[28] See D*e Martelaarsspiegel*, by the Dordt Anabaptist predecessor Van Braght, a classic book in which many accounts of the sufferings of Anabaptist martyrs are recorded (1st ed., 1660; 1685 improved and enlarged reprint, with 104 prints by Jan Luyken). http://plautdietsch.22web.org/documents/martiera-ep.pdf?i=1

On May 16, 1569, Willems was led to the stake near Asperen and burned. Though the man was now dead, the spirit of non-violence and humanity that graced him lived on. The town of Asperen even has a street named after him.[29]

2.3 A brief history of Anabaptist origins

The Anabaptist movement of Menno Simons thus continued peacefully, joining in confession and thought with a number of early Anabaptists from Switzerland and southern Germany—such as Conrad Grebel, Felix Mantz, George Blaurock and Michael Sattler.[30] These early Anabaptists taught that the church of Christ consisted of believers who, through baptism, shared in the new life that the Lord bestowed. Life with Christ made the Christian share in a radically new history. The life history of a believer was thus human and "divine" history at the same time. The Christian had a dual identity, where Christlikeness and his personal identity were interwoven.[31]

Mennonites did distinguish themselves from their spiritual relatives by their strongly penitential orientation. An austere lifestyle, great emphasis on obedience and penance, even gave the impression of a movement that was still entirely in the Catholic context of the time. In any case, when Menno Simons thought of the notion of *discipleship*, he was thinking more of obedience in faith, suffering and fear of God than of the modern idea of voluntary following and personal victory.[32] Believer's baptism expressed, first and foremost, obedience to Christ and with it a willingness to suffer for the name of the Lord. In baptism, each

---

[29] See also the historical drama *Dirk's Exodus* by James C. Juhnke.
[30] Anabaptism has a complex genesis, and not all names associated with it were advocates of non-violence. One can distinguish a Swiss, a South German/Austrian and a North German/Hollandic root. Naturally, these have interactions. See C. Arnold Snyder, *Anabaptist History and Theology*, rev. student ed. (Kitchener: Pandora Press, 1997), 5, 111.
[31] See Olof de Vries, *Leer en praxis van de vroege dopers uitgelegd als een theologie van de geschiedenis* (Utrecht: Rijksuniversiteit, 1982), 153–154.
[32] Marjan Blok, "Discipleship in Menno Simons' *Dat Fundament*: An Exercise in Anabaptist Theology," in *Menno Simons: A Reappraisal*, ed. Gerald R. Brunk (Harrisonburg: Eastern Mennonite College, 1992), 105–129. See also Visser, "Mennonites and Baptists in the Netherlands," 305.

believer was allowed to consciously experience God's history in following Jesus. In this sense, Anabaptists had a strong awareness of the history God was sharing with the church. It was a history of following Christ that would never lead to great worldly success.

Baptism was about a historical imitation of the Son of God, not a complicated theological construct that substituted baptism for circumcision. Anabaptists had difficulty with the many theological abstractions that established churches, whether Roman Catholic or Protestant, used in their teaching and confessions. For example, in their view, the doctrine of predestination was so abstract that it seemed largely removed from the daily practice of life with Christ. In delving into predestination, one spoke of eternal decrees, thereby entering a path of speculative theology. Surely, a Christian could not do much with the *idea* of a super-historical election in his daily life with God? Anabaptists therefore, emphasized the *practical-historical* character of salvation.

Outside of ordinary life, there was no possibility of participating in God's salvation. Anabaptists were therefore critical of the academic theological constructs of reformers such as Luther, Zwingli and Calvin. How could anyone be a Christian solely by election? Did not this Reformed doctrine encourage false security and false safety? Surely, Jesus warned us that the tree is recognized by its fruit? What use is election if there is little or no fruit? Were Lutherans and Calvinists not reversing the truths of faith?

Zwingli and his students

The discussion of the historical character of salvation was at the root of the origins of the Swiss Anabaptist denomination. Beginning in 1521, the Zürich reformer Huldrych Zwingli (1484–1531) had gathered around him a group of students with whom he read classical writings. These included works by the philosopher Plato. With this initiative, we clearly see the humanistic spirit of Zwingli's reformed thinking coming to the fore (and again the influence of Erasmus). By rereading the classics, including the gospel, Western civilization had to be brought back to its historical sources. This common feeling determined the humanist agenda.[33]

---

[33] This Christian humanism must be distinguished from later humanism. The Christian humanists were not concerned with "man" in himself but with who this man

Huldrych Zwingli (1484–1531)   Conrad Grebel (1498–1526)

Over the years, Zwingli's daily early morning study meetings became increasingly popular (Fridays were kept free) and were characterized as moments of "Prophezei."³⁴

A young promising student named Conrad Grebel (1498–1526) also joined the study group. Grebel, son of a wealthy patrician, had received a scholarly education in Vienna and Paris and had returned to Zürich in 1520, where he studied Greek language and literature under Zwingli. The following year, Grebel joined the Reformation and broke with his Roman Catholic background and family.

---

was before God outside the usual church channels. For this reflection they went *ad fontes* (back to the old Christian sources).

34 See C.A. Tukker, "Zwingli en de Nederlanden," in *Zwingli in vierderlei perspectief*, ed. W. Balke, W. van't Spijker, C.A. Tukker, K.M. Witteveen (Utrecht: De Banier, 1984), 119–123. First the Vulgate was read, then the Hebrew text and the Greek translation (of an Old Testament passage) were studied and commented on. Finally, someone gave an application. Everyone could ask questions and participate in the discussion. The meetings lasted one hour.

In and around Zürich, there was a ferment of unrest and expectation in those days.[35] The fire of the Reformation took hold and stirred many people. At first all hope was placed on Zwingli, priest and preacher of the great cathedral in Zürich.

By the end of 1522, Zwingli had resigned his ecclesiastical office and become a city pastor, falling under the direct responsibility of the city council. The converted priest was well on his way to winning over local politicians to his Reformation views. The expectations of Zwingli's circle were also high. The reformer's sermons were sharp and pointed, especially where the abuses of the church were concerned. In his plans for reform, Zwingli relied primarily on the "weapon" of conciliar discussion. When church policy issues needed to be discussed, a town hall meeting was usually called, where free debate with fellow townspeople and other interested parties could take place. Sometimes, hundreds of invited guests would gather, in order to reach consensus. Yet, it was the city council which, after discussion, always retained final responsibility and power of decision. Zwingli hoped in this way—and he was a good debater—to work out the Reformation gradually.

Separation

Conrad Grebel and dozens of like-minded people did not deviate from their teacher, but after a few years they became severely disappointed in the reformer. It even came to an open rift between Zwingli and some young students, who felt their teacher did not support his own plans for reform consistently enough.[36]

Early in 1523, turmoil arose in the countryside around Zürich over the duty to give up tithes to the omnipresent Catholic Church. The Church had so far always collected tithes from the people and had instructed priests to strictly observe this rule. Especially among the peasantry, who were predominantly poor and did not understand why the church needed wealth, the idea arose that

---

[35] See Snyder, *Anabaptist History and Theology*, 103–104, and especially (also for the sequel) "Swiss Anabaptism: The Beginnings," in *A Companion to Anabaptism and Spiritualism, 1521–1700*, Brill's Companions to the Christian Tradition 6, ed. John D. Roth, James M. Stayer (Leiden: Brill, 2007), 45–81.

[36] See H. Veldman, *Huldrych Zwingli: Hervormer van kerk en samenleving* (Goes: Oosterbaan & Le Cointre, 1984), 87.

believers should not have to contribute to the upkeep of a clergy who would not listen to Scripture.

The unrest was not innocent, and the Zürich City Council had to come to a policy decision. Now it came down to standing firm, even for Zwingli, and showing that Reformation positions had inner urgency. Although Zwingli was convincing in his argument, in June the city council decided otherwise and Zwingli had to resign himself to this decision. It was felt that the time was not yet ripe for radical measures, such as the abolition of the church tithe law. The other Swiss cantons even threatened military intervention. The reformer may have been disappointed himself, and there is no indication that Zwingli's and Grebel's views were diverging at the time.

However, Zwingli, Grebel and the non-conformist rebellious people inside and outside the city did not give in easily. The next debate scheduled for October 1523 concerned the celebration of the Mass and the use of images of saints in church services. Here and there radical reformers had already been proactive, and several church buildings were made free of images. Everything that had to do with saint worship was removed and demolished. The public discussion was to clarify these actions and determine what decision the city council should take. The question for many was whether the spirit of the Reformation would now achieve victory or whether it would again end in defeat.

During this second Zürich religious discussion, Zwingli was assisted by Balthasar Hubmaier (1480–1528), the reformer from Waldshut. Hubmaier, like Zwingli, defended the idea that Holy Communion was a meal of remembrance and that there could be no question of a so-called *transubstantiation* (the literal change of bread and wine into the body and blood of Christ). Both teachers also refuted from Scripture the liturgical use of images of saints, as well as personal prayer to saints. Even here, Zwingli was in line with the other champions of the Reformation, and even now he was convincing. And yet, although Zwingli no longer wanted to make concessions, he was once again forced to hold back. The city council, fearing a civil war (there was a threat from other Swiss districts), did not dare to change its mind and abolish the Catholic mass and the worship of images.

Zwingli's vision was still clear. The teacher was convinced that the government had no right to judge Scripture, and that its authority extended no further than to examine how best to implement the results of religious discussions in a political sense. But the local government of Zürich had no desire to impose the Reformation on those who disagreed. The city council preferred to remain conservative rather than risk a bloody revolution. For the fanatical reformers, this decision meant that an unacceptable brake was put on the magisterial reformation. This was also the opinion of Hubmaier, and he too would later break with Zwingli.

This group of radicals believed Zwingli had taken too much of a middle course after the strategic religious conference of October 1523, at which over 900 delegates were present. The reformer wanted to "run with the hare and hunt with the hounds." Zwingli, as the spiritual shepherd of the flock, did not want to run faster than the rear of the flock. Grebel and others, so to speak, wanted to lead the flock by setting the pace. In December 1523, Zwingli split with many of his enthusiastic fellow clergymen for this reason. There are indications that the bitterness occurred only in the week shortly before Christmas 1523. What had happened?

After the religious discussion in October of that year, it had been decided by the competent city council that prior to the abolition of the Mass and the use of statues in church buildings, a tract on the why and how of this decision should be prepared in the name of the city council. The purpose of this was to make Reformation thought understandable and accessible to every citizen in the city. Zwingli drafted the text, which was proclaimed as the official position of the Zürich magistracy on November 17, 1523. Meanwhile, everyone was called upon to maintain the necessary calm and quiet.

About three weeks later, the city was again rocked by violent reactions against the customary Catholic Mass. A pile of liturgical books had been put out with the trash, and some chaplains from Zwingli's district refused to celebrate the usual Mass any longer, because each time the people present began to whistle and hiss. It seemed as though the unrest was not inconvenient for Zwingli either, because now the city council had to rethink the timetable for ecclesiastical changes. In any case, it had now become obvious that a good portion of the people preferred to see the classical Mass abolished. The council therefore convened a committee of wise men to give *Ratschlag* (advice). Zwingli was also among these wise men. Shortly after December 10, 1523, the commission came out with a new proposal that, had it been implemented as it was, would have radically altered the course of Protestant church history.

The commission of three wise men decided to introduce a reformatory form of Communion on Christmas Day 1523. After all, it was no longer possible to wait to introduce what the people of God seemed to need so badly: the true worship of God in church celebrations. The commission of wise men was resolute in this. At the same time, the commission called for tolerance. A tolerant attitude was advocated toward those who had not yet reached that point. Priests who still wanted to celebrate Mass in the old style should be able to do so. They were not to be hindered in their work. However, it was clear they would not be replaced after their retirement. Conversely, believers could not be forced to take communion against their will. Believers had to be free to take their own position on this sensitive issue.

It is unfortunate that the city council did not immediately adopt the advice of the committee of wise men in its entirety. The text was passed on to a broader committee, which included the three drafters, but where they held a minority position. The discussion now had to continue with no fewer than eight counsellors and three ecclesiastical prelates. After the deliberations, the assembly came out with a text, again drafted by Zwingli, which differed subtly in wording from the previous one. While they agreed with the earlier text, they were also focused on compromise. The intention to renew the liturgy during the coming Christmas celebration was weakened. The text was clearly a fruit of the forced search for consensus.

On December 19, therefore, the city council rejected both proposals and quietly stuck to the old, and so the time-honoured Mass remained unchanged. Both parties, radical reformers and moderate reformers, could not reach an agreement, so it was thought better to turn back than to face an end of chaos and revolution in the city. It is noteworthy that Zwingli did not oppose this decision; he exerted no pressure to turn the tide and apparently resigned himself to the situation. As a result, the Mass in

Zürich would be performed for at least one more year.

Apparently Zwingli had changed his mind between December 10 and 19.[37] Added to this was the fact that Zwingli repeatedly allowed himself to be made spokesman for a consensus that was fundamentally at odds with ideas he shared with friends in private. How could this leader ever accept compromise if what he said was true, namely that the Roman Church was a false church and that celebrating the Catholic Mass was tantamount to the sin of idolatry? How could a teacher who taught this with dry eyes and without a trace of indignation keep accepting the status quo?

Believer's baptism

We cannot separate the discussion on waiting or moving quickly from the question of how radical reformers viewed the constitution of the kingdom of God and the kingdom of man. In general, Anabaptists thought more from an awareness of the reality of salvation (the "standing in salvation"). Christ had risen; the old had passed and the new had come.[38] This meant that the world as we knew it, the governments and social order and all manmade structures and relationships would disappear through God's intervention in Christ.[39] The old world had to make way for the new life of God, which was already taking shape in the true church that imitated Christ in everything. That this view sounded quite revolutionary to the ears of Zürich's local politicians was understandable. The political establishment did not seem to be taken seriously by Grebel and his friends in the bright light of God's coming kingdom.

Grebel, moreover, became convinced that following Christ implied the practice of believer's baptism. Those who repented and went the way of Christ had to break with the old—and it was precisely this radical change that was signified by baptism. Baptism by faith made the life of the baptized one pass into the life of Jesus. Baptism thus marked a spiritual transition. Christ included the person to be baptized in his story of the cross and resurrection, and thus the latter entered a new path of life. This new path

---

[37] This is doubted by Robert C. Walton, "Was There a Turning Point of the Zwinglian Reformation?" *The Mennonite Quarterly Review* 42 (1, 1968): 45–56.
[38] 2 Corinthians 5:17.
[39] 1 Corinthians 7:31, "For the outward appearance of this world is passing away."

followed Christ and consistently placed the Christian back into the old world as a stranger, as an alien. Although the Christian was returned by God to the existing world, he was definitely not the same person he had been. He now had a part in the story of Christ. He was "in Christ" and Christ was in him.

This did not mean that daily life for Anabaptists was all about the "already," although this is often how they were perceived. The view of Anabaptists that they thought they were *already* in heaven and were complacent was a caricature. Anabaptists also lived with the unrelenting "not yet" (the unfulfilled salvation).

Hence, among other things, Grebel was against the use of the sword—he felt the sword was not available to Christians. They have to take the way of imperfection and the cross. The symbolic *cross* was a constant reminder of the imperfection and temporality of existence. Life as a Christian was also spent in that imperfection, in sickness and in worry, in a congregation that was always on her way to God. Anabaptist Christians were also bound by this imperfect life, but for Grebel this did not take away from the fact that the new life of God presented itself in the midst of the old. After all, through the resurrection power of Christ, it was possible to choose a new way of thinking and acting in the midst of impermanence and the brokenness of life.

The Anabaptists were also accused of contrasting the New Testament too strongly with the Old Testament. The dispensation of Christ replaced and set aside the Old Testament. It was now the new that was in vogue. But this one-sidedness cannot be discerned from the texts of men like Grebel, Mantz, Sattler, Denck and Hut.[40] On the contrary, they made extensive use of the Old Testament. However, the old, because of its imperfection, was entirely dominated by the new with these Anabaptists. The Old Testament was a foreshadowing of the New, for it could not be that God had moved through two different histories.

The history of God was the history of Christ, foretold in the Old Testament and identified and revealed in the New Testament. Without participating in this one history, there was no salvation

---

40 De Vries, *Leer en praxis van de vroege dopers*, 153–154. See especially Stuart Murray, *Biblical Interpretation in the Anabaptist Tradition*, Studies in the Believers Church Tradition 3 (Kitchener: Pandora Press, 2000).

or redemption, not for the single person and therefore not for the church. Baptists therefore wanted the historicity of the gospel and salvation to remain intact. Salvation was always lived out in Spirit-transformed lives and could not be reduced to mere theological positions of faith. This is why the daily following of Jesus was so important to Anabaptists. A Christian was not recognized by his conviction, faith or Bible knowledge, but by how he or she walked like Christ. No doubt Lutherans and Calvinists would (mostly) agree, but this conviction received greater emphasis in Anabaptism.

The split between Conrad Grebel and Huldrych Zwingli was now final. In January 1525, Grebel, Blaurock and others, met in Zürich in the house of Felix Mantz on Neugasse, near the Grossmünster church. At the religious meeting on January 17, their request to the city council to be allowed to freely baptize on the grounds of faith had been firmly rejected. A daughter had been born in Grebel's house and the father categorically refused to have the child baptized. On the evening of January 21, they were discussing the prohibition of baptism. Suddenly, the ex-priest George Blaurock (1491–1529) stood up from his chair and asked the attending Conrad Grebel to baptize him (by pouring, not by immersion). Grebel agreed and performed the first believer's baptism of those days. Blaurock then baptized the other attendees.[41] On this historic evening, the first Anabaptist "cell" (a self-reproducing core group) was formed on the mainland. In the ensuing years, the community of Anabaptists would spread like an oil slick all across Europe. With the outward appearance of the community of newly baptized, Anabaptism was closely watched and fiercely opposed by the Zürich authorities.

Grebel was resolute in his aversion to violence, a position he shared with many Anabaptists. Any use of outward force to get another to conform was rejected. Only God could convince people, and human rules of faith often lacked "waiting for the Lord." The guidelines for this were given by Christ himself in Matthew 18, in the passage that talks about Christian *discipline*. For example, Jesus never instructed that a sinner should be punished corporally, intimidated or manipulated. A sinner needed to

---

[41] Veldman, *Huldrych Zwingli*, 89–90.

be addressed by God, but his conscience was not served or seared by threats and corporal punishment.[42] Only God could speak words at the level of his conscience and could change his heart—punishments and threats did not reach that depth. Grebel's tone here differed substantially from that of, for example, Thomas Müntzer (c. 1489–1525), with whom he was sometimes erroneously mentioned in the same breath.[43]

The concept of freedom

The year 1525 would forever go down in history as the year in which the Anabaptist movement arose and the peasant revolt took place, as if those two events were two sides of the same coin. But were the Anabaptists really to blame for the peasant revolt? In the first place, we cannot speak of only one peasant war. In the second half of the 1520s, no less than five revolts, separated in time and region, broke out.[44] In the second place, in the peasant revolt, the Reformation had to deal with a brainchild that it had produced itself. Indeed, the peasants who revolted invoked some of the fundamental values of the Reformation. They therefore hoped Luther would take the lead in the armed struggle. The reformer refused, however, because he wanted nothing to do with mixing the gospel with political programs.[45] For Luther, church and government were two separate but equal realms or kingdoms through which the Lord let his light shine in the world.[46]

On the other hand, it could not be denied that Luther's actions had awakened among the people a sense of freedom that would not be limited to the spiritual sphere. The Reformation principles also touched upon a certain form of social emancipation. How

---

42 See De Vries, *Leer en praxis van de vroege dopers*, 27.

43 Thomas Müntzer was originally a supporter of Luther but alienated from him when he took up the sword. Müntzer was one of the leaders of the peasant revolt. He was beheaded in 1525.

44 The Anabaptist movement therefore has several social faces, see Claus-Peter Clasen, *Anabaptism: A Social History, 1525–1618, Switzerland, Austria, Moravia, South and Central Germany* (Ithaca-London: Cornell University Press, 1972). See also Williams, *The Radical Reformation*, 137–174.

45 M.A. van den Berg, *Niet het zwaard maar het Woord. Luther en Müntzer in de Boerenoorlog van 1525* (Kampen: De Groot Goudriaan, 1990), 17.

46 Luther's doctrine of the two kingdoms is discussed in more detail in §4.1. Luther further sharpened this idea after 1525. See Van den Berg, *Niet het zwaard maar het Woord*, 18.

could it be otherwise? Surely, God was not only interested in personal faith? The liberty idea of the Reformation evoked expectations that reached beyond the heart and made critical questions regarding the existing socio-political order. At the very least, the understanding of the Word of God created a desire to experience it freely, without being judged by higher authorities. In any case, the conclusion is justified "that the Reformation, although it cannot be blamed for the Peasants' War, was undoubtedly one of the causes of the new revival and the great expansion of the peasant movement, albeit unconsciously and unintentionally."[47]

The years of the Peasants' Revolt were eventful years, strongly driven by an apocalyptic (end-time) orientation. One was aware of living in "the last days." This was also true of Luther. The end of the world was expected and feared. All kinds of prophets ventured into predictions and time calculations. Judgement day could come at any time.

Well known in those days was the ironic saying:

He who does not in 1523 lose his life,
nor in 1524 in the waters perish
nor beaten to death in 1525,
he great miracles can publish.[48]

Apocalyptic speculations and expectations were constantly in the air, so to speak. The end of the world was expected, and therefore there was also a need for atonement among the masses. Existing churches had a great deal of focus on the penitentials. In addition, the unstable social and economic conditions, as well as the haunting plague, made the average medievalist open to apocalyptic scenarios. It was not just radical Anabaptists who were susceptible—a certain susceptibility to end-time conspiracies prevailed everywhere. We can imagine that on the waves of this apocalyptic tide, all kinds of prophetic figures came and went.

The Reformation movement that swept through Europe in the sixteenth century was more than a transformation of the Catholic dogma of atonement (man is not saved by his own works). It also

---

[47] Van den Berg, *Niet het zwaard maar het Woord*, 18.
[48] Van den Berg, *Niet het zwaard maar het Woord*, 18.

meant an apocalyptic-prophetic correction of the church. The church was to be led back to the Word, and with it, back to its own "pre-eminence." The earthly church would soon cease to exist. The message got through: the existing Catholic Church was not the final form of the kingdom of God, and the Church was by no means the kingdom itself. And it was regrettable that this wave of correction at some point had stalled, short of reaching the final goal. The Reformation was never completely finished, especially with regard to church doctrine; many opportunities were missed. When we think of a Reformation slogan such as the "priesthood of all believers," for example, we do not think of the typical ministerial church that arose in Western Europe in the course of the post-Reformation centuries. We now want to look a little deeper into the revolutionary component of the Reformation.

Andreas Karlstadt

One of the revolutionaries who was originally close to Luther's heart was theologian Andreas Karlstadt (1485–1541).[49] Karlstadt had been Luther's teacher at Wittenberg and had encouraged the young Martin Luther to get his doctorate degree. Until 1523, the two theologians were even colleagues; during that time, there was a cordial and friendly relationship. Not long after, however, Luther was widely praised as the great and celebrated reformer, while Karlstadt was associated with spiritual fanaticism, sedition and subversive resistance. How could this be so? What had happened? It is certain that Karlstadt became interested in Luther's ideas as a result of the spiritual changes he observed in Luther. At Luther's

Andreas Karlstadt
(1485–1541)

---

[49] See Williams, *The Radical Reformation*, 110–120.

urging, Karlstadt bought an edition of Augustine's works, for example, and immersed himself in the writings of this church father. In the spring of 1517, this began to have an effect and Karlstadt also began to look at the question of grace and justice with different eyes.

His conviction grew that Scripture presented not so much God's righteousness as a *demanding* righteousness, but as a *bestowing* righteousness, in and through faith in Christ. In the Catholic tradition, the notion of "God's righteousness" was mostly interpreted as a righteousness God demanded of people.[50] This implied they had to know God's laws accurately and live by the rules, because only on the basis of punctual obedience would God accept them as redeemed.

Luther had recognized that this way of reasoning led to a form of works-righteousness and self-salvation that could drive believers to despair. A person would only be acceptable to God if he obeyed the law as much as possible. The law was thus relegated to a divine strangulation contract, full of fear and threat. Luther knew this from personal experience. As an Augustinian monk, he had worked relentlessly—but unsuccessfully—to banish sin from his life. Only when he recognized that God *accepted* the sinner, and *gave* him the faith to throw himself upon Christ for his salvation, did peace come. Luther could not accomplish what Christ had already done for him. Christ took the punishment for the transgressions of men. That is why he died on the cross. He did what no one else could do. No man could ever die for his sins and live eternally with God.

Those who were set on the unsavoury path of self-righteousness most likely ended their spiritual quest in desperation and despair. No one could ever muster what God demanded. He is the holy and eternal One. Therefore, God did not demand without first giving. Luther and Karlstadt read with Augustine that God wanted to give man in grace what he asked of him. In his *Confessions*, the church father spoke the familiar words, "Give what You command, and then command what You will."[51] Thus, Luther

---

[50] For example, in Micah 6:8, "He has told you, O man, what is good; and what does the Lord require of you but to do justice, and to love kindness, and to walk humbly with your God?" See also Romans 3:21 and 4:22.
[51] Augustine, *Confessions* 10, 29, 40.

and Karlstadt learned to receive from God what they could then give back to him in faith. God thus bestowed the righteousness he asked for.

Paul spoke clear words about this in his letter to the church at Corinth:

> Therefore, we are ambassadors for Christ, God making his appeal through us. We implore you on behalf of Christ, be reconciled to God. For our sake he made him to be sin who knew no sin, so that in him we might become the righteousness of God.[52]

God offered reconciliation through Jesus and could do so because Jesus had become sin for sinful people. Christ, as the sinless Son of God, bore the punishment of others so that anyone who believed this wholeheartedly, could be seen as righteous. Here we see the "joyful exchange" (*fröhliche Wechsel* or *fröhliche Tausch*) that Luther spoke of.[53] Jesus took the place of sinful people so that sinners could come into Jesus' position. But the exchange never worked automatically; it required faith, for only by faith were people justified. "For we hold that one is justified by faith apart from works of the law," Paul stated.[54] This is where Luther's *sola fide* (*allein durch den Glauben*[55]) came from.

Karlstadt also began to teach that righteousness was a gift from God. However, he was careful in his statements. Luther was initially more fanatical and progressive with respect to the progress of the Reformation than his teacher.[56] Luther was sometimes downright impatient. In any case, Karlstadt was also excommunicated by the pope in 1520.

---

[52] 2 Corinthians 5:20–21.
[53] Luther, *Von der Freiheit eines Christenmenschen* §12: "Hier erhebt sich nun der fröhliche Wechse" in *Martin Luther. Aufbruch zur Reformation*, ed. Karin Bornkamm, Gerhard Ebeling (Leipzig: Insel Vlg., 1995), 246. Would Luther have taken the expression from the early Christian letter *Ad Diognetum* 9.5: 'O sweet exchange!' (*ō tēs glukeias apallagēs*)? Metaphorically, *sweet* can also be translated as *pleasing* or *delicious*.
[54] Romans 3:28.
[55] Thus the Lutheran Bible translates, "So halten wir es nun, daß der Mensch gerecht werde ohne des Gesetzes Werke, allein durch den Glauben."
[56] Snyder, *Anabaptist History and Theology*, 47–54.

Initially, both teachers seemed to be united on Reformed principles, but as time went on, great differences of opinion arose over how the Reformation should proceed. For Karlstadt, the changes could not go fast enough. Luther may have been impatient, but he did not want to run faster than was socially and politically acceptable. He did not want to antagonize the government that was protecting him. Karlstadt had other plans. When Luther was taken to safety at Wartburg near Eisenach by troops of Frederick the Wise, Elector of Saxony (1463–1525) immediately after the Reichstag at Worms[57] in April 1521, Karlstadt temporarily took over Luther's pastorate at Wittenberg. A few months later, an iconoclasm (destruction of icons) broke out which Karlstadt advocated and defended.

The months when Karlstadt was in charge of the reforms at Wittenberg were tumultuous. He wanted all monastic vows, for men and for women, considered as null and void. Public disputes were organized that regularly ended in riots. Disputes also arose over the removal of statues from churches. Church buildings were damaged, and Karlstadt allowed this all to happen.

Frederick the Wise, however, made it clear to the spiritual leader that under no circumstances were changes to the Eucharist to be made. On Christmas Eve 1522, disputes again broke out. The following day, Karlstadt held an "evangelical" worship service on Christmas Day with about 2,000 people in attendance. Radical enthusiasm spread rapidly, resulting in a chain reaction. Karlstadt, after all, had the city council on his side. The council issued a decree that liturgical changes had to be implemented without exceptions: the Mass was to be celebrated in the German language, both bread and wine were to be offered at the Eucharist,[58] the Mass for the dead was abolished and images of saints were resolutely removed from the church.

---

[57] At Worms, Luther was asked to recant his Reformation texts (books, tracts). Luther refused, and after a few days he reportedly spoke the words, "Hier steh ich, ich kann nicht anders" before the full Reichstag. Luther had come with safe conduct and could leave with safe conduct. Nevertheless, he was "arrested" by his protectors on the return trip and taken to safety. See Bakhuizen van den Brink, *Handbook of Church History*, 3:40–41.

[58] The custom was that during communion only the host (whether or not baptized in wine) was handed out.

Zwickau prophets

The upheavals in Wittenberg were attended by some notable figures who visited the city during this stormy time and were part of a group of "Zwickau prophets" (Zwickau is in Saxony in Germany).[59] Nicholas Storch, Thomas Dreschel and Markus Stübner are mentioned in the records. The latter was a committed disciple of Thomas Müntzer.[60] The prophets had arrived in Wittenberg in 1521 and had influenced Karlstadt. They had developed radical views about how the Christian church should function, when Christ's return would occur and how God revealed himself to people. They also believed Christians should live in complete fellowship and were—in principle—all equal.[61] To distinguish between Christians on the basis of origin, education or offices was, according to the Zwickau prophets, against the will of God. In their view, learned knowledge of Scripture or theology was more of a hindrance than a blessing. The fulness of the Spirit was necessary, nothing more. And through the working of the Spirit, every believer could receive revelations and make known the will of God, for he gave dreams and visions without the need for studying Scripture or receiving formal training.

The Zwickau prophets looked with contempt upon all academic study and Bible belief. In order to be saved by God, one had to abandon knowledge-oriented reading and even forget the first letters of the alphabet. That is why this prophetic direction is sometimes referred to as "Abecedarianism." The practice of theology was, according to the prophets, a form of idolatry. Luther, who was strongly opposed to this kind of over-spiritualism, said sarcastically about Karlstadt that he had gobbled up the Holy Spirit "with feathers and all" (the Spirit as a dove).[62] Karlstadt

---

[59] Zwickau was the place where Thomas Müntzer was a pastor and where a peculiar guild of prophets arose. Storch exerted great influence on Müntzer. Müntzer's spirituality and fanaticism caused him to be expelled from Zwickau in due course.

[60] See Williams, *The Radical Reformation*, 120–136.

[61] Carter Lindberg, "There Should Be No Beggars Among Christians: Karlstadt, Luther, and the Origins Of Protestant Poor Relief," *Church History* 46/3 (1977): 313–334.

[62] *D. Martin Luther's Werke*, 18. Band (Weimar: Herman Böhlaus Nachfolger; 1964), 66.17–20: "der den heiligen Geist mit feddern und mit all gefressen habe." See Thomas A. Fudge, "Icarus of Basel? Oecolampadius and the Early Swiss Reformation," *Journal of Religious History* 21/ 3 (1997): 268–284.

eventually rejected his doctoral degree and began to earn his living as a porter in the streets of Wittenberg.

When Frederick the Wise learned of the revolution, the Elector intervened harshly and the decisions of the misguided city council were annulled. Shortly thereafter, in March 1522, Luther returned to Wittenberg and the prophets were expelled from the city. For eight days in a row, beginning on March 9 (on Invocavit Sunday, the first Sunday in Lent), Luther preached a penetrating message on the core values of the Christian faith, such as love, patience and freedom, and called on Wittenbergers to have faith in the changing power of God's Word. After all, violence could not bring the desired changes—only the proper understanding of Scripture could. These eight sermons were a great success, and Karlstadt's leadership role was thus over. A year later, he was confirmed as pastor in the small town of Orlamünde, but Luther —his former friend!—managed to get him expelled from this place, and even from the province of Saxony.

Spiritualists and Thomas Müntzer

The history of Karlstadt shows how the Protestant renewal movement became divided within itself by the emerging spiritualism. Spiritualism was a radical form of reformed thinking that placed more value on the direct whisperings of the Spirit than on external means such as the Bible, church, sacraments, ministers and teaching. For the spiritualist, direct inspiration from the Spirit was an inner experience, available to all Christians, that required no outside help. Karlstadt still held to Scripture as an important and necessary book of revelation, but he was convinced that no one could understand anything of Scripture without the direct prompting of the Spirit. Reading what was before the eyes prevented the reader from truly understanding what was being read.

The Zwickau prophet Thomas Müntzer drastically extended Karlstadt's spiritual lines of thought. He claimed that God also gave Spirit-guided revelations outside of Scripture. God, in his view, did not need the Bible at all to reveal his will. Too much concentration on the written word only led to Pharisaism. Nor was Scripture needed to test dreams, visions and "words" for their truth and purity. The Spirit-filled inner self could make that assessment, independently of the written Word of God.

Müntzer did not develop these controversial ideas on his own. As a pastor in Zwickau, he had to deal with proletarian rebellion resulting from the miserable living conditions and economic recession in the German countryside. Zwickau was a place with many poor artisans and wage labourers, who worked mainly in the textile industry. Nicholas Storch and Thomas Drechsel were also involved with the cloth trade. One day, Storch received a vision, which he himself referred to as an "inner Word" or an "inner light" from God. Drechsel also received visions. It was Storch in particular who managed to get Müntzer on the spiritualistic track with his radical claims and apocalyptic visions. This enabled Müntzer to become one of the most important "architects" of the peasant war.

Müntzer began his spiritual career as a committed Lutheran. On Luther's recommendation he was ordained as an evangelical pastor in Zwickau in 1520, after which the preacher soon took a firm stand against Luther and his *sola fide*. The formulation "by faith alone" was too simple for Müntzer. Was there not more to be done at the heart? Was not Luther preaching a message of cheap grace? According to Müntzer, one was only a Christian when the Spirit had accomplished a transforming work in the heart. The new life the Spirit awakened only came about through deep spiritual woe, and was accompanied by intense inner suffering from sin and the world. Only those who received this suffering could be called "elect." They were the *sheep* that the Lord would soon separate from the *goats*.[63] Müntzer believed the *goats*—the high church clergy—proclaimed a false faith.

Müntzer claimed to have insight into the characteristics of true Christianity and wanted to furnish the church of Zwickau with them. Morals in Zwickau had traditionally been quite loose, and the prophetic renewal was to point out the sins of the people and bring them to penance and repentance. Müntzer's ideal of repentance was largely derived from ideas in the early church, which led to a separation from the sinful world that someone like Luther was trying to avoid. Luther was much more concerned with the church's unfailing connection to creation and the world. Müntzer's accentuation made him move away from Luther more and more.

---

[63] See Ezekiel 34:17 and Matthew 25:32–33.

Hermann Mühlpfort (1486–1534), mayor of Zwickau and a personal friend of Luther's, interpreted the radical movement as an outright provocation against the incumbent church authority. Müntzer mocked all Luther had accomplished; church and liturgical renewal with restoration of the authority of the Word alone would not suffice. The city council, however, was quite annoyed with all the mocking. The prophets had even appointed twelve apostles after Jesus' example, as if they were the core of the new people of God, and moreover women were put on equal footing with men and allowed to prophesy and speak in the congregation. These were unsettling signs for Lutheran authority. The prophetic following grew in the process, and Luther saw the gains of the Reformation in Zwickau as seriously threatened. This led to some fierce confrontations in the city, on the basis of which the government finally felt compelled to intervene. In late April 1521, fifty-five Christians were arrested and Thomas Müntzer was expelled from Zwickau.

However, this intervention from above had a counterproductive effect on the civil government. In the face of repression, the Zwickau Radical Party continued to grow in numbers. Luther was fed up with it and planned to go to Zwickau in person to put things in order. Before that happened, Luther agreed to talk to the prophet Markus Stübner[64] and learn about his views personally.

At the beginning of 1522, less than two years after Müntzer's appointment to Zwickau, a meeting took place in Wittenberg which would have far-reaching consequences for the direction the Reformation would take in the following years.[65] The Zwickau prophet Stübner arrived in Wittenberg to convey a prophetic "word" from God to the reformer Martin Luther. Luther barely listened to the man and began to insult him. The reformer attributed the prophecies to a heightened state of spiritual imagination. Luther also reproached the prophets for mistaking demonic inspirations for revelations from God. When Stübner then suggested that not everyone was given to understand the contents of the visions, Luther ignited in a blind rage. Finally, he had his

---

64 Markus Stübner was the only *scholar* among the prophets; he knew Luther.
65 See Dieter Potzel, "Thomas Müntzer und die Zwickauer Propheten. Auf den Spuren von Jesus, von Luther verfolgt," *Der Theologe* 10 (1998).

guest thrown out of the door with the words, "I'll smack your Spirit on the snout!"[66] This moment of confrontation probably also made him decide to actively fight the Zwickau Renewal and to act against it in person.

At the same time, the people of Zwickau became convinced and divided by Luther's action. The vast majority lined up behind the Wittenberg preacher, and the Zwickau radicals were put under great pressure to abandon their convictions. The prophetic movement was thus socially and spiritually stifled and could not help but fall apart. Nevertheless, Luther was not satisfied with the success of Zwickau alone. The reformer also visited Leipzig, Erfurt, Weimar and other places where similar situations arose. Luther had Müntzer's followers dispersed and persecuted wherever they went looking for such radical renewal.

The reformer accused the radicals of contempt for the authorities and for the Scriptures (putting the "inner light" above the Word of God), and he was largely right. Nevertheless, the authorities did not succeed in mapping and tracking down all the fleeing and hiding *Schwärmer*,[67] as they were called. The social abuses remained, such as exploitation of serf peasants, compulsory serfdom and church taxes, and it was inevitable that sooner or later another fuse would be lit in the waiting powder keg. Eventually, hope for real improvements in the name of God would lead to a broad-based revolt.

Less than three years after Luther's victory in Zwickau, the time had come. Peasants in the regions of Upper Swabia, the Black Forest and Stülingen (1524, Waldshut and others), Thuringia, the Harz (1524/1525, Eisenach, Zwickau), Franconia (1525, Rothenburg and others), Saarland, Palatinate (1525) and Tyrol (1525/1526) revolted in large numbers. Tens of thousands of peasants demanded improvement of their living conditions and believed God would bring a turn in their fortunes.

Thomas Müntzer proceeded to promote armed struggle in Mühlhausen and incited the combative peasants to violence with flaming apocalyptic visions. Violence was now permissible, because Gód wanted it; after all, the coming of Christ and the

---

[66] "Eurem Geist hau' ich auf die Schnauze!"
[67] The term *Schwärmer* refers to the old term *enthusiasts*, meaning *fanatics* or *dreamers*.

judgement were near. Müntzer believed the peasant revolt would herald the end of the fifth kingdom in the book of Daniel. This fifth kingdom was an empire of "iron and clay," a kingdom divided within itself, which would be destroyed by "a stone, cut out by no human hand" and overthrowing everything in its path.[68] Müntzer saw in this the hand of God. The stone had been wrenched loose by God and was unstoppable in its advance. The stone even became "a great mountain, which filled all the earth!"[69] So, it was with the peasant movement—it was the beginning of the coming of God's kingdom on earth and would overthrow everything that stood in its way, even by force of arms. In doing so, Müntzer consciously deviated from the principle of non-violence proclaimed by early Christianity, the church to which he mirrored himself.

When the revolt broke out in May 1525, Thomas Müntzer believed he had a leading role to play in the divine finale of world history. The peasants had to take on the trained soldiers of the army of Count Filips van Hessen (1504–1567).[70] Humanly speaking, this was an unequal battle, but the peasants reckoned on the judgemental action of God. Alas, the confrontations and battles ended in terrible tragedy. Some 6,000 peasants lost their lives at Frankenhausen. To expect God's intervention in this way was to make a terrible miscalculation. Thomas Müntzer himself ran away and was found hiding in an attic in Frankenhausen and arrested. Not long after, the spiritual leader was tortured and beheaded in Mühlhausen. The life of perhaps Luther's most determined opponent came to a sad end.[71]

Luther regretted the use of the army, but eventually reconciled himself to it. In all, about 70,000 to 100,000 peasants died between 1524 and 1526. Of course, not all of them could be counted as notorious Anabaptist radicals or spiritualists. But the social unrest and peasant uprisings provided a context in which

---

[68] Daniel 2:34, 45.
[69] Daniel 2:35.
[70] Filips van Hessen, nicknamed "der Grossmütige," was the grandfather of Anna of Saxony, the second wife of Prince William of Orange. Incidentally, he vehemently opposed his granddaughter's marriage to the prince.
[71] For an in-depth study of the enigmatic figure of Thomas Müntzer, I refer to Ulrich Bubenheimer, *Thomas Müntzer: Herkunft und Bildung*, Studies in Medieval and Reformation Thought 46 (Leiden: Brill, 1989).

some important Anabaptist themes could become relevant and attractive. For most Anabaptists, social, economic and moral reform were an integral part of a desired religious reformation. For Luther, this was less the case.

For example, in addition to social equalization, the peasants desired that each village or region could choose its own pastor and that the chosen pastor would be maintained by the community and be accountable to that community. Luther was adamantly opposed to this and believed it was responsible to fight rebellious peasants and, if necessary, to kill them. Whoever was killed in the service of God and the government, in his opinion, died a blessed death.

Luther, therefore, placed ultimate responsibility for the death of the peasants on the Lord God himself: "I struck down all the peasants in the riot. All their blood is on my head, but I pass it on to the Lord God. He has instructed me to speak of it in this way."[72]

The reformer knew himself to be guided by God in his tragic decisions. In retrospect, it is better to say that Luther believed he was acting at God's behest, but that he was also guided by his own views on the division of labour between church and government (see Appendix 1). His views on this can certainly be questioned. The massacre of a generation of peasants cannot simply be justified by a spiritual appeal to God. This does not alter the fact that, in my opinion, the reformer remains a worthy father of faith as a part of the Reformation heritage.

Sola fide insufficient

For most Anabaptists, the Lutheran Reformation positions were too one-sided, too unreal and sometimes too complicated. As indicated, "faith alone" (*sola fide*) was too minimal, too reductionist and, according to Anabaptists, promoted a dichotomy of faith and life. Luther spoke of the right hand and the left hand of God. With the right hand, God ruled the church and carried Christendom. With the left hand, God ruled the governments

---

[72] *Tischreden* (Weimarer Ausgabe), 5. Band. 2911 a–b (Weimar: Herman Böhlaus Nachfolger; 1967), 75–76: „Ich habe im Aufruhr alle paur erschlagen; alle ihre blut ist auff meinem halß. Aber ich weiße es auf unsern herrn Gott; der hatt mir solchs befholen zu reden".

and punished the evil and rewarded the good. For Luther, both hands ultimately came together in God. In him the distinction between church and world fell away.

In Luther's day, incidentally, the latter was quite common; church and government largely coincided in people's experience: the government interfered with the church in everything and the church meddled with political affairs. Yet Anabaptists saw a grim dichotomy in Lutheranism. The world was divided into "two regiments": the territory of the government and the territory of the church. The church left it up to the government to make pronouncements on social issues and did not want to get in the way of the government in doing so. As a result, the church tended to retreat into its spiritual territory and preached a gospel that had little to do with the headlines of the day. The church had no intention of getting involved in politics and readily acquiesced in government decisions.

The worldview of the Anabaptists was more *realistic* in a philosophical sense, that is, the visible and invisible worlds coincided more, in both their thinking and experience. In this respect, the Anabaptist worldview still closely matched the perception of reality of the late medievalist. The spiritual world was always present in the visible and tangible, and expressed itself therein. Nothing of the experiential reality thus stood alone. Nothing was simply "neutral." The existing reality belonged either to the realm of God or the devil. It was that simple. There was free movement possible between earth, heaven and hell, and the dividing lines between the three were not easy to draw for ordinary people.[73] Daily life was therefore a plaything of the powers from both above and below.

The medievalist was aware a fierce battle between light and darkness was being waged above, in the heavenly realms; earthly life below was but a pale reflection of it. Everyday life was, so to speak, porous and transparently down to the world of God and the devil. Signals from the heavenly spheres and from the caverns of darkness and misery constantly came through. This reality was at once fascinating and frightening. Fear, therefore, played a major role in the perception of life in the sixteenth century. At

---

[73] Snyder, *Anabaptist History and Theology*, 25.

any moment one could be struck by a devilish curse or a punishment from God.

The thin border between the superhuman and the subhuman also included the assumption that no separation could be made between the inner world of the heart and the outer world of the hands. In other words, what you believe and confess deep inside must come out and become observable for everyone. The medieval ideal was to live a life of ascetic detachment and thus escape the temptations of the evil world. The only way to overcome evil lay in the way of worldly avoidance and in the contempt of all the world had to offer in terms of pleasantries. A true Christian was characterized by *contemptus mundi*, that is, by contempt for and rejection of the evil world. Those who succeeded in this were highly respected. The medievalist had an outspoken contempt for the Christian who held beautiful spiritual theories, but in the meantime enriched himself by all kinds of duplicity and underhanded gain.

Anabaptist Christians, therefore, were not actually living with a new worldview.[74] We can say their way of life was closely aligned with the spiritual ideal that had been present among the people of Europe for centuries. The Lutheran separation of belief and work was correct and biblical in itself, but it came across to some as if Luther's God was not so concerned about *how* you believed, as long as you believed (and of course Luther never meant it that way). In the Anabaptist tradition, the inner conviction and the outworking of it were more in line. That someone believed was certainly not enough for God, because this faith only appeared pure when one could see *how* this faith worked out in newness of life. By the fruit, one came to recognize the tree.[75] The newness from *within* had to be reflected in an *external* newness or else there could be nothing new inside. This is how the reasoning went, and it sounded more natural to the man of the sixteenth century than it does to the Christian of the twenty-first. We have

---

74 See R. Seeberg, *Lehrbuch der Dogmengeschichte*, Band IV,1 (Graz: Akademische Druck- und Verlagsanstalt, 1953), 31: "Diese Ideale bieten nicht viel Neues dar. Sie nehmen die mannigfachen spätmittelalterlichen Tendenzen zu einer Reform der Kirche auf und versuchen die mystische Frömmigkeit zum Mittel dieser Reformtendenzen zu gestalten."
75 Matthew 7:20; 12:33.

become accustomed to rational irony and skepticism when it comes to visible fidelity to Christ.

The difference between Luther and the Anabaptists had to do with Luther's view that one and the same Christian could be *both righteous and a sinner at the same time (simul iustus et peccator)*.[76] After all, did not the assertion create the impression that a Christian, after being justified by grace, was doomed to still go through life as a sinner?[77] Yes, believed Luther, but in this process the Christian would have to learn by trial and error to live fully as a righteous person; and in this trial and error God was graciously near the believer.[78]

To Anabaptist ears, Luther's thoughts on justification sounded suspicious and incomprehensible.[79] Surely a Christian could not simply resign himself to his sinfulness. Nor could he resign himself to violence, the sword or other injustices. Luther seemed to resign himself to it. And of course, on the one hand, he was right. The most committed Christian still makes mistakes. No one in this life would ever be *completely* free of their sinful nature. And yet, from an Anabaptist point of view, this observation was incomplete. There was too little reckoning with the powerful and persistent grace of God. The Christian life was certainly a life of repentance and weeping over sins, but also a life of victory and visible change.

Anabaptist Christians, so to speak, reckoned more with "a victorious Christian life" and marked spiritual change by practicing baptism upon confession of faith. This baptism was one of the most hated expressions of the Anabaptist faith in the Reformation era. Shortly after the Zwickau upheaval, Luther's close associate Philip Melanchthon (1497–1560) even managed to have Anabaptists imprisoned and put to death as declared opponents of infant baptism. In this way, the reformers wanted to prevent further spread of rebaptism.

---

[76] "Voll sunde und an sunde seynd." See J.T. Bakker, *Coram Deo. Bijdrage tot de onderzoek van de structuur van Luther's theologie* (Kampen: Kok, 1956), 100–111; See also Walther Koehler, *Dogmengeschichte als Geschichte des christlichen Selbstbewusstseins. Das Zeitalter der Reformation* (Zürich: Max Niehans Verlag, 1951), 340.

[77] See Anthony N.S. Lane, *Justification by Faith in Catholic-Protestant Dialogue: An Evangelical Assessment* (London: T&T Clark, 2002), 171–173.

[78] Seeberg, *Lehrbuch der Dogmengeschichte*, Band IV,1, 132.

[79] See Rollin Stely Armour, *Anabaptist Baptism, A Representative Study*, Studies in Anabaptist and Mennonite History (Eugene: Wipf & Stock, 1998), 135–136.

2.4 Excursus 1: Believer's baptism

Christian baptism has often been controversial in the history of the church. Questions such as who may baptize, when to baptize, how to baptize and how often to baptize regularly played out. Differences about baptism have often caused Christians to turn their backs on each other. They did not really listen to each other; there was no dialog. The question is whether the great reformers of the sixteenth century ever understood the Anabaptists and vice versa. Usually, caricatures were made of dissenters, and parodies and clichés are hard to resist. What view did most Anabaptists have of baptism? Why was it so important to them that they were willing to die for it? Here we come to some central tenets and basic values of Anabaptist theology. For the sake of clarity, we will first give a brief summary of the basic ideas of believer's baptism.[80] After that, they will collectively be examined in more detail.

Basic ideas

(1) In Anabaptist theology, the ritual of baptism had everything to do with the question of *how* a person entered the Christian life and in what quality of life the Christian life was lived. In doing so, Anabaptists approached this issue from a different perspective, distancing themselves from the prevailing sacramental view of baptism and from Protestantism, both of which defended infant baptism.

Fundamental to the Anabaptist view of baptism was the idea that baptism was a kind of rite of passage. The person being baptized embraced a sign, expressing that he or she was rejecting and renouncing the old sinful life and receiving the new life of Christ. The old life was the life ruled by sin and ignorance. Baptism expressed that sin and ignorance no longer ruled, but had been *overruled* by the grace and Spirit of Christ. Perhaps this is best compared to the example of a traffic light and a police officer. If a traffic light is red and the traffic officer makes the familiar gesture to the motorist to drive on, then he can, indeed he must, drive on. The main rule of stopping on red is then overruled by the

---

[80] See Walter Klaassen, ed., *Anabaptism in Outline: Selected Primary Sources*, Classics of the Radical Reformation 3 (Waterloo: Herald Press, 1981), 162–163.

officer's gesture, that is to say, set aside by a higher authority. In this way the Christian could and must get moving and obey a higher authority, even if the world's lights were red. For example, he had to learn to "drive past" sin and no longer pay attention to it. God's agent showed him the way.[81]

(2) To qualify for baptism, a Christian needed to seriously consider the *meaning* and *purpose* of baptism. One did not get baptized lightly. Anabaptists assumed that Christians should come to baptism voluntarily and were able to respond to God's invitation with their hearts. Their view of man differed somewhat from Luther's. According to Luther, a person could not choose freely because his will was not free. In simple everyday choices man was free of course, but not when it came to the ability to choose between good and evil. Then the will was bound.[82] The fact that people were saved was therefore entirely due to God. Baptism could not be chosen, unless one wanted to give credit to oneself.

In Anabaptist theology, as with Luther (and Calvin), the natural bondage of the human will was fully taken into account. In themselves and of themselves, people were not free. Yet, Anabaptists reckoned more strongly than Luther did with the possibility that God's grace could set people's will free from bondage. Under the proclamation of the gospel, God's Spirit was working on the soul of the listener and appealing to his will. After all, God was the One who worked the "will and the work" in people.[83] This working of the Spirit was usually called God's *preparatory* or *preliminary grace*. This grace thus worked toward salvation and was aimed at making the will so free that a person came to surrender of his own accord and at the same time chose life with God. This choice was his supreme choice and at the same time was 100 per cent predetermined by God. The choice

---

[81] By this I mean Jesus. To "learn to pass over sin" requires submitting mind, feeling and will to Christ.

[82] Philippians 2:13: "for it is God who works in you, both to will and to work for his good pleasure."

[83] See W. Janse, *Free or Forced? Erasmus, Luther and Augustine on the Free Choice of Will*, Willem de Zwijger Foundation, Reformatorische Stemmen (Amsterdam: Buijten & Schipperheijn, 2004), 24–37. Luther responded to Erasmus' *De servo arbitrio* (1526) with his own *De servo arbitrio* (see Augustine's *De libero arbitrio*). Janse rightly notes that the distinct views are complementary rather than completely mutually exclusive.

to be baptized was thus one of the first fruits of the liberated will to go God's way and honour him in everything.

Regarding man, the difference in view between Luther and the Anabaptists was not great. Rather, there was a difference in emphasis.

(3) Third, baptism was also a powerful ritual of initiation (an initiation rite, thus also a rite of passage).[84] In addition to being a parting ritual, faith baptism was also an image of "becoming part of something." The apostle Paul wrote, "For in one Spirit we were all baptized into one body—Jews or Greeks, slaves or free—and all were made to drink of one Spirit."[85] Baptism symbolized being added to the body of Christ, which was the congregation of believers. This communal aspect was and still is of great importance in Anabaptist theology, for the baptized person expressed by his baptism that he was going the way of Christ and wanted to be supported by the congregation. He needed other Christians to find his way and stay on the way of God. Therefore, the principle of discipline was an absolute necessity in Anabaptist church doctrine.

Christian life in the Anabaptist tradition largely revolved around the congregation. Honouring God was first and foremost a communal event. The Christian community had its own place in the thinking and confession of the proponents of the radical Reformation. In the congregation, people looked out for each other, read the Scriptures together and relieved each other's needs. The early Anabaptist community also characterized itself as a suffering and persecuted congregation; she was a martyred church. Therefore, they not only spoke of baptism with water but also of baptism with blood.[86] As a community of Christians, they wanted above all to be a visible congregation who lived in peace, holiness and isolation. Making one's faith visible was essential to this. The baptismal ritual was more or less the starting signal for a

---

[84] See Wright, *Free Church, Free State*, 71.
[85] 1 Corinthians 12:13.
[86] In this respect, too, the Anabaptist church sought to emulate the early Christian church. Ancient Christian writings already speak of blood baptism. See for example the *Passio Perpetuae et Felicitatis* 21:2. It also occurs with Tertullian, as well as with Cyprian, Origen, Cyril of Jerusalem, Basil of Caesarea, Gregory of Nazianzus and Chrysostom.

believer to follow in the footsteps of the Lord as a follower of Christ. Personal lifestyle was therefore constantly the subject of thorough examination. In the congregation, people spoke frankly to one another about this.[87]

Symbolic visibility and unification

Making the faith visible is meaningful and necessary, but at the same time it has one major drawback. Every form of making matters of faith visible carries with it the seeds of legalism, sectarianism and schisms. It is all too easy to read piety and righteousness into the specific walk of a particular group of Christians, without asking whether that piety also has other expressions. Can two people not be equally devoted and devout, while one reads from the Bible every day and the other once a month? When it comes to wanting to measure someone's spirituality, is not the creation of lists of behavioural indicators very wrong? Does not externalization of personal faith foster division among Christians? And what about camouflaging a lack of spirituality with a sauce of pious outward show? Can a congregation not fall victim to lists of outward appearances that are hypocritical, because they subtly shift attention from the inner world of the heart to the outer world of behaviour? Does not the stress on the visible in this way also foster a false sense of security?

On the one hand, false security and moralism should be avoided as much as possible in the church of Christ. On the other hand, no church can escape having its own lists of identity markers that delimit and characterize the communal spirituality. A certain amount of self-exposure is necessary to know who is *inside* and who is *outside*. Whether it is infant baptism, the celebration of the Lord's Supper, the uttering of a confession or praying before dinner, every church has its own instruments for knowing who *really* belongs and who does not. In the Anabaptist movement, faith baptism was the primary indication that someone had truly come to the way of Christ. As a matter of course, the person baptized then gradually adopted the other behavioural characteristics of the community.

---

[87] For further elaboration, see Chapter 3..

We have seen that in the tradition of the radical Reformation, faith baptism sought to bear witness to at least three spiritual facts. Baptism was:

1. a farewell ritual,
2. a voluntary ritual, and
3. an initiatory ritual.

In sum, baptism marked a transition to a new reality. Baptismal symbolism expressed that the person baptized had passed from death to life. In faith he had partaken of a spiritual *rebirth*, a renewal of head and heart about which Scripture spoke with regularity. The texts on this subject were very clear to the Anabaptists. What were these texts and thoughts? We will now discuss, very briefly, some of them.

The rebirth was explained by Paul in direct connection with the word *bath*. The apostle spoke of the "bath of regeneration," where the figurative word *bath* referred symbolically to the renewal of the Holy Spirit:

> But when the goodness and loving kindness of God our Savior appeared, he saved us, not because of works done by us in righteousness, but according to his own mercy, by the *washing of regeneration* and renewal of the Holy Spirit, whom he poured out on us richly through Jesus Christ our Savior.[88]

Rebirth as a "water bath" was seen as a breakthrough of new life from God. The conscience had been *washed* and sanctified,[89] so to speak, by the forgiveness of God and had undergone a renewal that placed the life of the person being baptized in a completely new perspective. He knew himself to be participant of a new creation.[90] God's future was taking shape and one had become part of the "powers of the age to come."[91] The future was thus present in faith. This is how Anabaptist Christians experienced

---

[88] Titus 3:4–6. Italics added.
[89] 1 Corinthians 6:11; Hebrews 10:22.
[90] See 2 Corinthians 5:17 and Galatians 6:15.
[91] Hebrews 6:5.

life with God and how millions of Christians still experience it. Hearing the Word of God produced an inner "water bath" that had an intense and life-changing effect and anticipated things to come.[92]

The apostle Peter compared the baptismal ritual to the rescue of Noah and his family in the ark. Noah was commissioned by God to build an ark. This huge ship led him and his family through the chaotic powers of storm and flood to a new world. When the flood was over, Noah's family had a new opportunity. The history of Noah's salvation was seen by Peter as a foreshadowing of the sign of baptism. The flood and the miracle of salvation pointed beyond itself, so to speak, to the history of Jesus. Noah had a good conscience and could therefore be saved. The one who was baptized had come to know Christ and, through God's forgiveness and grace, also had a cleansed conscience. Through forgiveness he lived in communion with God and the baptismal ceremony was the symbolic expression of this, for the ritual was (and is) in every respect an expression of prayer.

> For Christ also suffered once for sins, the righteous for the unrighteous, that he might bring us to God, being put to death in the flesh but made alive in the spirit, in which he went and proclaimed to the spirits in prison, because they formerly did not obey, when God's patience waited in the days of Noah, while the ark was being prepared, in which a few, that is, eight persons, were brought safely through water. Baptism, which corresponds to this, now saves you, not as a removal of dirt from the body but as an appeal to God for a good conscience.[93]

---

[92] See Ephesians 5:26, "that he might sanctify her, having cleansed her by the washing of water with the word." Here Paul uses the same word for "washing" as in Titus 3:5 ("washing of regeneration"). "Washing of regeneration" and "washing of the word" go together in Scripture. After all, regeneration is awakened by the Word. The Word is likened to "seed" that awakens and sprouts new life (1 Pet 1:23).

[93] 1 Peter 3:18–21. The ESV translates with "an appeal to God for a good conscience" (3:21). The arguments for this are strong, see P.H.R. van Houwelingen, *Peter, Circular letter from Babylon*, CNT (Kampen: Kok, 1991), 140–144. Yet I choose the translation "but is a prayer of a clear conscience to God." The comparison with Noah is flawed if baptism is a prayer *for* a clear conscience and not *of* a clear conscience. Noah already had a clear conscience when he began to build the ark. Besides, verse 3:16 already

The miracle of regeneration was not only described in Scripture with terminology derived from water. The association was also made with germinating seed. The Word of God was a *seed* that germinated in heart and mind and produced a spiritual birth. The first letter of Peter indicated this with the words:

> ... since you have been born again, not of perishable seed but of imperishable, through the living and abiding word of God.[94]

According to Peter, regeneration was not a work of men but of God. Spiritual renewal was wrought through words that germinate like seeds and produce new life. Hearts and minds change because God's Word starts a process of deepening reflection and confrontation leading to redemptive insight. These new insights, in turn, lead to other views and convictions that become firmly anchored in head and heart. Their thinking is restructured and reoriented. This was the core meaning of conversion.[95] Conversion expressed a new way of thinking and acting.

Paul wrote, "Be transformed by the renewal of your mind,"[96] and, "If then you have been raised with Christ, seek the things that are above, where Christ is, seated at the right hand of God. Set your minds on things that are above, not on things that are on earth."[97] For Anabaptist Christians, the world of "above" had opened up wonderfully.

The ritual of baptism thus expressed a profound cleansing and renewal of thought and conscience. This spiritual change was called, among other things, *rebirth* in the New Testament and was definitely necessary in this life in order to look forward with confidence to Christ's kingship.[98] Anabaptist Christians experienced spiritual rebirth intensely, and looked for ways to shape the new

---

presupposes the "good conscience" of Noah (3:16 and 21 both have *suneidesis agathe*). Why pray for what is already there?
[94] 1 Peter 1:23.
[95] *Conversion* is a reversal brought about by change and renewal of mind (Gr. *metanoia*).
[96] Romans 12:2.
[97] Colossians 3:1–2.
[98] "Truly, truly, I say to you, unless one is born again he cannot see the kingdom of God" (John 3:3).

spiritual reality in dealing with others, and in mutual community. They wanted to live as changed people. Had not Paul said that those who were baptized have "put on (like clothes) Christ"?[99]

In a symbolic sense, being "clothed with Christ" meant a Christian looked different inside and out from other people. The difference was to be demonstrable and provable. Moreover, this could give rise to the hope that changes would spread noticeably and also have *social* consequences. The gospel of God's kingdom was a power that was hardly noticed at first, but then suddenly could turn the world upside down. This is how Jesus constantly spoke of it in his parables. At first glance, the kingdom of God seemed small and insignificant and was like a seed or a little lump of leaven. Yet the power of this small leaven was exceedingly great. In time, the leaven appeared to have touched and affected everything in its path, and the small seed brought forth a great tree that dwarfed all other crops.[100]

Christians of the radical Reformation saw the power of the gospel in exactly this way. God's grace and forgiveness were a reality that produced a new quality of life. Faith baptism symbolized this reality. Indeed, the sign of baptism referred to death and resurrection. The baptismal ritual was comparable to a funeral. Paul wrote, "We were buried therefore with him by baptism into death."[101] Christians were baptized into the death of Jesus. Symbolically, they went under in a tomb (poured over with water) which, as a metaphor, referred to an inner reality. They went down with him into death, to appear alive and well in his resurrection. In this sense, baptism spoke a powerful language. Baptized Christians lived each day with the death and resurrection of Christ in their minds and hearts.

Thereafter, the conviction grew that the resurrection was winning over death and the Christian was changing into the image of Christ in love and devotion.[102] The memory of the baptismal water helped them do this. Baptism was therefore a marking moment, not just as a marking memory, an event that brought

---

[99] Galatians 3:27.
[100] See Matthew 13:31–33.
[101] Romans 6:4. See also Colossians 2:12, "having been buried with him in baptism."
[102] Romans 8:29 and 2 Corinthians 3:18.

them into connection with Christ in a unique way, and therefore blessed them. This requires a brief explanation.

As a ritual, baptism had not only symbolic and referential power. There was more going on when the person being baptized stood in or near the baptismal water. Something really happened during baptism. Something was happening to the person being baptized.

First of all, baptism was to be seen as a repetition of Jesus' baptism. When Jesus began his ministry among men, he had John baptize him in the Jordan River. Jesus did not need that baptism for himself. He was the Son of God and did not need to repent of sins, for John's baptism was a baptism of repentance.[103] Yet, Jesus allowed himself to be baptized to do what he needed to do. He said to John, "Let it be so now, for thus it is fitting for us to fulfill all righteousness."[104] Jesus' baptism was necessary because the Father asked it of him. Jesus came to identify with his people in everything, including their sins. With his baptism, Jesus showed what people had to do to come to terms with God. They had to repent and be baptized. Thus, the beginning and the end of Jesus' ministry were connected, for also on the cross Jesus identified himself with people's sins.[105] Baptism and the death on the cross were related. Those who were baptized symbolically repeated a crucial moment of Jesus' path. He or she was, so to speak, "following Jesus" and "following in his footsteps."

Second, when receiving the sign of baptism, Jesus' life and the life of the person being baptized merged in a spiritual sense. Just as Jesus was baptized and died 2,000 years ago, so at the moment of baptism the person being baptized followed him closely, as it were. There was faithful narrative identification, so to speak.[106] Both narratives touched each other and, as it were, slid into each other. Jesus' history was suddenly present and was as concrete as the history of the person being baptized. Jesus' history repeated itself, as it were, and Jesus himself was now actually there to

---

[103] Matthew 3:11.
[104] Matthew 3:15.
[105] By the way, the death of Jesus is also called a "baptism." See Mark 10:38–39 and Luke 12:50.
[106] James William McClendon, *Systematic Theology, Vol. 1: Ethics* (Nashville: Abingdon Press, 2002), 265-269.

baptize the baptized.[107] In this sense, baptism was literally and figuratively Jesus' touch. Jesus' baptism brought about a wave that after hundreds of years also reached the baptized in the sixteenth and seventeenth centuries (and us) and in which the baptized still felt and experienced the movement of Christ. This wave of closeness and comfort also manifested itself where disciples of Christ bore the reproach of the Lord in facing persecution.

Third and last, baptism was a presentation of the *eschaton* (the world's end) and baptized Christians lived as people who drastically changed the course of their lives in the face of the end. Jesus' death and resurrection marked the end of the visible world. Paul believed that with Christ's death on the cross, the world had also been crucified and was coming to an end.[108] Both the death of Jesus and the resurrection of the Lord were a sign of the end. After all, the resurrection of the dead was something that could only be expected at the world's end. Jesus was, so to speak, the firstfruit to rise from the dead; the rest would soon follow.

Baptism not only confronted the person to be baptized with his own death in the death of Christ, but also placed him in expectation of the resurrection and eternal life. Baptism anticipated the future and made one taste the new already. The baptismal ritual grasped anticipation of things to come. With the mind's eye, they were already presenting themselves in baptism.

We have already indicated that in the Anabaptist tradition the voluntary nature of the baptismal ritual was emphasized. Baptism could only be administered if the person being baptized indicated it himself and was ready for it (and with the congregation's approval). He was baptized on his professed (and demonstrated) faith and then welcomed and admitted into the congregation on

---

[107] There is recapitulation, see James William McClendon, *Systematic Theology, Vol. 2: Doctrine* (Nashville: Abingdon Press, 1994), 386–393. Those who baptize do so in the name of Jesus (Jesus himself did not baptize; his disciples baptized on his behalf. See John 3:22, 26 and 4:1–2) and represent him in such a way that he is there (see Matt 10:40). A sent one must be received as the sender himself. See also Henk Bakker, "Powerful Practices: Celebrating God's Farewell to the Powers That Be," in *Baptist Sacramentalism 3*, ed. Anthony R. Cross and Philip E. Thompson (Eugene: Pickwick Publications, 2020), 259–279, and "The Roaring Side of the Ministry: A Turn to Sacramentalism," *Perspectives in Religious Studies* 38/4 (2011), 403–426.
[108] Galatians 6:14 and 1 Corinthians 7:31.

his faith.[109] Baptism was a sign that he received in grace, but which he himself had to long for with all his heart. This desire he did not have by nature, for it was a fruit of the working grace of God himself. God's love and grace acted on man's will and prepared him to receive forgiveness and rebirth.

In itself, the idea of *preparatory grace* did not differ much from the Reformation one. However, Anabaptists generally viewed the issue of free will differently. As mentioned, according to Luther the free will of man was a fiction. Free will would not exist. His opponent Karlstadt thought otherwise. According to Karlstadt, the human will could be free if it lived in surrender to the will of God. This life in surrender was called by him *Gelassenheit*[110] and was an active form of subordination of one's desires and ambitions to God. Living in surrender to God also meant a life of active devotion. In the process, man was not disengaged and put on hold, but rather was allowed to give himself wholly to the kingdom of God in the service of God.

In the eyes of Anabaptists, people were not morally evil in every respect. According to Balthasar Hubmaier, by God's grace there was also some good in man. He believed that through Christ's incarnation and sacrifice, man's fallen will had been restored in power. Every human being had been created in God's image, and in Adam every human being had fallen and was equally shackled in sin. Through the sacrifice of Jesus Christ, the second Adam, man's fall had come to look differently. It was certainly not the case that every human being was automatically saved as a result. By no means. However, according to Hubmaier, every person was now free to accept or reject salvation in Christ. Jesus' coming, his life, death and resurrection from the dead, had restored humankind, fallen in Adam, to the extent that the human will could respond of its own accord in light of the gospel. People could either surrender to that grace or turn away from it.[111]

---

109 Such a church is in the "believers' church" tradition. See Donald F. Durnbaugh, *The Believers' Church: The History and Character of Radical Protestantism* (1968; Eugene: Wipf & Stock, 2003).
110 Snyder, *Anabaptist History and Theology*, 51.
111 In many ways, the Anabaptists' view of man's free will resembles that of the early church. Justin Martyr, for example, clearly explains why man must have his own freedom of choice, see *Apologia* I 43,3ff ("if mankind does not have the capacity by free

2.5 Balthasar Hubmaier

Easter morning, April 16, 1525, was a special day in the town of Waldshut, Austria. On that feast day and the days that followed, pastor Balthasar Hubmaier baptized as many as 300 professing Christians. One after the other came to the conviction to request believer's baptism.

People were not yet being baptized by immersion at this point. Hubmaier used a water-filled milk bucket that had been placed on the baptismal font for the occasion.[112] Hubmaier himself had been baptized the previous day by Wilhelm Reublin (1484–c.1559), along with sixty others.

Balthasar Hubmaier
(1480–1528)

The city had already fallen into disrepute because of its reformatory sympathies and its involvement in the peasant uprising. Now that hundreds of citizens turned out to follow Hubmaier in his radical vision of baptism as well, the churches of Waldshut must have shaken to their foundations. The atmosphere in Waldshut's churches had changed in a short time and there was talk of a broad-based spiritual turnaround.

In order to get a clearer picture of this, it is necessary to take a brief look at Hubmaier's previous years in Waldshut and Regensburg. We will also follow Hubmaier in the last years of his life.

---

choice to avoid the shameful and to choose the good, then it is not responsible for any deeds").
[112] See Armour, *Anabaptist Baptism*, 19, see also 20–57.

Regensburg

Hubmaier had not been a priest in Waldshut for very long when he decided to be baptized on profession of his faith. Prior to that, he had been a priest of the Catholic Church in Regensburg for some time (1516–1521).[113] Hubmaier was a celebrated speaker and administrator in those years, having received his education from the famous Catholic theologian Johann Eck (1486–1543) in Freiburg.[114] Subsequently, he had earned his doctorate at the University at Ingolstadt; Eck was proud of his student. For Hubmaier, humanly-speaking, a brilliant career lay ahead of him. In Regensburg, he preached in the local cathedral, managed to attract the common people and wholeheartedly supported the anti-Jewish sentiment that prevailed in Regensburg. Indeed, the Jews of Regensburg experienced perhaps the blackest pages of local history in the early years of Hubmaier's ministry.

The Jewish population of Regensburg was one of the oldest and foremost Jewish communities in Germany. Jews had been living in Regensburg since the mid-tenth century. For centuries, Jewish merchants managed to successfully market their wares in the city. Their trade flourished and the Jewish community of Regensburg achieved fame and prestige. During the eleventh and twelfth centuries, the Jewish city of Regensburg was considered the spiritual centre of European Jewry. Famous rabbis studied and taught there. Miraculously, the Jews of Regensburg were spared the massacres of 1298, 1336–1338 and 1348–1350,[115] with the latter attacks breaking out in response to the spreading plague. The Jews were accused of poisoning local water sources and were said to have the Black Death on their conscience.

During the fifteenth century, the relationship between Jews and Christians in Regensburg deteriorated. The economic and political situation changed rapidly and, in addition, accusations

---

[113] Waldshut is located in southern Germany on the Rhine, on the border of Germany and Switzerland, between Lake Constance and Basel. Regensburg lies approximately 350 km northeast of Waldshut, 100 km above München.

[114] Johannes Eck was the notorious opponent of Luther. When Karlstadt could not win over Eck in academic disputes in July 1519, Luther took his place.

[115] The Jews of Regensburg benefited greatly from the political wrangling between the emperor, some counts and the city's ecclesiastical and political authorities in those years. All sorts of power changes had turned attention away from the Jewish population.

of ritual murder by Jews began to circulate. Beginning in 1475, the Christian population of Regensburg wanted to get rid of "their" Jews, and several attempts were made at the end of the fifteenth and beginning of the sixteenth centuries. In the end, in February 1519, the plan succeeded when, partly at the instigation of Hubmaier, the Jews of Regensburg were expelled from the city. The Jewish quarter and synagogue were destroyed.

While the synagogue of Regensburg was being razed to the ground, one of the stonemasons there was struck by falling debris. The man had—it seemed—died, but shortly after nightfall, he was found to have miraculously recovered; the dead man had miraculously come to life. News of this spread quickly and resulted in the Virgin Mary being widely venerated as the benefactress of this miracle.

The miracle was seized upon with both hands, and it was decided to build a chapel in honour of the mother of Jesus next to the stone heap and to emphasize how much it had pleased the Virgin that the Jews had been expelled and the Jewish house of worship destroyed. The wooden chapel was dedicated "To the beautiful Mary" (*Zur Schönen Maria*) and became a popular place of pilgrimage in the years to come where, as tradition went, many miracles had occurred since its construction. In the year 1520 alone, some 100,000 devoted pilgrims visited the new place of worship. The beloved Regensburg city preacher Balthasar Hubmaier spoke with fire and conviction at the dedication of the chapel and, by his own account, could recount as many as forty-five miracles that had taken place since the Jews' eviction. At the time, the theologian did not show any understanding of Reformation principles, which were slowly but surely gaining ground. This would soon change.

Waldshut

At the end of 1520, Hubmaier left the city of Regensburg. The reason for his departure was a dispute over the patronage of the holy chapel. The Dominican monastery of Regensburg had seen its income and prestige decline and spent on the worship of the Beautiful Mary. The monks were furious and disappointed, while Hubmaier had not succeeded in successfully mediating between the local authorities and the monks.

Beginning in January 1521, Hubmaier began to delve into the writings of Luther. The "Luther issue" was ubiquitous at the time.[116] In the spring of 1521, Hubmaier left for Waldshut-on-the-Rhine (Austria), not far from the great Swiss town of Zürich, where in those same days Zwingli had laid the foundation for reforms.

For several reasons, the spring of 1521 was an important period. Many things were happening. Luther was being summoned to the Reichstag and Zwingli was beginning to seek to win the city of Zürich for the Reformation. It was also when Thomas Müntzer was expelled from Zwickau.

Hubmaier became pastor of the church at Waldshut, where he soon clashed with the Bishop of Constance. The clash could not have been avoided, as the spiritual atmosphere in the church of Waldshut began to change drastically. Hubmaier had become convinced that faith in Christ meant a true Christian had to put his faith into practice. His view of the Eucharist also began to change. The Reformation spirit began to win the Waldshut pastor's heart for Christ and would make Hubmaier an entirely different person. The old Hubmaier could hardly to be recognized in the new one.

It did not yet occur to Hubmaier to be baptized on the basis of this new faith. Possibly the thought of a "rebaptism" even stood in his way at that time. This too would change in the course of the following years. In 1522, Hubmaier met the humanist musician and writer Heinrich Glarean (1488–1563) in Basel,[117] as well as the well-known humanist Erasmus. The following year in Zürich, he made the acquaintance of Huldrych Zwingli and was definitively won over to the cause of the Reformation. We have already pointed out the contribution Hubmaier had in Zürich in the second religious discussion of October 1523. His contribution showed how much he had grown away from the Catholic faith in the previous two years. With fervour, he defended Zwingli's position that the celebration of the Lord's Supper did not fundamentally involve a transformation of bread and wine. The sacrament was no more, but also no less, than a meal of remembrance

---

116 On January 3, 1521, Rome made the decision by ecclesiastical law to banish Luther.
117 Heinrich Glarean had a great influence on Conrad Grebel as a teacher.

where Christians commemorated the death of Christ on the cross. Hubmaier also expressed the view that the use of images of saints was a form of idolatry. He called for obedience to Scripture and wished to purge the church liturgy of all these forms of paganism.

It is certain that by October 1523 Hubmaier was already of the opinion that infant baptism was not according to Scripture either, and that he rejected it. Although he may have had doubts about infant baptism as early as 1520, we know from an account of a conversation between Hubmaier and Zwingli in May 1523 that both reformers agreed that children should not be baptized. Walking along the canals of Zürich, Zwingli and Hubmaier discussed the existing practice of infant baptism and both theologians evaluated this practice in the light of Scripture. According to the latter, there was clear agreement on the need to first instruct believers in the faith before they could be baptized.

Only on the basis of their faith and regeneration could Christians receive the sign of baptism, and Zwingli, according to Hubmaier, agreed with this wholeheartedly.[118] This was how things had been in the early church, and to this practice the Catholic Church had to return.

There are doubts about the accuracy of Hubmaier's account of his conversation with Zwingli. Yet there is no reason to believe Hubmaier was selective in his recollections. After all, Zwingli himself admitted to having once been "misled by (Anabaptist) error and to have thought it better then not to baptize children before they had reached the years of discernment."[119] Hubmaier, in later correspondence with the reformer, referred to his conversation with him and the assertion that children should not be baptized until they had received sufficient knowledge of the faith,

---

[118] See Gunnar Westin and Torsten Bergsten, ed., *Balthasar Hubmaier: Schriften*, Quellen und Forschungen zur Reformationsgeschichte 29, Quellen zur Geschichte der Täufer 9 (Gütersloh: Gerd Mohn, 1962), 186; Leonhard von Muralt and Walter Smid, ed., *Quellen zur Geschichte der Täufer in der Schweiz*, I. Band: Zürich (Zürich: Theologischer Verlag, 1974), no. 179, 195; Torsten Bergsten, *Balthasar Hubmaier: Seine Stellung zu Reformation und Täufertum, 1521–1528*, Acta Universitatis Upsaliensis: Studia historico-ecclesiastica Upsaliensia 3 (Kassel: J.G. Oncken Verlag, 1961), 120–248.

[119] Emil Egli et al., ed., *Huldreich Zwinglis sämtliche Werke*, Band 4. *Teil: Von der Taufe, von der Wiedertaufe und von der Kindertaufe*, Corpus reformatorum (Leipzig: Verlag von M. Heinsius Nachfolger, 1927), 228.

but it seemed that the latter had changed his mind. For a snort time Zwingli had been of the opinion that the New Testament did not teach infant baptism. On reflection, however, he equated Jewish circumcision and Christian baptism more closely, and chose to maintain infant baptism. Zwingli was concered that otherwise the unity of the Old and New Testaments would be sacrificed. And, indeed, the Anabaptists had been accused of wanting to abolish the Old Testament.[120]

After growing resentment between the radicals and Zwingli, Zwingli tried to save what could be saved. Repeated conversations and the writing of various tracts were of no avail. All attempts at persuasion and reconciliation in 1524 failed. After the third religious meeting on January 17, 1525, things fell irreversibly into a deadlock. The local government had decided all newborn children should be baptized within eight days. Those who refused baptism for their child could be punished with banishment. The Anabaptists now knew that they were no longer welcome in Zürich. We are already aware of what happened then.

Four days after the painful debate (on January 21), Grebel and Blaurock and others were together in the home of Felix Mantz and Blaurock asked Grebel to baptize him. That evening became the hour of Anabaptism's birth. Shortly thereafter, Blaurock and Manz and twenty-five more were arrested and imprisoned. After their release, and also after a new dispute with Zwingli (on March 20, 1525), opinions remained far apart. Now, all the radicals who did not possess Zürich citizenship were expelled from the city.

Hubmaier had previously returned to Waldshut, where he enjoyed the approval of the local government to reform the church. From surrounding towns, however, Hubmaier's movements were closely followed and a confrontation was sought.

In December 1523, some church representatives visited Waldshut and an official accusation was made against Hubmaier. The Catholic Church charged the reformer with being part of a Lutheran sect, and with misinterpreting Scripture in his sermons. The city council stood up for Hubmaier and refused to hand over

---

[120] See notes 152 and 153. See Murray, *Biblical Interpretation in the Anabaptist Tradition*, 97–121.

its preacher to the Bishop of Constance. The deputation then gave the council fourteen days to reconsider. Within a week, the city council drafted a letter making it clear to church officials that Hubmaier was completely innocent and that he explained the Scriptures clearly and correctly. At the time the case fizzled out, because Austria had to fight against France and had too much on its plate to carry out the threats toward Waldshut. In July 1524, an attack on Waldshut was decided upon, but due to the circumstances, this was never carried out.

Religious conversation and the eighteen theses

Meanwhile, Hubmaier was not passively standing by. In April 1524, he organized a closed religious discussion in Waldshut to engage in conversation with a variety of invitees. This was not an open invitation to debate with various parties on issues where a city council would make decisions. This is how it had happened in Zürich, so Hubmaier modified his approach. He and the Christians of Waldshut, wanted to peacefully open and discuss the Scriptures with regard to some essential spiritual principles. The invitation was addressed primarily to the clergy of Waldshut and the surrounding area. It is not clear whether the conversation actually took place.

Hubmaier was definitely a reformer. His eighteen theses have become widely known and mark a reform process from which some early principles of Anabaptism would emerge within a short time. We provide here a translation of the full text.[121]

> Eighteen assertions concerning the Christian life and wherein this life consists, defended at Waldshut by Dr. Balthasar Friedberger[122] in the year 1524.
>
> I, Balthasar Friedberger, doctor and pastor at Waldshut, wish all the brothers of my order and its head grace and peace in Christ Jesus our Lord.

---

[121] Westin and Bergsten, ed., *Balthasar Hubmaier: Writings*, 71–74.
[122] Hubmaier was born in Friedberg and used the name Friedberger as his surname quite often.

Beloved brethren, it is an ancient custom from the time of the apostles that when the faith is threatened, all who desire to speak the Word of God and have a Christian way of reasoning should be called together to examine the Scriptures. This is done to take the utmost care to feed the Christian flock according to the Word of God. Such an assembly was called a *synod* or *chapter* or *brotherhood*. In light of recent anxious times, this kind of gathering can give our Christian believers dignity and good cheer in no small measure. After all, we are supposed to feed not only our bodies with food and drink, but also our souls, so as to be of greater service to the flock and to feed them in peace and unity with the Word of God. To this end, all contentious talk and scolding should be set aside.

Therefore, I bind you, laity and confreres,[123] with ties of brotherly love and with the sanctity of Christian peace through the name of our Lord Jesus Christ, to consider the propositions formulated here by me as research questions on a biblical foundation. At the next meeting of the Chapter, which will take place at Waldshut, you can discuss this with me calmly and fraternally.

And then, in order not to waste our time unnecessarily with trivialities and thereby jeopardize our good record: please bring your Bibles, or else, should you not have any, bring your books for High Mass with you, so that we may share the God-given words of Christian teaching as much as possible. As far as it is within my power, I will not send you away from the fraternal table without having refreshed you with spiritual food and spiritual drink. Godspeed to you all in the name of Jesus Christ our Saviour.

1. Only faith makes us godly in the sight of God.

2. This faith is the acceptance of the grace of God, for he has redeemed us through the sacrifice of his only Son.

---

[123] Meaning *colleagues*.

This excludes all nominal Christians, who have only historical knowledge of God.

3. This faith does not look on idly but extends to God in gratitude and in charity and all kinds of good works to fellow men. All works of penance are to be rejected, such as the burning of candles or using palm branches and holy water.

4. All the works that God has commanded us to do are good. The deeds he has forbidden are evil. The latter category includes such things as eating fish on Lent, abstaining from meat, and wearing the monk's hood.[124]

5. The Mass is not a sacrificial ritual, but a remembrance of the death of Christ. Therefore, the Mass may not be celebrated as a sacrifice, either for the living or for the dead. It follows that the plans of those who are engaged in cunning and deceit will come crashing down.[125]

6. As often as a meal of remembrance is celebrated, the death of our Lord is proclaimed, as we all confess it with the heart and with the tongue. A celebration of the Mass in which silence is required is therefore out of the question.[126]

7. Statues and paintings are of no value. Therefore, you should no longer trust in wood and stone but in the living and suffering God.

8. Since each Christian believes for himself and is baptized for himself, each one must see for himself with Scripture in hand and judge whether he is properly nourished by his pastor.

---

[124] According to Hubmaier, these types of ritual fasts and the many abstentions of monastic life were not in Scripture.

[125] The church knew how to make money from the celebration of Mass for the dead, but also for the living. After all, one had to pay for it.

[126] Hubmaier argues here for a clear preaching of the gospel during the celebration.

9. Since Christ alone died for our sins and we are all baptized in his name, he must be the only Intercessor and Mediator for us. All pilgrimages now come crashing down.

10. It is far better to read only one verse of a psalm in one's own national language which one understands than to sing five whole songs in an unknown language, which is not understood by the church. Now all kinds of morning services, prayer meetings, readings, vespers, compline, and vigils come crashing down.[127]

11. All teaching that is not of God exists for nothing and will be torn out by the roots. Now the disciples of Aristotle perish, as do the Thomists, the Scotists, those of Bonaventure and those of Occam, and every doctrine that does not arise from the Word of God.

12. The time is coming and is now that no one is considered a true priest except he who proclaims the Word of God. This does away with such things as the Mass, the votive Mass, the use of reliquaries and the dedication of services to others.[128]

13. It is the duty of church members to provide food and clothing appropriately for those who proclaim the Word of God to them, and furthermore to take them into protection. Here the following, among others, cease to exist: government-paid clergy, retired money lenders, faith guilds, the priesthood *in absentia*, impostors, and rabble-rousers.

14. Let those who fear purgatory and those who have God "in the belly" go find the tomb of Moses. It will be some time before they find it.

---

[127] Latin was the church language, and so the common people did not understand much of it. It was their *hocus pocus pilatus pas* (fairy tale magic spell), from *hoc est corpus meus and sub Pontio Pilato passus est* ("This is my body... (which) suffered under Pontius Pilate"), phrases from the priest's mouth.
[128] The votive mass is a service that is fulfilled as a vow by someone. This also cost money. Often at certain services, relics (eg. of saints) were taken from cupboards and carried around.

15. So that priests and others might hide their carnal sins, Barabbas was set free and Christ killed.

16. To demand virtue to be achieved by human effort is no different than ordering someone to fly without wings.

17. He who conceals the Word of God, or twists it for temporary gain, betrays the grace of God, as did the ruddy Esau for a dish of lentils. But Christ will reject him.

18. Whoever does not try to earn his bread with sweat on his face is cursed and is not worthy of the food he eats. Now all slackers are put to death, no matter who they are. The truth is immortal."[129]

Hubmaier's eighteen articles left a powerful mark on the development of early Anabaptist thought in the area of Switzerland and southern Germany.

Although these theses are not overtly Anabaptist, the attentive reader will recognize in some of them concepts that would later play a prominent role in Anabaptist theology. Most of the propositions are reformatory and anti-Roman Catholic in content (theses 1, 2, 5, 6, 7, 9,[130] 10, 11 and 16). In particular, proposition 8 and 3a are indications of early Anabaptist leanings. "Since each Christian believes for himself and is baptized for himself, each one must see for himself with Scripture in hand and judge whether he is properly nourished by his pastor."[131] Believer's baptism is more or less implicitly mentioned here already. We also see how central to life and thought the Scriptures had become for Hubmaier. A biblical foundation was an absolute principle for Southern German Swiss Anabaptists. Human traditions and considerations had only a derived authority.

---

[129] This originally read, "*Die warheyt ist untödlich.*" In light of persecutions, Hubmaier probably means to say that truth is ineradicable.
[130] Thesis 9 ends remarkably with "all pilgrimages now plummet to the ground." Hubmaier, as the former mouthpiece of the Chapel for the "Beautiful Mary," knew better than anyone what he was expressing with these words.
[131] "Wie ein yeder Christ für sich selbst glaubt und getaufft wirt, also soll ein yeder sehen unnd urteylen durch die geschrifft, ob er recht von seynem hyrten gespeyßt und getrenckt werde," Westin and Bergsten, ed., *Balthasar Hubmaier: Writings*, 73.

We recognize early radical convictions in proposition 3a as well: "This faith does not look on idly but extends to God in gratitude and in charity and all kinds of good works to fellow men." No doubt Luther would have largely agreed with the statement. Faith without works is a dead faith.[132] But we have noted that in radical circles, Luther's *sola fide* was not central. Faith did not mean merely spiritual deliverance alone. Whoever said "faith" also meant liberating speech and action. In Hubmaier's wording that "faith does not look on idly" we see something of the criticism which developed in radical circles against both Luther and Zwingli. Faith was not to wait and idly watch but was to extend itself in charity and good works toward fellow men.

In the resistance, to Schaffhausen, returning to Zürich

Two months after Hubmaier's convocation, the Austrian army decided to postpone its attack on Waldshut. According to reports, this was because of a lack of manpower, but this was most likely not the only reason for postponement. When it became known that an attack on Waldshut was imminent, the town was sealed off and occupied by disgruntled farmers from the surrounding area. Hundreds of armed, indignant peasants marched into town to— if necessary—take on the prince's troops. This turned out to be the "breaching of a dike," because in a short time thousands of peasants spread out over several regions to resist the authorities.

The districts of Stühlingen and Upper Swabia turned into hotbeds of resistance and became the scene of the first major peasant uprising in southern Germany and the Black Forest. The unrest spread at lightning speed and Balthasar Hubmaier also began to take part in the resistance. His role in the uprising was not entirely clear, but it is certain that Hubmaier supported the rebellious peasants and—on several instances—provided them with the necessary weapons. It is also assumed that he wrote a number of texts at the time in which he openly declared his support for the rebellious peasants. The peasants were, as it were,

---

[132] "Solcher glaub mag nit müssig geen, sunder muß außbrechen gegen Gott in dancksagung und gegen den menschen in allerley werck bruederlichern liebe. Hie werden alle butzenwerck nider getossen als kertzen, palmen und weyhwasser," Westin and Bergsten, ed., *Balthasar Hubmaier: Writings*, 72.

useful agents for church and government. Hubmaier advocated reforms that offered the peasants social and economic prospects.

On September 1, 1524, Hubmaier fled to nearby Schaffhausen, which was also committed to the Reformation. Hubmaier felt somewhat responsible and thus guilty that the safety of Waldshut was threatened, and therefore he thought it better to take refuge for an indefinite period of time.

At Schaffhausen, the teacher wrote some important tracts, including his well-known main work *Von Ketzern und ihren Verbrennern* (*On heretics and those who burn them*). In this work, Hubmaier wanted to rid himself of the stigma of "heretic" for he certainly did not see himself as a deviant Christian. A heretic was one who resisted and distorted the light of Scripture. Hubmaier, on the other hand, repeatedly called for discussion and conversation, always with the intention of closely examining and talking through the Scriptures. The government, in particular, appeared to be mostly unwilling to do this.

In the reformer's view, it was therefore unjust to declare him a heretic when a debate on the content of Scripture could not be held. Hubmaier constantly stated that he was eager to learn from others, advocating a degree of restraint and tolerance in conflicting matters of faith. Surely a government could not prematurely judge and proceed to prosecute on religious matters? Moreover, Hubmaier believed that opposing views and customs could be profitable for mutual edification. First, carefully listen to each other and honestly try to understand each other before you pass judgement.

Hubmaier openly expressed his respect and reverence for the government. He did not want to be accused, under any circumstances, of hatred toward his superiors. His critical questions addressed to the government were too fundamental for that; they were not to be confused with gut feelings. He was too much of a theologian and reformer and gentleman for that. Hubmaier distanced himself from any social unrest that was served up under the guise of Christian language and so-called Christian justice.

The frustrating part of Hubmaier's history in Waldshut was that he was not heard by the Catholic authorities. Hubmaier's respect for the ruler was severely tested, when the ruler refused to listen and proceeded to persecute him anyway. Hubmaier believed the government had no right to pass judgement on matters of faith anyway. Incidentally, many other Reformed Christians told him exactly the same thing.

According to Hubmaier, the government's task was to punish those who committed evil.[133] After all, that's how it was written in Scripture:

> Would you have no fear of the one who is in authority? Then do what is good, and you will receive his approval, for he is God's servant for your good. But if you do wrong, be afraid, for he does not bear the sword in vain. For he is the servant of God, an avenger who carries out God's wrath on the wrongdoer. Therefore one must be in subjection, not only to avoid God's wrath but also for the sake of conscience.[134]

But the authorities in Waldshut were not talking about true heretics: false believers who propagated wrong ideas about God and Christ and were therefore unreliable citizens. The government's duty was to catch thieves, tax evaders, rapists and murderers, but not to use soldiers on groups of Christians who, for example, taught different views of Christian life and church.

Nor was the government allowed to resort to repression and persecution when Christians rebelled against church abuses and socio-economic exploitation. Then, according to Hubmaier, there had to be talk and a search for what was "just and according to the Scriptures." If the government thought it had to separate the wheat from the chaff or pull the weeds out of the fields early, it was in flagrant violation of God's order and was putting itself in the place of God. Christ himself said in the parable of the wheat and the weeds, "Let both grow together until the harvest."[135] He was exhorting patience. Judging the faith of others was in the first instance a matter for God and only in the second instance a possibility for the church to make use of (in disciplinary matters). The government had no business there, unless practices to subvert the state were taking place.

In the fall of 1524, Hubmaier returned to Waldshut via Zürich. At Zürich, because of his record, the reformer was received with

---

[133] De Vries, *Leer en praxis van de vroege dopers*, 20.
[134] Romans 13:3–5.
[135] Matthew 13:30.

due honour and spoke with the local town pastor Zwingli. Hubmaier's tenacity had by now become proverbial to the radicals in Zürich. His presence in the city was enough for some to put their money where their mouth was and proceed to a limited iconoclasm.

Zürich was a veritable powder keg in late fall 1524. The tragic rift between Zwingli and Grebel (and his followers) was almost inevitable by then. Hubmaier must have tried to convince Zwingli of the importance of the Reformation "momentum." Now was the time to move on and fully recognize the movement of the Spirit. For Hubmaier, these were so-called "kairotic" times (God-given moments), as they were for Grebel, Sattler, Mantz and Reublin. When Hubmaier was back in Waldshut, he was probably more determined than ever to continue the Reformation with a firm hand.

Baptized

Early in 1525, Hubmaier married Elsbeth Hügline (d. 1528), the woman who would tirelessly assist him with wisdom and decisiveness in the hard times that were coming. While the third Zürich religious meeting came to nothing on January 17 and the so-called "radicals" were rebaptized four days later, Hubmaier also decided to take an even clearer stance than before. The pastor decided not to baptize any more children, unless they were seriously ill or unless the parents really insisted. However, newborn children were given a special blessing.

In this cautious approach to the baptismal issue, we recognize once again the respect Hubmaier wanted to show to dissenters who did not share his opinion. He operated cautiously, somewhat in the spirit of Zwingli, but in the spring of 1525, Hubmaier took a profound step forward on the path he had embarked upon. It was to prove a decisive step, whereby all previous caution was abandoned, and this would radically change the spiritual scene of Waldshut.

We know Hubmaier confessed himself to the radical Anabaptists no sooner than April 1525. He was forty-five years old at the time. After the evening of January 21, 1525, on which the first Anabaptist "cell" opened in Zürich, a series of events was set in motion that would lead to Hubmaier's believer's baptism of faith three months later.

Wilhelm Reublin was among those who were expelled from the city of Zürich at the end of January due to "rebaptism." The expellees dispersed into the surroundings of Zürich, and made sure that the baptism of faith was widely known. It was hoped this would bring all potential Anabaptists to their feet against the Zwinglians, and form a united front against Zürich. Anabaptists, for example, moved to nearby Zollikon (South of Zürich) and to Basel and Bern (Westward), St. Gallen and Appenzell (Eastward). Likewise, people trekked north, including to Schaffhausen, Hallau and Waldshut.[136] The news spread quickly, but so did, of course, the indignation at the expulsion. We can imagine their ejection from Zürich was like lighting a fuse on a powder keg. Peasants and other marginalized citizens rebelled and threatened to disrupt public order.

Conrad Grebel and Wilhelm Reublin paid several visits to Waldshut in March 1525. They explained their decisions to Hubmaier and tried to convince him to join forces with them. A month later, when Reublin was again in Waldshut, on Easter Sunday, April 14, he baptized Balthasar Hubmaier and with him sixty others. During the rest of Easter week, Hubmaier himself baptized 300 more. On the Monday after Easter, Holy Communion was celebrated in a simple manner. Foot washing was also introduced.[137]

Although during the spring a large portion of the Waldshut people had been baptized on expression of personal faith, Hubmaier was disappointed with the results. There appeared to be little enthusiasm for actually implementing his reformation program. The reformer ran into a wall of fear and reluctance among many. During this time, he wrote two important works, one on the Christian life[138] and the other on Christian baptism.[139]

---

[136] Snyder, *Anabaptist History and Theology*, 107.
[137] The washing of feet was also seen as an institution of Jesus. See John 13:14–17: "you also ought to wash one another's feet. For I have given you an example, that you also should do just as I have done to you.... blessed are you if you do them." The words are at least as strong as those of the institutions of baptism and the Lord's Supper.
[138] Balthasar Hubmaier, *Ain Summ aintz gantzen Christlichen lebens. Durch Baldasaren Frydberger, Predicant yetz zu Waldßhütt, verzeichnet an die drey Kirchen Regensburg, Jngolstat und Frydberg, seinen lieben herren, briedern vnd schwestern in gott dem herren. Sonderlich ain bericht den kinder Touff vnd das Nachttmal belangent* (1525).
[139] *Von dem christlichen Tauff der Gläubigen* (1525).

Both tracts are considered foundational to the Anabaptist cause in the sixteenth century.

Most leading Anabaptists did not get around to writing. Their lives were too chaotic for that. Only a few managed to commit their thoughts and convictions to paper. Hubmaier was one of them. His versatility and scholarly curiosity helped him do so. He was one of the few early Anabaptists to publish an account of the baptism of faith. Hubmaier's book on baptism was both a standard work and a reference work in its day. It was especially popular among Swiss and Southern German Anabaptists. Soon violent reactions from Zwingli and Calvin followed.

Hubmaier's argument on baptism was easy to follow and was based primarily on a clear discussion of numerous New Testament texts. His conclusion was that biblical passages did not call for the baptism of children, but for the repentance and faith of people who could be held responsible for the arrangement of their lives. Only when faith in Christ could be established was baptism allowed.

Those who believed in Christ's death and resurrection, and wanted to follow him in dependence, shared in the forgiveness and new life of God. Hubmaier had been able to experience this himself during his stay at Waldshut. By faith he was given part in the power of a new kind of life that had been opened up by Christ as a decisive phase in the history of salvation.[140]

Apprehended

In the second half of 1525, the rebellious peasants in the German-Swiss border region gradually lost ground and, on December 5, Waldshut was taken by force by Austrian soldiers. Hubmaier was seriously ill at this time. Despite his illness he was forced to escape to Zürich. His farewell to the brothers and sisters at Waldshut was intense and painful.

When Zwingli learned that Hubmaier had arrived in Zürich, he feared there would be a new rebellion in the city and he had the refugee-reformer arrested. The peace in Zürich was shaky and fragile. Because of an Anabaptist like Hubmaier, serious trouble could easily break out again. A council was formed to

---

[140] De Vries, *Leer en praxis van de vroege dopers*, 13.

question the arrestee about his doctrines. All sorts of rumours circulated about Hubmaier. It was said, for example, that he taught that Christians were not allowed to own property but should live in community of property. Also, Christians could not work in government service because the worldly government could not be on the side of God's kingdom. It was also said he would claim he was without sin. Fortunately, Hubmaier was able to refute all of these allegations.

When Hubmaier asked for a debate, he got one. In the company of nine other scholars, swords were crossed with Zwingli. Hubmaier himself had been able to select four of the experts present. During the discussion, the still-ill Anabaptist brought forward Zwingli's own statements in which he claimed children should not be baptized until they had received sufficient instruction in the faith. Zwingli denied these and believed he had been misunderstood. Hubmaier was also exhorted to recant his views on baptism.

On pain of extradition to the Austrian authorities, Hubmaier was required to prepare a text and read it publicly on Friday, December 29, in the large Fraumünster church, following Zwingli's sermon. At this point, the physically weak teacher had no choice but to agree. Hubmaier was going through a deep depression, spiritually and physically.

When it came time for Hubmaier to read his text in the Fraumünster church on January 7, 1526, he could not get the words out of his mouth. His first words were, "O what agony and sorrow have I experienced last night over the points I have formulated. I therefore declare here and now: 'I cannot and will not recant.'"[141] Hubmaier then began to explain why infant baptism was contrary to New Testament teaching. Zwingli immediately intervened and reminded Hubmaier of the agreement made. When Hubmaier still refused, he was taken away and led to the torture chambers. After months of repeated beatings, Hubmaier was once again ready to "stage" a so-called recantation. In three churches, the tormented reformer uttered his text, after which he was allowed to quietly leave the Swiss city at the end of April 1526. The Anabaptist was drained and humiliated. He had gone

---

[141] Estep, *The Anabaptist Story*, 92.

off terribly in the eyes of both the local Zwinglians and his "own" Anabaptists. Some felt betrayed by their master; others felt sorry for him.

Moravia and martyrdom

Immediately after leaving, Hubmaier picked up the thread of his Anabaptist faith. Torture and intimidation could not break his inner convictions after all, although the memory of the moments of weakness continued to haunt Hubmaier. The tone of his expositions now changed forever. He sounded less triumphalist and more aware of his hidden imperfections. In a succinct defense of faith written in 1526, the troubled leader wrote,

> I might err, I am but a man, but a heretic I cannot be because I am constantly seeking to understand the Word of God....
> O God, forgive me my weakness.

For a short time Hubmaier stayed in Augsburg, where he baptized Hans Denck (1495–1527), among others. Denck would become a valuable spiritual leader for the Anabaptist movement. From Augsburg, the Hubmaier family travelled on to Nikolsburg in Moravia, some 150 kilometres north of Vienna, a true sanctuary for Anabaptist Christians, in the middle of Bohemia (now in the Czech Republic). The influence of the famous Johannes Hus (1369–1415) was still noticeable in that region.[142]

The stay at Nikolsburg was initially a relief. Hubmaier could write and publish there, and also enjoyed the sympathy of Leonhard von Liechtenstein (1482–1534), baron and administrator of Moravia. Hubmaier even baptized von Lichtenstein. Within a year, Hubmaier would baptize some 6,000 believers; his ministry was expanding in a big way.

More than 10,000 Anabaptists migrated to Moravia in those years, and with their faith they also brought their diversity. In Nikolsburg, Hubmaier met Hans Hut (1490–1527), who, as an Anabaptist, thought strongly along the lines of Thomas Müntzer. Von Lichtenstein was concerned about the anti-state spirit of Hut

---

[142] Johannes Hus can be seen as a precursor of the Reformation. The Czech reformer was burned at Prague in 1415. His ideas influenced Luther, among others.

and his followers and urged an open conversation with the Anabaptists. Hut saw himself as an end-time prophet and predicted that the kingdom of God would dawn in 1528.

In May 1527, a religious conversation took place in which Hut and Hubmaier engaged in a vigorous debate. While Hut used chiliastic rhetoric to attack worldly governments, Hubmaier defended the vital place God had assigned to the state. Christians even had the duty to enlist in military service and to pay taxes for the armed forces. Christians were also allowed to work in government service as civil servants, according to Hubmaier.[143] After the discussion, von Lichtenstein had Hans Hut arrested, and it was clear to everyone that Hubmaier had become a moderate Anabaptist. The reformer from Waldshut was clearly distinguishing himself in his last years as a moderate.

Meanwhile, in February 1527, King Ferdinand I (1503–1564), a sworn enemy of Anabaptism and certainly of Balthasar Hubmaier, had also become king of Bohemia.[144] Ferdinand was eager to have Hubmaier extradited and quickly began to urge von Lichtenstein to do so. When it became clear to the latter that he could only keep power over Moravia if he betrayed Hubmaier and his wife, it was easy for him to make up his mind. Balthasar and Elsbeth Hubmaier were escorted to Vienna, where they were immediately apprehended by the Austrian authorities. From Vienna, the Hubmaiers were transferred to the Kreuzenstein state prison near Korneuburg on the Danube (about 15 km north of Vienna).

At Hubmaier's request, he was allowed to write an account of his faith. In January 1528, the tract *Rechenschaft meines Glaubens* (*An account of my faith*) was handed over to Ferdinand I. Ferdinand recognized in the articulation a number of Catholic convictions, such as attention to free will and the absence of radical eschatology. But he found it deficient in the areas of baptism and the Lord's Supper, upon which Hubmaier was given the opportunity to supplement the text on a number of

---

[143] Hubmaier is inconsistent in his support of the positive role of government. See De Vries, *Leer en praxis van de vroege dopers*, 21.
[144] Ferdinand I, the brother of Charles V, was archduke of Austria and became emperor of the Holy Roman Empire in 1558. He became king of Bohemia and Hungary in 1527. Philip II was king of Spain and the Netherlands.

Kreuzenstein Castle, near Korneuburg, Austria

points. The ammended text was submitted but was still not convincing enough for the king. A complete revocation of old positions had been requested. Hubmaier was then again taken to Vienna and interrogated before the dreaded tribunal of heretics. Even under torture, he stood his ground: he would not revoke believer's baptism.

On March 10, 1528, Hubmaier, a founding father of Swiss and Austrian Anabaptism, was led to the stake in Vienna and publicly burned for his participation in the peasant uprising of October 1524. His wife had to look on and she urged her husband to remain faithful to God until the end. When the wood started to burn, he asked the bystanders to pray for him.

One of the eyewitnesses gave a brief account of the execution and indicated that Hubmaier clung to his heresy like an unyielding rock. In a Swiss dialect, Hubmaier spoke, "O gracious God, forgive my sins in my severe torture." To all those present he said, "O dear brethren, if I have hurt anyone, by words or deeds, let him forgive me for the sake of my God who is full of mercy. I forgive everyone who has done me harm." When his clothes were taken off, he said, "From You, too, O God, the clothes were taken off. My clothes I gladly leave here and I pray You, preserve my spirit and my soul!" Then Hubmaier spoke in Latin: *in manus tuas, Domine, commendo spiritum meum* ("Father, into your hands I commit my spirit!").[145] As sulfur and gunpowder were rubbed into his beard, he spoke the words, "Yes, brine me well, brine me well." After this he raised his head and said, "O dear brothers and sisters, pray God that he grant me perseverance in this suffering." Finally, as his beard caught fire, the man cried out to Jesus. Hubmaier died of suffocation in the smoke.[146] Three days later, his wife Elsbeth was drowned in the Danube with a rope and stone around her neck.

The history of Balthasar Hubmaier cannot be understood unless both the strength and weakness of his faith are considered. The above events relate the documented faith of a man who wanted to follow Christ radically, and in doing so regularly fell short. But his ideals of faith did not suffer, rather his self-image did. Indeed, rebirth is a great renewing force, but on this side of the *eschaton* it always faces limitations. Hubmaier learned all too well the limits of salvation on this side of the grave.

As a theologian and reformer, Hubmaier has been underappreciated for too long. Fortunately, this has changed over the past few decades. Austrian Baptists consider Hubmaier to be Austria's first Baptist.[147] In 1928, some international Baptist unions commemorated the 400th anniversary of Hubmaier's death as a martyr for his Anabaptist convictions. On June 11, 2003, at the Vienna Stubentor,[148] where the stake once stood, a memorial plaque in memory of Hubmaier was erected by the Austrian government. With this gesture, the person of the Anabaptist Balthasar Hubmaier was publicly rehabilitated;[149] may the same be done for his wife.

---

[145] Luke 23:46.
[146] This eyewitness was Stephen Sprügel, the dean of the faculty of philosophy at the University of Vienna. Sprügel was no supporter of Hubmaier and therefore will have given a fairly objective account. See Estep, *The Anabaptist Story*, 103.
[147] A plaque commemorating Hubmaier hangs in the oldest Baptist church in Mollardgasse, Vienna.
[148] Bath House Gate, now a metro station
[149] For those who want to read more about Hubmaier: Torsten Bergsten, "Balthasar Hubmaier: Anabaptist Theologian and Martyr," in *Balthasar Hubmaier: Theologian of Anabaptism*, ed. William R. Estep (Valley Forge, PA: Judson Press, 1978); Daniel Liechty, *Early Anabaptist Spirituality: Selected Writings* (New York: Paulist Press, 1994);

2.6 Schleitheim

One year prior to Hubmaier's death, on the very day that Grand Duke Ferdinand I was crowned King of Bohemia and Hungary, a group of Anabaptists secretly met at Schleitheim near Schaffhausen in order to openly and unanimously endorse a common declaration of faith.[150] The Swiss Anabaptists desired to have their own confession of faith. On February 24, 1527, the conference adopted in great unity the text that has come to be called the *Schleitheim Confession*, in which seven articles of faith are confessed. The articles proved to be very formative and representative of Anabaptist thought and belief in Switzerland, southern Germany and Austria. Hubmaier differed with the *Schleitheim Confession* on a few points, but could have endorsed most of it without question.

Since the influence of this confession has been decisive for the development of Anabaptism in Germany and the surrounding area, we would like to take a moment to consider its contents. The *Schleitheim Confession* articulated a way of believing and living that is closely associated with Michael Sattler (1490–1527) and those surrounding him. We also want to address Michael Sattler, after first explaining the core ideas of the *Schleitheim Confession*.[151]

Need for a confession

The *Schleitheim Confession* came about at a crucial moment in the early history of South German and Swiss Anabaptism. In January 1527, it became clear the Anabaptist movement was in danger of being automatically identified with resistance, violence and rebellious peasants. Anyone who said "Anabaptists" was

---

Eddie Louis Mabry, *Balthasar Hubmaier's Doctrine of the Church* (Lanham: University Press of America, 1994); James Stayer, *The German Peasants' War and Anabaptist Community of Goods* (Montreal: McGill-Queen's University Press, 1991); David C. Steinmetz, *Reformers in the Wings: From Geiler von Kaysersberg to Theodore Beza* (Oxford: Oxford University Press, 2001), 138–145; George H. Williams and Angel M. Mergal, ed., *Spiritual and Anabaptist Writers*, Library of Christian Classics (Philadelphia: Westminster John Knox Press, 1957).
[150] See Williams, *The Radical Reformation*, 288–313.
[151] See (also for the sequel) James M. Stayer, "Swiss-Southern German Anabaptism," in *A Companion to Anabaptism and Spiritualism, 1521–1700*, Brill's Companions to the Christian Tradition 6, ed. John D. Roth and James M. Stayer (Leiden: Brill, 2007), 83–117.

The *Schleitheim Confession*

talking about vengeful people who carried the sword. Anabaptists were being stigmatized and persecuted as villains.[152] The fact that almost all Anabaptists believed just the opposite was difficult to understand in the established Catholic and also Protestant churches. In order to rid themselves of this threatening stigma, the Anabaptist delegates in Schleitheim declared their fundamental opposition to violence and the use of the sword. This widely supported statement was also intended to prevent the new movement from resorting to weapons and revolution if there was a power vacuum. For some Anabaptists, this obviously meant a radical change of course.

---

[152] Reformed churches of Dutch background typically adhere to the *Belgic Confession* of Guido de Brès. In article 36, "Of the Magistrates," it declares: "Wherefore we detest the Anabaptists and other seditious people, and in general all those who reject the higher powers and magistrates, and would subvert justice, introduce community of goods, and confound that decency and good order which God hath established among men."

A possible power vacuum was not unthinkable. After all, the main leaders of Anabaptism from its beginning, Conrad Grebel and Felix Mantz, had already died. After the historic evening in January 1525, Grebel had spent twenty months alternating between travelling and being detained as an Anabaptist preacher. Physically weak as he was, he eventually succumbed to the effects of the plague in the summer of 1526.

Mantz had been put to death by drowning on Saturday afternoon, January 5, 1527. He was the first Anabaptist to be officially sentenced to death and executed in reformist Zürich.[153] In the very city where he had sat at Zwingli's feet, he was taken in a boat close to the city hall to a fishing hut in the middle of the Limmat. His hands and feet were bound (with his arms pulled over his knees and a stick passed under his knees) and dumped into the water. Countless people watched from shore, for Mantz was the most popular Anabaptist of the time. He only lived to be 28, as did Grebel.

Thus, in January 1527, the young Anabaptist movement was missing its two most important leaders. In addition, Blaurock was in Tyrol and Hubmaier in Moravia. Other names of importance, such as Wilhelm Reublin or Johannes Brötli, did not have sufficient leadership qualities to bind the growing number of Anabaptists together and give them a face.[154] Therefore, shortly after Mantz's death, some determined and somewhat distressed delegates of Anabaptist congregations had met secretly with Michael Sattler at Schleitheim (Schlaten am Randen).

Sattler had drafted a statement of faith that had been read by most Anabaptists and was intended to prevent the movement from being structurally misrepresented. It also sought to guard against further radicalization and polarization. The latter could have meant the end of the fledgling Anabaptist church in the area of Lake Constance. The statement of faith would make clear to everyone that the religious content of the Anabaptist movement was in no way dangerous or subversive to the state.

In the confession, Sattler called on Anabaptist believers to separate themselves from the extremists among them. The

---

[153] von Muralt and Smid, ed., *Quellen zur Geschichte der Täufer in der Schweiz*, §204, 224–226.
[154] Estep, *The Anabaptist Story*, 64.

movement was sickened by radical elements who abused their freedom in Christ. They thought they could have the freedom to follow an "inner Word" outside the commandment of Scripture, and thereby sow unrest and division. Following an "inner Word" or an "inner light" was a common occurrence among Anabaptist Christians, and was roundly criticized by Sattler as dangerous.

Some of these *spiritualists* at the time included Karlstadt, Schwenckfeld and Müntzer. For them, the written Word of God was less important than the immediate personal revelation of the Spirit in one's own heart and soul. After all, they claimed, what was written was essentially only "a dead letter." The written Word was readily placed underneath a mystical personal word. Anabaptists such as Grebel, Mantz and Sattler could not support the revolutionary apocalyptic enthusiasm of the spiritualists. This obtrusive and sometimes even violent enthusiasm was too far removed from Scripture, in which God clearly indicated the path of non-violence and peace. The words of Conrad Grebel in a letter to Thomas Müntzer were well known:

> Likewise, one should not protect the gospel and its adherents with the sword—nor oneself.... They do not wield the worldly sword, do not make war, because for them killing has completely ceased.[155]

The *Schleitheim Confession* had seven sections:

1. Baptism
2. Excommunication
3. Ehe Lord's Supper
4. Separation from abominations
5. Pastors in the congregation
6. The sword
7. The oath

---

[155] "Man soll ouch das evangelium und sine annemer nit schirmen mit dem schwert oder sy sich selbs.... Sy gebruchend ouch weder weltlichs schwert noch krieg, dann by inen ist das tötten gar abgetan," von Muralt and Smid, ed., *Quellen zur Geschichte der Täufer in der Schweiz*, I, 17.

In concise style it explained that (1) baptism was to be administered to everyone who had been taught about repentance and life renewal, who knew about the forgiveness of sins and wanted to "walk in the resurrection of Jesus Christ."[156]

In this text we again see the Anabaptist view of Christian ethics. It was possible for Christians who lived out of the forgiveness of Christ to grow upward in their lifestyle toward the image of Christ. After all, that is how Scripture described the Christian's calling.

Paul testified:

> And we all, with unveiled face, beholding the glory of the Lord, are being transformed into the same image from one degree of glory to another. For this comes from the Lord who is the Spirit.[157]

> For those whom he foreknew he also predestined to be conformed to the image of his Son, in order that he might be the firstborn among many brothers.[158]

This was not only about the final destination of a Christian, but also about the daily change he was undergoing—especially in times of suffering and tribulation—in his mind and spirit.[159] Baptism symbolized death with Christ and a daily walk in resurrection and newness of life.

The congregation was to be a community in which each member was watched over and was encouraged to live a pure life, and in which for this reason (2) discipline was recognized and applied as an instrument to that end. Naturally, the well-known passage on church discipline from the Gospel of Matthew (18:15–17) was relied upon for this purpose. This included that (3) the Lord's Supper could only be celebrated with Christians who walked together in the light of and with God and had the same vision of baptism. Christians therefore (4) had to keep away from everything the world held in its evil and darkness. Light could not

---

[156] "...und allen denen, die wandeln wollen in der Auferstehung Jesus Christi." See McClendon, *Systematic Theology*, 1:246–249.
[157] 2 Corinthians 3:18.
[158] Romans 8:29.
[159] See also 2 Corinthians 4:16–18 ("our inner self is being renewed day by day").

have fellowship with darkness. This fourth article ended with an early reference to worldly violence. If the Christian was to keep away from all that was unchristian and diabolical, then sword and clash of arms were immediately off the table.[160]

Before Sattler went into detail about the prohibition of carrying the sword, he first indicated that (5) the shepherd of the spiritual flock should, according to Paul's rule, enjoy a good reputation. He was to be "above reproach."[161] He also had to educate the congregation in life and doctrine in such a way that he silenced the slanderers "outside." Such virtuous pastors had the privilege of making a living by their service; if necessary, they were maintained by their own church members.

The sword

In the final two articles, Sattler addressed the Christian ethics of the sword and of the oath. In particular, the ethic of the sword weighed heavily for them. For this reason, we have translated Article 6 in its entirety.[162]

> Six: On the sword we have agreed as follows. The sword is a measure of God that is outside the perfection of Christ.[163] It punishes and kills the wicked man and shelters and protects the good man. In the law, the sword is commanded to punish and kill the wicked. The worldly authorities were created to use the sword. Yet in the perfection of Christ, discipline is applied only to warn and exclude the sinner, not by killing the body but only by admonishing and demanding to sin no more.
>
> Now the question is being asked by many who do not accept Christ's will for us whether, for the shelter and protection of

---

160 "So werden dann auch zweifellos die unchristlichen, ja teuflischen Waffen der Gewalt von uns fallen, als da sind Schwert, Harnisch und dergleichen und jede Anwendung davon, sei es für Freunde oder gegen die Feinde—kraft des Wortes Christi: Ihr sollt dem Übel nicht widerstehen (Matt. 5:39)."
161 1 Timothy 3:2.
162 The German text is taken from the MennoPedia, available on the Internet.
163 See Hebrews 7:19, "(for the law made nothing perfect); but on the other hand, a better hope is introduced, through which we draw near to God."

the good and for the sake of love, a Christian cannot or should not carry the sword? In reply we—in unison—offer the following. Christ teaches and commands us to learn from him, for he is meek and humble of heart. Thus, we find rest for our souls.[164] Now, Christ does not say in connection with a pagan woman arrested for adultery that she should be stoned according to his Father's law; but he does say, "As the Father has commanded me, so I do." He warns her according to the law of compassion and forgiveness not to continue sinning: "Go, and from now on sin no more!"[165]

A second question about the sword is whether a Christian may judge between unbelievers who have worldly disputes and conflicts with one another. The answer to that is this: Christ did not want to judge between two brothers concerning an inheritance issue and spoke out against it.[166] This is how we too are supposed to act.

A third question concerning the sword is whether a Christian may enter into public service if he is appointed to do so. To this question we answer as follows: When it seemed that Christ would be made king, he withdrew[167] and did not discern his Father's institution.[168] Thus, we too must do likewise and follow after him. Then we will not walk in darkness. After all, he himself says, "If anyone would come after me, let him deny himself and take up his cross and follow me."[169] He himself forbids the means of power of the sword, saying,

---

[164] Matthew 11:29.
[165] John 8:11.
[166] See Luke 12:14, "Man, who made me a judge or arbitrator over you?"
[167] John 6:15.
[168] There is a translation issue here. The German reads: "und hat die Ordnung seines Vaters nicht berücksichtigt." Lumpkin translates with "and did not view it as the arrangement of His Father" (*Baptist Confessions of Faith*, 8), but a better English translation is "and did not discern the ordinance of His Father." Either Jesus did not discern becoming king at the behest of men as the "Ordnung des Vaters berücksichtigt" or kingship itself, although kingship itself was an institution of God in the Old Testament. The latter statement does more justice to the German text (see the first lines of Article 6).
[169] Matthew 16:24.

"You know that the rulers of the Gentiles lord it over them…. (Yet,) it shall not be so among you."[170]

Furthermore, Paul says, "those whom he foreknew he also predestined to be conformed to the image of his Son."[171] Peter also says, "Christ suffered," not reigned, "leaving you an example, so that you might follow in his steps."[172]

Finally, on the following grounds, it may be noted that it is not befitting for a Christian to hold a government position. The governmental power is carnal; that of the Christian is spiritual. Its houses and residences are fused with this world. Those of the Christian are in heaven. Their citizenship is of this world, the citizenship of the Christian is in heaven.[173] The weapons of the former for battle and war are human and are directed against the flesh. The weapons of Christians are spiritual and are directed against power of the devil.[174] The people of the world are armed with spears and iron but Christians are equipped with the armor of God, with truth, righteousness, peace, faith, salvation and the Word of God. In short, as Christ, our Head thinks, so the members of Christ's body should always reason like him, lest there be divisions in the body and it perish.[175] After all, any kingdom divided against itself will be destroyed.[176] Now, since Christ is as he is described, the members of his body also ought to be so, that the body may remain unblemished and one, and it may unfold and build itself up.[177]

For the Anabaptist Christian, carrying the sword was outside of resurrection life with Christ. In his confession, the sword as an institution of God stood outside the perfection of Christ (*Das*

---

[170] Matthew 20:25.
[171] Romans 8:29.
[172] See 1 Peter 2:21. The words "nicht geherrscht" are not from 1 Peter and were inserted by Sattler himself or by someone else.
[173] Philippians 3:20; see also Ephesians 2:12,19.
[174] See 2 Corinthians 10:3–4.
[175] 1 Corinthians 12:25.
[176] Matthew 12:25.
[177] Ephesians 4:16; Colossians 2:19.

Schwert ist eine Gottesordnung außerhalb der Vollkommenheit Christi). It was not that Sattler thereby misunderstood government and the sword as an institution of God. Certainly not. Anabaptists could not be accused of any kind of Marcionism. Marcion was a second-century Christian who could not imagine that the creative and legislative God of the Old Testament was also the heavenly Father of Jesus Christ. What—in his view—seemed perfectly obvious according to a simple reading of the New Testament, namely, that Jesus Christ was born in Israel as the Son of God and lived and thought as a Jew in all things, and that he was basically scrupulous in his observance of the law. It was therefore absolutely inconceivable in the thinking and believing of the Greek-Pontic renewer of the faith. He saw an unbridgeable gap between the old dispensation of the law, which ended in failure, and the new dispensation that replaced the old. It was, so to speak, for Marcion, done with the law; the old had passed away and the new had taken its place.[178] Christians were above the law[179] and that was the last word on it, Marcion thought.

Anabaptist theology could not generally be charged with a Marcionite spirit.[180] The Old Testament was fully taught and preached by most Anabaptists. However, the old dispensation stood entirely in the light of the fulfilment brought by the Son of God, and to demonstrate this, Anabaptists did not hesitate to strongly spiritualize (typologically) the Old Testament.[181] After all, it could not be denied that the New Testament was its fulfillment. Jesus, however, had not abolished the law,[182] but had set himself as the standard next to and above the law. He alone could say: "You have heard that it was said..., but I say to you...."[183] No one but the Son of God could make this kind of statement. Jesus embodied the law, fulfilled the law as the perfect Son of Israel and tied the law strictly to living in obedience to him. Keeping

---

[178] 2 Corinthians 5:17.
[179] Romans 6:14.
[180] See Murray, *Biblical Interpretation in the Anabaptist Tradition*, 119.
[181] The Reformers did not quite get there either. Luther was not far from the Anabaptist view with his hermeneutical thesis *"was Christum treibet."* Calvin made so little distinction between Old and New Testaments that the Jewish theocracy continued.
[182] Matthew 5:17–20.
[183] Matthew 5:21–22, 27–28, 31–32, 33–34, 38–39, 43–44.

the law now became "going the way of Christ." Those who followed Jesus would, by God's grace, fulfil the law. Following Jesus was lawkeeping at the highest level. Jesus himself had become the living law. He did not set aside his Father's law, but elevated the law in all its glory to a rule of life, which could only be realized through a "life in him." The law was, is and remained eternal, just like Christ. Whoever fulfilled Jesus' command to "come after Me" was also fulfilling the law.[184]

Sattler had never thought of doing this in his own strength. To fulfil the law in imitation of Christ required the grace and power of the Holy Spirit. This is how Paul put it: "For God has…condemned sin in the flesh, in order that the righteous requirement of the law might be fulfilled in us, who walk not according to the flesh but according to the Spirit."[185] So, walking by the Spirit, that is, walking after Jesus, in a direct sense also meant fulfilling the law requirements of God. In summary, the commandments of God for Paul came down to this: "Owe no one anything, except to love each other, for the one who loves another has fulfilled the law." Whoever loved others was thereby fulfilling the law.[186] Therefore, Paul could write to the Galatians that the law was not "against" people who pursued love, joy and peace.[187] Jesus thus taught to walk scrupulously in his footsteps and in doing so, step by step, to look upon our neighbour with love, joy and peace.[188]

Government and repression

We can imagine these considerations, which offer clear indications of a well-defined Christian ethic, caused Anabaptist Christians great difficulty in the way governments imposed their own morality on citizens. Especially where issues of punishment and

---

[184] See Arjan Plaisier, "Geweld en het Oude Testament," in *Wie het zwaard opneemt. Klassiek-theologisch licht over een vreeswekkend thema*, Utrechtse Cahiers, ed. Arjan Plaisier, Guus Labooy, Willem-Henri den Hartog and Nico den Bok (Zoetermeer: Boekencentrum, 2007), 25.
[185] Romans 8:3–4.
[186] See Romans 13:8–10. See Galatians 5:14: "For the whole law is fulfilled in one word: 'You shall love your neighbor as yourself.'"
[187] Galatians 5:22–23: "But the fruit of the Spirit is love, joy, peace, patience, kindness, goodness, faithfulness, gentleness, self-control; against such things there is no law."
[188] Interestingly, these first three characteristics of the fruit of the Spirit (love, joy, peace) come so clearly from Christ in John's gospel: "my peace I give to you" (John 14:27), "abide in my love" (15:9) and "that my joy may be in you" (15:11).

violence were concerned. In Sattler's view, governments were a pertinent superfluity for Christians who walked in the footsteps of Jesus. The state was there to punish the sinner, not to interfere with Christians who sought to pursue the principle of love in everything. A punitive government was a blessing when evildoers were apprehended,[189] but not when it sought to serve the church of Christ. In the spiritual world of faith and confession, kings, emperors and mayors had no jurisdiction.[190] A government that thought it had authority over the hearts of people overestimated itself. And not only that: it also made a big mistake. In the realm of man's inner conscience, every act and choice that was forced was nothing more than pretense. Enforced convictions could not be true convictions, for they were not sincere and heartfelt. The heart could not come to new insights through threats or torture, unless they were fearful insights. And this was precisely what governments did as a matter of course; they forced their policies on the citizenry and the people obeyed out of fear.

Sattler noted in the *Schleitheim Confession* that among Christians, application of biblical discipline sufficed *(In der Volkommenheit Christi aber wird der Bann gebraucht)*. Christians were taught not to be rough or hostile with each other and there was to be no violence between Christians. Therefore, Sattler noted:

> But in the perfection of Christ, the discipline is applied, only to warn and exclude the sinner, not by killing the body but merely by warning and enjoining to sin no more.

Christ himself set the example in this, Sattler believed. When a sinful woman who had been caught in adultery was brought to him, Jesus did not allow her to be stoned to death.[191] According to the law of Moses, stoning was apparently an option in this situation, but Jesus did not go along with this. We might say that Jesus "overruled" the prevailing view of the law at the time. The Lord refused to decide on the sword. The only one qualified to

---

[189] Surely it is now established that Anabaptists did not preach rejection of the state, see Hans J. Hillerbrand, "The Anabaptist View of the State," *The Mennonite Quarterly Review* 32 (2, 1958): 88.
[190] Hillerbrand, "The Anabaptist View of the State," 89.
[191] John 8:3–11.

cast the "first stone" was Jesus himself, for he was without sin. The comment, "Let he who is without sin throw the first stone!" was enough to make anyone who wanted the woman dead to walk away. Only Jesus remained standing. He was sinless, and he left the stones on the ground.

Whoever thought he was following Jesus could not, according to Sattler, reach for the sword. This we had to learn in obedience from the loving Lord, he wrote. Violence was not an option for Christians, at least, if they wanted to follow Jesus in everything, because the Lord was meek and humble of heart. For this reason, Anabaptists also could not participate in worldly justice and could not serve in government service. Always attached to secular jurisdiction and government functions were decisions and decrees that a convinced Christian could not agree to. Christians were citizens of a kingdom in heaven, and in this realm different laws and rules applied than on earth. However, Christians did live by the principle of the Sermon on the Mount: "Thy will be done, even as it is done in heaven, so also on earth" (KJV).[192] They lived out the life of the Lord of the Sermon on the Mount. The Spirit of God gave it shape and form through the people of Christ. If grace and peace reigned in heaven, then it was in the will of God to make the earth a kingdom of peace,[193] and Christians belonged in the forefront of that. They were the people of God's compassion. They had experienced God's grace and forgiveness in the very fibre of their being.

Here is where a fundamental distinction between Anabaptist and Protestant views became apparent. Although the Reformers were advocates of a certain freedom of faith, as soon as the personal faith of Anabaptists became public in character and was perceived as disturbing the peace, these believers were ordered to leave the city or province. In such a situation, they had to leave by force and leave hearth and home behind. Luther, Calvin, Zwingli and others had no doubt that government had the duty and authority to externally settle impending conflicts over matters of faith in this way. Formally, civil government carried the authority and they determined whether or not minority gatherings were

---

[192] Matthew 6:10. The Sermon on the Mount covers the teaching in Matthew 5 to 7.
[193] See the description in Isaiah 2:1–5 and 11:1–10.

allowed. They were therefore empowered to intervene if "deviant" baptismal rites were performed or if the liturgy imposed from above was not consistently adhered to. Governments could refuse to provide a spiritual roof over the head of "troublesome" believers. For the first reformers, this was a foregone conclusion (although Luther moved beyond this). Of course, in their view, the state had this authority, and it had to use it. In this respect the state was *defensor fidei* (defender of the faith) and had to come to the aid of the true Christian faith where necessary.

Of course, the state did not stop at regulating matters of faith externally. External faith always touched the invisible capillaries of internal faith. Faith suppression was therefore never just an external matter. The internal was involved, and it was a false comfort to forbid someone to believe his public faith and not his private faith. If someone could formally believe what he wanted, he had to be able to express it with heart and soul. There was no faith without some form of visible piety. If an Anabaptist Christian was allowed to keep his Anabaptist heart, but was not allowed to baptize or be baptized, that form of freedom of faith amounted to nothing. If Anabaptists were not allowed to join together in prayer, open the Scriptures and celebrate the Lord's Supper, then the Reformed mind lacked a proper understanding of the Sermon on the Mount.

We are not talking about whether or not governments should intervene in social disturbances or during social unrest. When militant radicals wanted to seize power, as in Münster, governments had no choice but to intervene. This intervention, however, was quite different from hunting down peace-loving Anabaptists, bringing them to trial or expelling them from the country on pain of treason.

Sattler's death

The Anabaptist soul was profoundly non-violent. The *Schleitheim Confession* breathed this out through all its pores, and encouraged believers to chose a non-violent path. Sattler and many others with him wanted to make clear to the world they were not dangerous revolutionaries. They were not interested in a social upheaval that needed to be enforced by violence. Anabaptism was—above all—an inner revolution, with possible major consequences for the living environment. But Anabaptism began with the free decision to follow Christ. A revolution of grace could result from that, but it was not to be made with hands, and certainly not by force.

Unfortunately, Michael Sattler, almost certainly the drafter of *Schleitheim Confession*, would not be heard. He, who was so opposed to violence, would be killed by brute force. After the one-day conference at Schleitheim had ended on February 24, 1527, and everyone went their separate ways, it became clear the Roman Catholic authorities had been aware of the secret meeting. Sattler and his wife Margaret, along with a number of other men and women, were arrested and imprisoned. It was immediately clear to the authorities that Sattler was a key figure in the Anabaptist movement. The handwritten confession was found in his possession.

The trial against Michael Sattler began on May 17. He managed to defend himself competently and courageously. This was very much against the wishes of his interrogators, who gradually became more agitated and hateful, for—in their view—Sattler did not recognize the authority of the rulers in matters of faith. He based his opinion on Scripture, but was laughed at by his judges. They shook their heads, and as the town clerk of Ensisheim pulled his sword half out of its scabbard he exclaimed: "Believe me, the executioner will argue with you, and if he doesn't, I'll try you myself with the sword!"[194]

Rarely has someone been killed in a more disgusting manner than Michael Sattler. On May 20, he was led to the market square of Rottenburg and a piece of his tongue was cut off. Then, with red-hot pliers, pieces of meat were scorched from his body and he was tied to a cart and led to the other side of the square. On the way, the scorching and mutilation was repeated no less than five times. Michael Sattler himself was not to be dismayed and he prayed for those who persecuted him, as the Lord of the Sermon on the Mount had taught him. Finally, he was bound to a ladder

---

[194] von Muralt and Smid, ed., *Quellen zur Geschichte der Täufer in der Schweiz*, I, §224, 250–252: "Darzu der herrenn fursprech, der statschriber von Einshen, sprach: Der diebhenkenn, der müßte mit im disputieren. Und zech sin schwert halb uß der scheid, sagt: 'So er nitt, wil ich dich selbs mit dissemm schwert richtenn.'" See C. Arnold Snyder, *The Life and Thought of Michael Sattler*, Studies in Anabaptist and Mennonite History 27 (Scottdale: Herald Press, 1984), 100–104.

and pushed into the waiting fire at the place of execution. Still conscious, Sattler prayed an intense prayer and gave a message of comfort to the brothers and sisters present. It was agreed that Sattler would raise his two index fingers if the death of a martyr would be bearable. This he did, and he died with the words of Christ on his lips, "Father, I commend my spirit into your hands." Sattler died that day with three others. His wife was drowned eight days later in the Neckar River.

One of the accusations against Sattler was his claim that the Turks, who regularly stood at the gates of Vienna in the sixteenth century, did not need to be fought, and that if there was to be fighting he would be on the side of the Turks rather than on the side of the Christians.[195] The reason for this provocation will be clear. Sattler would be ashamed to be counted among Christians who were out to kill their neighbours. After all, Christians under arms were not worthy of the name. One could apparently not expect anything else from Muslims, but one should expect something else from Christians. After all, Jesus was explicit about non-violence.[196]

On the other hand, it was easy to understand that Sattler's views were considered rather dangerous to the state. At a time when the Turkish threat was permanently present and violence was quite normal, views advocating non-violence could obviously be seen as foolish and subversive.

2.7 Excursus 2: The Sermon on the Mount

Baptists have a special fascination with the Sermon on the Mount.[197] The reason is obvious: the compact and penetrating speech of Jesus gives a blueprint on the essentials that should characterize and identify a follower of Jesus.[198] One of those

---

[195] For the text, see Klaassen, ed., *Anabaptism in Outline*, 270.
[196] See A. Plaisier, "Geweld en het Nieuwe Testament," in Plaisier, et al, ed., *Wie het zwaard opneemt*, 30: "Jesus did not use violence against people. He calls his followers to do the same."
[197] Balke, *Calvijn*, 329.
[198] J. van Bruggen speaks of a "constitution for all times," in van Bruggen, *De Bergrede, reisgids voor christenen* (Kampen: Kok, 1985), 5.

The burning of eight Anabaptists in Amsterdam in 1549

characteristics is that a disciple of Jesus is not violent.[199] His body and mind should not be "in a state of war."[200]

The texts of the Sermon on the Mount are complex and not easy to understand, but they have a charge that has made these words of Jesus known worldwide. Jesus' stance on violence stands

---

[199] See Sam Janse, *De tegenstem van Jezus. Over geweld in het Nieuwe Testament* (Zoetermeer: Boekencentrum, 2006). See the response by Erik Peels, "'Mijn oog kent geen medelijden.' Agressie en geweld in het Oude Testament," *Wapenveld* 56/5 (2006): 17–29; "Liever langer luisteren. Antwoord aan dr. S. Janse," *Wapenveld* 56/6 (2006): 24–29; "Want onze God is een verterend vuur: het bijbels Godsbeeld van Oud naar Nieuw," *Kontekstueel* 21/4 (2007): 14–20; "Opdat wij geen lust tot het kwade zouden hebben," *Wapenveld* 57/1 (2007): 31–37.

[200] See especially Richard B. Hays, *The Moral Vision of the New Testament: Community, Cross, New Creation. A Contemporary Introduction to New Testament Ethics* (New York: HarperCollins, 1996), 317–346. See also Glen Stassen and David P. Gushee, *Kingdom Ethics: Following Jesus in Contemporary Context* (Downers Grove: IVP, 2003), 149–193, and the articles in Willard M. Swartley, *The Love of Enemy and Nonretaliation in the New Testament*, Studies in Peace and Scripture, Institute of Mennonite Studies (Louisville: John Knox Press, 1992).

out for most people. Christians worldwide are therefore expected to forgive their enemies and if they are slapped on the right cheek, they are to turn the left cheek.[201] They pray for their enemies and they are infinitely forgiving.[202] In the early church, we see how powerfully these texts were worked out. The Gospel of Matthew, more than the other gospels, shaped the lifestyle of the first generations of Christians.[203] The Sermon on the Mount was "popular" among Christians, so to speak, even though the content was not easy to digest. The path that the Lord of the Sermon on the Mount pointed out was attractive in a way, but it demanded the most from the Christian who wanted to be a salting salt and a light shining in the world.[204] Humanly speaking, Jesus demanded a certain degree of perfection. Thus, the statements on the Law of Moses end with the observation, "You therefore must be perfect, as your heavenly Father is perfect."[205] Although no human being will achieve perfection in this life, Jesus encouraged his disciples to be focused on the spiritual ideal of the Sermon on the Mount. This involves a firm spirituality connected to a committed life orientation.

Of course, no Christian can achieve and fulfil the standard of the Sermon on the Mount in their own strength. Without the gracious indwelling and help of the Holy Spirit, this is out of the question. The Spirit therefore teaches Christians a new spirituality for which the Sermon on the Mount sets the basic outlines. This contact with God in Christ makes a Christian come "in a state of receiving," so to speak, and is carried out in extraordinary ways.

Jesus teaches his followers to pray and fast, and know that their heavenly Father knows what they need.[206] He cares for them and does not give them stones for loaves of bread or snakes for fish.[207] They learn to continually "knock on God's door" and

---

[201] Matthew 5:39.
[202] Matthew 5:44.
[203] See Henk Bakker, "Convictional Theology as Mapping Moral Space," *Baptistic Theologies* 6/1 (2014): 81–97.
[204] Matthew 5:13–14.
[205] Matthew 5:48.
[206] Matthew 6:8.
[207] Matthew 7:9–10.

know that sooner or later he will open it.[208] Above all, followers of Christ know that God the Father comforts and blesses them.

This brings us to the famous so-called "Beatitudes" in Matthew 5:1–12. God, through Jesus, declares all his disciples happy, glorious and blessed. But anyone who scans the passage notices that they seem to be about disciples who, humanly speaking, should not be so joyful. After all, what is joyful about being "poor in spirit," "grieving" and "being persecuted"?[209] Why should a Christian rejoice when he is being scorned, persecuted and defamed with lies?[210] Yet Jesus claims that a disciple who undergoes such things may indeed rejoice because his "reward" in heaven is great.[211] On earth, he may be less than vermin in the eyes of some; to God, he is precious. The new spirituality that Jesus teaches makes Christians look at the principle of *joy* with different eyes.[212] The kingdom of God turns things around. Where the Lord of the Sermon on the Mount is glorified as King, the world experiences "a revolution."

It is remarkable that Jesus ends the series of beatitudes with the statement: "your reward is great in heaven, for so they persecuted the prophets who were before you."[213] Those who read Matthew's Gospel carefully will notice that the evangelist has a certain preference for the figure of the *prophet*. The Sermon on the Mount therefore seems to be primarily about the person of the prophet. With the designation *prophet* we do not mean the prophets of the Old Testament, nor all kinds of new prophets or preachers who are doing well and who have been successful and are proud of themselves. Matthew is not talking about so-called prosperity preachers, who see everything they touch and speak out turn to gold. At the centre of Matthew's Gospel is the preacher, who—by human standards—is a failure.[214]

---

[208] Matthew 7:7-8.
[209] Matthew 5:3,4,10.
[210] Matthew 5:11.
[211] Matthew 5:12a.
[212] See Van Bruggen, *De Bergrede*, 16–22.
[213] Matthew 5:12b.
[214] See U. Luz, *Das Evangelium nach Matthäus, Vol. 2: Mt 8–17*, EKK (Zürich: Benziger, 1990), 392: "Die Leser...kennen die deuteronomistische Tradition vom Ungehorsam Israels, das allezeit seine Propheten verfolgt und ermordet hat. Die Anspielung auf sie

He seems to fail because he is rejected time and time again and barely manages to get his message across. Surely, the central mission of a prophet is to speak and portray the words of God, and to be heard. Matthew's preacher hardly gets a hearing and has to deal constantly with opposition, rejection and even persecution. The figure of the apostle Peter is a model for this.[215]

The Sermon on the Mount seems to be a kind of manual for Jesus' disciples as they go out to preach the kingdom of God. They will experience hard times.[216] They are sent to make peace, yet usually they encounter hardness and heartlessness.[217] Jesus urges them not to give up, and to be light and salt.[218] They must learn to go a second mile and step beyond their own limits in many ways,[219] for with Jesus it is not "an eye for an eye and a tooth for a tooth." The right of retribution expires for those sent by him.[220] Those who follow Jesus and expect his kingdom will have to break radically with violence.[221] When Jesus sends his disciples, he sends them like sheep among wolves, for they will be handed over to authorities and hated and punished.[222] However, whoever does not reject the prophet, and opens the door for him and offers him a cup of water, will receive peace and "the wages of a prophet."[223]

It is remarkable that, for Jesus, the disciple who is sent out is an itinerant preacher or prophet. All the disciples of Jesus together

---

ist das wichtigste matthäische Interpretament." *Zie ook Didachè*, 10–13. In and around Antioch lived Christian communities with a strong focus on prophecies.
[215] See Michael J. Wilkins, *The Concept of Disciple In Matthew's Gospel*, SuppNovTest 59 (Leiden: Brill, 1988), 209–216.
[216] Luz writes: "Die ausgesandten Propheten und Weisen machen in Israel furchtbare Erfahrungen.... Auf alle Fälle werden Verfolgungen nicht alle Mitglieder der Gemeinde, sondern vor allem die missionarisch tätigen Wanderradikalen getroffen haben," Luz, *Das Evangelium nach Matthäus, Vol. 3: Mt 18–25*, EKK (Zürich: Benziger, 1997), 371–372.
[217] Matthew 5:9–10.
[218] Matthew 5:47.
[219] Matthew 5:40–42.
[220] See Luz, *Das Evangelium nach Matthäus*, 1:296–298. Concerning the church, Luz says, based on the Sermon on the Mount: "In ihr gilt die Forderung nach Gewaltverzicht... Gewaltfahrung ist für sie in der Verfolgung etwas Reales, Verzicht auf Widerstand ein Konkreter Auftrag. Er ist möglich, weil Jesus selbst diesen Weg gegangen ist" (298).
[221] Van Bruggen, *De Bergrede*, 50.
[222] Matthew 10:16–22.
[223] Matthew 10:12–13, 40–42.

form an out-going *prophetic* movement. They bring and embody a counterculture, the culture of the kingdom of God.

After Jesus' death and resurrection, the Lord sent his disciples as preachers to all nations. The churches that arose from them were apostolic, and in that sense also prophetic churches.[224] The Lord's church is therefore, by definition, a prophetic community that adheres to the teachings of the Sermon on the Mount. The living out of the Sermon on the Mount makes up the truly prophetic content of a Christian community, not how many prophets walk around and how many visions they utter. A congregation that does not "live out" the Sermon on the Mount cannot be a prophetic congregation.

How can Christ's church be prophetic, be "light and salt," if it engages in the right of retribution (*ius talionis*)? A Christian who wants to see blood is no different than most people who do not know God, and do not reckon with the brokenness of life. Violence usually leads to spirals of violence, and in the long run hurts more innocent victims than thought possible ("an eye for an eye" makes the whole world blind.) In the eyes of Jesus, this way of thinking and acting is precisely a form of *lawlessness*, because one deeply refuses to follow after the Lord, and does not want to give up the right to self-preservation and violence. Peter was even called an "adversary" (Satan) by Jesus when he wanted to forbid Jesus following the way of suffering and self-denial. Jesus immediately ordered Peter to "get behind him" and take up his cross.[225]

There will be, according to Jesus, at the dawn of the heavenly kingdom, prophets who will invoke miracles and prophecies and to whom Jesus will say, "I never knew you; depart from me, you workers of lawlessness."[226] The issue, then, is not whether or not a Christian is proficient in his spiritual gifts. More important is whether he has remained faithful to the Lord of the Sermon on the Mount and whether, like Peter, he has not remained "in front of" (or confronting) Jesus, but has moved "behind" him. The questions in eternity will not be: How many prophecies have you

---

[224] Matthew 28:19.
[225] Matthew 16: 23–24: "Get behind me, Satan!... If anyone would come after me, let him deny himself and take up his cross and follow me."
[226] Matthew 7:21–23.

spoken and how many powers and healings have you performed? The real questions will be: Did you learn to grieve? Did you seek peace? Did you go beyond your own human limits to do so? Did you forgive and bless your enemies? Did you always seek fellowship with God in secret? Did you always seek God's kingdom first? Did you discover the speck in the other person's eye as well as the log in your own eye?[227]

Again, living in the grace of the Sermon on the Mount makes a Christian congregation a powerful, prophetic community, proclaiming the will of God in both their walk and talk. It does not matter how many prophets there are—there can be one or there can be 100—without being "poor in spirit"[228] and renouncing violence, the "spirit of prophecy" is not present.

The "spirit of prophecy," according to John, is the "testimony of Jesus,"[229] and by that the Scriptures do not mean simply *telling* the gospel. The words "testimony of Jesus" mean telling about Christ in a context that is focused on suffering (Gr. *marturia*).[230] Prophets testify to a truth that the world, and often the church, does not want to receive as truth. Therefore, prophets are usually not very welcome.

Throughout the books of faith, including various writings in the intertestamental period, runs a blood-red thread of resistance, from believers and pagans alike, to the prophetic messengers God sent to men time and time again. Each time they were rejected; rarely were they listened to attentively. This apparent failure has typified the prophet of God for many generations. Still, he stands as God's "whistleblower" on injustice, makes God's thoughts known and probably gets ignored and rejected. In most cases, therefore, this prophetic announcing of God's words is accompanied by a tormented conscience.[231]

---

[227] Matthew 5:4, 9, 44–45; 6:12, 14–15; 6:4, 6,18, 33; 7:5.
[228] Matthew 5:3a.
[229] Revelation 19:10.
[230] See Henk Bakker, *"Ze hebben lief, maar worden vervolgd," Radicaal christendom in de tweede eeuw en nu* (Zoetermeer: Boekencentrum, 2007), 188–189.
[231] See Henk Bakker, "'So On Earth': Liturgy From Heaven," in *Prayer and the Transformation of the Self in Early Christian Mystagogy*, ed. Hans van Loon, Giselle de Nie, Michiel Op de Coul and Peter van Egmond (Leuven: Peeters, 2018), 41–60.

2.8 Anabaptists and the Ottoman Muslims

These radical Protestants, the Anabaptists, were a prophetic people in the sixteenth and seventeenth centuries who were brutally silenced. Their prophetic message was one of spiritual renewal and non-violence.[232] Following in Jesus' footsteps, they wanted to be a community of radical peacemakers. It was only from this prophetic approach to the issue of "government and violence" that it is understandable why Michael Sattler and others did not want to use force against the incoming Muslims.

Nevertheless, most Anabaptist Christians saw nothing good in the war against the Muslims and believed that a true Christian should not defend his faith or cultural heritage with the sword. God had commanded us not to kill, and not to hate or slander our opponents. To prevent Muslims from taking Christian territory, God had given other means and opportunities. The right spiritual battle could decide the fight on earth: it was fought with non-violent resistance, only defensively, and in prayer rather than with axes and swords.

War council after the unsuccessful siege of Vienna, 1529

---

232 See Harold S. Bender, "The Anabaptist Vision" in *The Recovery of the Anabaptist Vision: A Sixteenth Anniversary Tribute to Harold S. Bender*, ed. F. Hershberger (Scottdale: Herald Press, 1962), 29–54. Bender's thesis that emphasis on "discipleship" was characteristic for the "Anabaptist vision" has been proven wrong. See Blok, "Discipleship in Menno Simons," 105–129, and John Horsch, "An Historical Survey of the Position of the Mennonite Church on Nonresistance," *The Mennonite Quarterly Review* 1 (1927): 5–22.

The Islamic armies, according to the Anabaptists, did not need to be destroyed. They should also be allowed to keep their own faith. According to Anabaptists, a faith that is *imposed* could never be a true faith.[233] Faith is only a true faith which, on the basis of content and arguments, is able to convince the individual in his spirit and conscience and bring him into communion with God. A process of spiritual conviction could only be authentic and genuine if it was characterized by a spirit of freedom and was voluntary from beginning to end.

For their sixteenth century context, Anabaptists took a decidedly revolutionary position on religious freedom. They believed that both Jews and Muslims should be left alone in their faith. What did the church of Christ gain from imposed uniformity? What was the point of forcing Jews to be baptized as pseudo-Christians? What was the point of fighting Muslims and then claiming Christianity was a better faith? Was Christianity better because the swords of Christians happened to be sharper? Fighting Christians, according to the Anabaptists, were not worthy of the name "Christian." Jews, Turks and Christians were to be free to profess and practice their own faith wherever they lived. Christians should not prohibit Turks from practicing their faith if they resided in a Christian country. An Anabaptist poem of unknown hand reads:

Christus thut niemand zwingen	Christ will not force a person
zu seiner Herrlichkeit,	into his realm of glory
Allein wirts dem gelingen	Only those succeed to enter
Der willig ist bereyt.	Who are willing and prepared.

Felix Manz, for example, articulated to the Zürich city council that no one should be forced to give up their personal faith. Let those who deviated from the Christian mainstream keep the faith they cherished (*die anderen irs gloubens lassenn plibenn*).[234] Hans Denck believed that in the name of God every person should be

---

[233] Both Erasmus and Sebastian Castellio (1515–1563) thought about the same.
[234] "Christ compels no one (to enter) to his salvation. Only he will succeed who is open to it of his own free will." Hillerbrand, "The Anabaptist View of the State," 91.

free to go over "foreign" territory or to settle there, even if the religious customs were quite different.[235]

> You should let another person live peacefully in your country or pass through it—whether he is a Turk or a pagan—without having to submit to the government for matters of faith. Is there anything we should desire more? I stand firm on what the prophet says about this. Every person from any nation may move freely back and forth in the name of his God. In other words, no one has to withhold this from another, whether a pagan, a Jew or a Christian. Every person should be allowed to move freely in any region in the name of his God. The peace that God gives in this way is also profitable for us.[236]

It was apparently common for Christians to not even allow dissenters to cross through Christian territory.

Anabaptist radicals such as Mantz, Denck and Hubmaier had been the first in human history to formulate the principle of religious freedom. They were far ahead of their contemporaries in their ideas on the subject. Even the reformers had not reached this point at the time. For Balthasar Hubmaier, heretic burners were greater heretics than their victims. They were the ones who twisted Scripture and gave it their own meaning. After all, Jesus had clearly said that the good seed and the weeds had to grow up together. Once the weeds had germinated, they could not be pulled out without damaging the good seed as well. Jesus, therefore, did not want premature intervention. Hubmaier therefore argued that whoever knowingly went against Christ's command and proceeded to burn heretics, fundamentally denied the Lord.

Moreover, whoever burned heretics or pagans was destroying people for whom Christ had died, and who might have come to new insights with patience and much prayer. Christians were

---

[235] Hillerbrand, "The Anabaptist View of the State," 9.
[236] Klaassen, ed., *Anabaptism in Outline*, 292; Hillerbrand, "The Anabaptist View of the State," 91, note 50: "Das auch je einer den andern, er sei Türck oder heyd glaub was er wöll, sicher wirt lassen ziehen unnd wonen, durch und inn seim landt.... Er soll keyner den andern, daz einer eyn heyd, ein jud, oder Christ were, lassen entgelte sunder durch alle landt eim jeglichen im namen seines Gots vergunnen zuo ziehen."

therefore not allowed to anticipate God's judgement. Hubmaier declared, "We cannot convince a Turk or a heretic with sword or fire. Only with patience and prayer can we succeed, and in exactly the same way we have to wait patiently for the judgement of God."[237] Hubmaier's words, sadly, have lost nothing of their relevance today.

The Anabaptists of the sixteenth century were peace-loving because Jesus was a peacemaker. Felix Mantz stated that Jesus never hated or wished away anyone. True disciples of Jesus consistently followed their Master in this. The way Jesus showed to deal with sworn enemies was the way of love and forgiveness. According to Mantz, only the love of God was able to deal with so-called enemies. Love would not harm them, but would divide and disperse them, and thus take the weapons out of their hands, completely without violence.[238] God's love was disarming and generally had a de-escalating effect in threatening situations. As difficult as it is not to enforce one's rights by force, Christians had to learn to deal with their own fundamental vulnerability and to act with God's forgiveness. This does not happen automatically, because forgiving requires a great deal.

Of course, Anabaptists knew that forgiving is not easy. Yet they were deeply convinced that God was asking them to step over themselves. This was what *self-denial* entailed. This was the pain of carrying the cross. Those who forgive often suffer more pain than those who ask for forgiveness

---

[237] Klaassen, ed., *Anabaptism in Outline*, 292.
[238] Klaassen, ed., *Anabaptism in Outline*, 268.

3

The character of the early Baptist church

Having followed the roots and character of Anabaptism, we will now return to the English refugee congregation of John Smyth and Thomas Helwys. We have indicated that around 1609 Smyth and some of his church wanted to join the Waterlander Mennonites in Amsterdam. His friend Helwys subsequently broke with him. At the same time, we have wondered what it was in the Mennonite tradition that might have appealed to Smyth, an English separatist. Why did the young Anabaptist seem to connect so well with this idiosyncratic tradition?

3.1 Menno Simons

Whatever the reason, Smyth did find among the Mennonites the ideal of an independent and holy congregation. The first Mennonites were more interested in life change (*reformatio vitae*) than doctrinal change (*reformatio doctrinae*), and they managed to maintain this preference for a long time.¹

In addition, the Waterlander congregation was a peaceful and tolerant community *par excellence*, with an open mind for the "inner Word" (God's speaking by his Spirit alongside Scripture), and with an outspoken aversion for the Reformed doctrine of election.²

It is certain, however, the Anabaptist element of non-violence, and the corresponding conception of freedom of faith and conscience,³ must have appealed to Smyth's heart. Menno Simons and the brothers Obbe Philipsz and Dirk Philipsz, as leaders of the Anabaptist movement in the northern Dutch provinces, had from the beginning spoken out strongly against the violent variant of Anabaptism.⁴ The three had a great deal of influence on non-violent and non-resistant Dutch Anabaptists in the mid-sixteenth century.⁵

Incidentally, Menno Simons did not prematurely reject the use of "the sword" by the government. Nor did he oppose the death penalty, imposed by a government appointed by God. The government was allowed to counter growing unbelief, albeit without pointless bloodshed.⁶ Simons and the Philipsz brothers did distance themselves from the grandiose visions of figures like Jan Matthijsz and Jan van Leiden. According to Simons, Christ was the only true King and an ordinary person was not called to this

---

¹ See Sjouke Voolstra, "Themes in the Early Theology of Menno Simons," in *Menno Simons: A Reappraisal*, ed. Gerald R. Brunk (Harrisonburg: Eastern Mennonite College, 1992), 37–55. See also Alfred R. van Wijk, *Plicht tot leren & plichten leren*, Vol. 1–2 (Kampen: Kok, 2007).

² J. Bakker, *John Smyth: De stichter van het Baptisme* (Diss. University of Utrecht, 1964; Wageningen: Veenman & Zonen, z.j.), 77.

³ Christian congregations and governments were not supposed to use corporal punishment to call dissenters to order.

⁴ Piet Visser, "Mennonites and Baptists in the Netherlands, 1535–1700," in *A Companion to Anabaptism and Spiritualism, 1521-1700*, Brill's Companions to the Christian Tradition 6, ed. John D. Roth, James M. Stayer (Leiden: Brill, 2007), 304.

⁵ The Münster Anabaptists were even expelled from the Anabaptist denomination, see William Estep, *The Anabaptist Story: An Introduction to Sixteenth-Century Anabaptism* (Grand Rapids: Eerdmans, 1996), 156–158, 163, 167–168. Cf. N. van der Zijpp, "Early Dutch Anabaptism," in *The Recovery of the Anabaptist Vision: A Sixteenth Anniversary Tribute to Harold S. Bender*, ed. F. Hershberger (Scottdale: Herald Press, 1962), 76.

⁶ For example, the Dutch Anabaptists supported William of Orange in his liberation of the Netherlands, see Visser, "Mennonites and Baptists in the Netherlands, 1535–1700," 318–319.

kingship. In this regard, Simons was spiritually on the side of preachers like Melchior Hoffman (1495–1543) and Hans Hut.[7] This requires some explanation.

Hoffman had once been an enthusiastic disciple of the reformer Martin Luther, yet as a preacher he had increasingly distanced himself from his teacher. Blessed with a great work ethic, he preached the gospel in almost all northern countries (such as Denmark and Sweden) and, as an "itinerant prophet," he stayed for extended periods in southern Strasbourg. He was baptized there on April 23, 1530, and joined the Anabaptist community. During the next three years, Hoffman repeatedly visited the Netherlands and northern Germany, speaking in Amsterdam, Leeuwarden and Emden, among other places, where the imminent return of Christ was proclaimed. Because of his great influence in the Netherlands, Hoffman, and only secondarily Simons, is also called the "father" of Dutch Anabaptism.[8]

Melchior Hoffman was in some ways a bigot, who saw himself as the prophet Elijah and predicted the return of Jesus in Strasbourg in 1533. In that city, he also made the request to be imprisoned, for he was sure his imprisonment would not last long. However, when liberation was delayed, the popular preacher even seemed to be forgotten. After a ten-year stay in prison, Hoffman died—in the eyes of many people—as a failed prophet.

In any case, Hoffman was a peace-loving apocalyptic, as was the German bookseller Hans Hut. Both Anabaptists opposed the use of violence to force the coming (*herbei zu zwingen*) of the kingdom of God. Initially, Hut was on the side of Thomas Müntzer, but after Hans Denck talked to him after the peasant revolt, he changed his mind. Hut continued (in 1528 that is) to believe the kingdom of God would soon dawn. He did preach the world's end as a sweeping revolution, but without the use of force and resistance. It was this strange mixture of defenseless passivity and hopeful, tense activism that characterized Hut's thinking.[9]

---

7 On the brothers Philipsz and Hoffman Augustijn, see *Reformatorica: Teksten uit de geschiedenis van het Nederlandse protestantisme*, ed. C. Augustijn, F.G.M. Broeyer, P. Visser, E.G.E. van der Wall (Zoetermeer: Meinema, 1996), 56–57, 60–62.
8 See George Huntston Williams, *The Radical Reformation*, Sixteenth Century Essays & Studies 15 (Kirksville: Sixteenth Century Journal Publishers, 1992), 524–551.
9 See Olof de Vries, *Leer en praxis van de vroege dopers uitgelegd als een theologie van de*

Hans Hut
(1490–1527)

On the one hand, according to him, Christians should be engaged in social and political activism; on the other hand, they should idly await the intervention of God. Man and God worked together, so to speak: man from below and God from above. Hut was not understood, not even by Denck and Hubmaier.

After his capture, Hut was interrogated and regularly tortured for almost four months. The authorities wanted to force him to recant his faith. Eventually, he died in Augsburg prison from suffocation after a fire broke out. Not satisfied with this, the authorities had Hut's lifeless body tied to a chair, his corpse condemned to "death" on December 7, 1527, and then placed on a stake and burned.

Menno Simons was a converted priest, who had been confirmed as an *elder* in the Anabaptist church by Obbe Philipsz through the laying on of hands. His ethical views and Christian expectations were closely aligned with Hoffman and Hut. It is not entirely clear which Anabaptist direction influenced Simons; in any case, his theological position was more eschatologically coloured than the Swiss and South German Anabaptists. Therefore, a comparison with Hoffman and Hut is appropriate here. At the same time, it must be said that the Northern and Southern Netherlands offered an entirely unique historical context within which an Anabaptist denomination, with its own distinctions, could emerge.[10] In the years 1539 to 1541, Simons stayed in

---

geschiedenis (Utrecht: Rijksuniversiteit, 1982), 92–93.
[10] See N. van der Zijpp, "Early Dutch Anabaptism," in *The Recovery of the Anabaptist Vision*, ed. F. Hershberger, 69–82, and Cornelius Krahn, "Anabaptism and the Culture of the Netherlands," in *idem*, 219–236. See also Williams, *The Radical Reformation*,

Amsterdam, where he baptized and where he always managed to stay out of the hands of the authorities.

Mennonite Anabaptism developed in part as a reaction to the strong *spiritualism* present in the Northern Netherlands. This religious movement was especially popular among civil servants, merchants, artists and academics, who wanted to see the church changed.[11] For spiritualists, the truth was more a matter of personal inner life than of external factors of faith. Therefore, a spiritualist could also simply remain a member of the existing church, because outward forms and confessions were, so to speak, "non-essential."

One of the most influential spiritualists was David Joris (1501–1556).[12] According to Joris, churches, church services, baptism, the Lord's Supper and discipline were superfluous and believing was a purely inner affair. It was even possible to bring the inner man to a state of perfection. Jesus was thereby reduced to no more than a moral-spiritual example. Following Jesus as an example could bring redemptive insights.

These views of Joris led to a drastic individualization and reduction of the Christian faith. We can therefore imagine that from both the Catholic and Reformed sides, a fierce stand was taken against this spiritualistic spirit.[13] The Dutch Anabaptists, in the person of none other than Obbe Philipsz, also had to deal with spiritualism. Obbe, although a fervent opponent of David Joris (he had once ordained Joris as an elder), distanced himself from the principles of Anabaptist church vision in 1640 and left the Anabaptist community. The church leader could no longer reconcile himself with the adopted congregationalist church form and blamed the Anabaptists for defiling the pure church idea

---

589–608, 723–753, 1566–1578, 1177–1191, and Sjouke Voolstra, *Menno Simons: His Image and His Message* (North Newton: Bethel College, 1997). Note especially Voolstra's emphasis on the penitential nature of Menno's thought.

[11] Herman J. Selderhuis, ed., *Handboek Nederlandse Kerkgeschiedenis* (Kampen: Kok, 2006), 250–252.

[12] On David Joris, see especially Gary K. Waite, *Spiritualizing the Crusade: David Joris in the Context of the Early Reform and Anabaptist Movements in the Netherlands, 1524–1543* (Waterloo: University of Waterloo, 1986), *David Joris and Dutch Anabaptism, 1524–1543* (Waterloo: Wilfrid Laurier University Press, 1990), and *The Anabaptist Writings of David Joris, 1535–1543* (Waterloo: Herald Press, 1994).

[13] See regarding Joris: ed. Augustijn, et al, *Reformatorica*, 62–72.

with visible idols such as ministry, ordinances and liturgy.[14] A spiritualist church vision such as this usually arose in circles where the approaching kingdom of God was considered so close that the building of a local congregation was seen as unnecessary or nonsensical.

Menno Simons and Dirk Philipsz certainly counted on the return of Christ, but they did not engage in speculations about spiritual perfection, inner truth and kingdom revelations.[15] Simon's sense was certainly more practical and modest in nature,[16] and for that very reason he and Philipsz placed great emphasis on the visibility of the church as the body of Christ on earth. The true Christian congregation, according to Simons, was one where:

1. pure doctrine was proclaimed,
2. the sacraments were administered according to Scripture,
3. the Word of God was wholeheartedly obeyed,
4. sincere mutual love was shown,
5. God and Christ were freely confessed, and
6. believers suffered for the sake of the Word of God.[17]

Simons also placed great emphasis on obedience to Scripture. Precisely those areas of faith that were considered *unimportant* by spiritualists were seen by Menno Simons and Dirk Philipsz as *vital* to a true Christian life of faith.

3.2 Excursus 3: Church discipline

Central to the characteristics of Anabaptists, particularly emerging from their views on obedience to Scripture and genuine mutual love, was their focus on congregational *discipline*. There was great attention to Christ's teaching on the discipline of faith. Not only was the Sermon on the Mount in the Gospel of

---

[14] Van der Zijpp, "Early Dutch Anabaptism," 77.
[15] See William Echard Keeny, *The Development of Dutch Anabaptist Thought and Practice from 1539–1564* (Nieuwkoop: De Graaf, 1968), 191.
[16] Visser, "Mennonites and Baptists in the Netherlands, 1535–1700," 304: "Na alle voorgaande profeten, met hun overdreven gevoel van eigenwaarde, was Menno een volstrekt gewone man van vlees en bloed."
[17] Van der Zijpp, "Early Dutch Anabaptism," 79.

Matthew a central teaching for Anabaptists, but also the eighteenth chapter of this Gospel—the passage on disciplinary procedure. Anabaptists wanted to be a holy community, and that meant strict adherence to these words of Jesus. If someone wanted to attend the meeting and remembered that a brother had something against him, he had to first go and reconcile with the other person.[18] Conversely, if someone had been hurt by a brother or sister, he had to go up to the person and discuss the situation.

In the early years of his ministry, Simons saw this arrangement primarily as acts of love. The offender was made aware of his mistakes and helped to change into the image of Christ.[19] Church discipline, so to speak, was centred on the service of love to one another. The community of love was essential to be able to survive as a Christian in the world. As a Christian, one simply could not live without a fellow brother or sister. For Anabaptists, the congregation and the mutual solidarity that comes with it, was (and is) necessary for salvation and sanctification. The congregation was a place of gracious reciprocity, where Christians were at the mercy of God's grace and each other's grace in a positive sense.[20]

Those who were not open to critical correction by a brother or sister did not yet realize how much they needed each other. To reject corrective words meant to reject the love of God in one another. Simons said (in the "Declaration of the Apostolic Bans") of him who rejects admonition: "It is more than plain that he... acts against Christian love."[21] After all, correction and admonition were not given out of self-interest, nor were they nurtured out of irritation or the need to lecture the transgressor. Jesus' intention in Matthew 18 was that those who were hurt should visit the offender in private to keep them from doing worse. Surely an offender could derail further. Therefore, a Christian who might have been hurt was expected to overcome himself and act out of concern. He had to put aside his own feelings for the sake of love and *go* and make an effort to *win back* the brother

---

18 Matthew 5:23–24.
19 Van der Zijpp, "Early Dutch Anabaptism," 80.
20 See Harold S. Bender, "The Anabaptist Vision," in *The Recovery of the Anabaptist Vision*, ed. F. Hershberger, 48–53.
21 Menno Simons, *Opera omnia theologica, or alle de Godtgeleerde wercken van Menno Symons* (Amsterdam: Johannes van Veen, 1681), 202, col. 1.

who might have gone off the rails.[22] He should not hate him, Simons said, but he was to practice "discipline in love" (*in der liefden straffen*) so that "his dear Brother would not derail farther and continue on the road to perdition, but to return him to the path of life" (*sijn lieve Broeder niet wijder en vervalle noch en verderve maer met alsulks te recht kome*).[23]

An Anabaptist understood that the disciplinary procedure was not a rod to punish and beat at will. The biblical process thus regulated the self-cleansing ability of a Christian community, and prevented silent reproaches from deteriorating into resentment and hatred. Simons' main idea was always that the Christian's heart should not harbour resentment and reproach, "for a righteous Christian does not harbour hatred."[24] He had to forgive again and again and insist on reconciliation, even if the offender refused to change,[25] although the latter could eventually lead to exclusion. Eventually there had to come a time to conclude that a notorious, incorrigible transgressor was refusing to follow Christ any longer.

The Anabaptist emphasis on patience and reconciliation in disciplinary matters was done with an appeal to Matthew 18. After all, Jesus' statement about the ultimate "exclusion" of an offender can be seen in the broader context of Matthew 18 as an emergency measure. Matthew 18 is a speech of Jesus in which the word church (Gr. *ekklēsia*) is used for a second time. The first time Jesus does so is in Matthew 16, where the building of the church is announced. In Matthew 18, Jesus continues his discourse on the Christian church and describes *essential features* of the community that grew up around the Lord. Matthew 16 makes it clear that Jesus "builds" his church with followers who carry their own cross. Matthew 18 discusses how things should work among themselves in that special community of those bearing the cross. Thus, Jesus clearly showed what distinguished the Christian congregation from other communities, for example the

---

[22] Matthew 18:12 and 15.
[23] "Revealing in love" so that "his dear brother does not fall deeper into destruction but comes out of it on the right path," Simons, *Opera omnia*, 201, col. 2.
[24] "For a righteous Christian knows no hatred," Simons, *Opera omnia*, 201, col. 2.
[25] Simons, *Opera omnia*, 202, col. 1.

synagogue in those days. The Christian community was soon perceived as a spiritual competitor of the synagogue.

According to Christ, Christian communities should excel at patience and expansive, God-qualified forgiveness. The community of Christ, so to speak, is full of forgiveness. Its essence, policy and calling are: to gather people in the grace and love of God that had appeared in Christ. Christians, therefore, were to be bridge builders in the name of Jesus. Let us briefly consider how the text and composition of Matthew 18 elaborates this element of forgiveness.[26]

The chapter begins with Jesus' disciples discussing the question of "who is the greatest" in God's kingdom. Jesus answers the question by calling a child to him, and reasoning from the child's position. Whoever does not become like a child and cannot consider himself *small* will not enter the kingdom of God. Whoever humbles himself will be able to be *great* in God's kingdom.

Then the direction of his conversation with his disciples takes a change. Jesus earnestly warns his disciples not to tempt such a child to sin. Whoever receives a child in Jesus' name receives the Lord himself, but whoever "tempts" or "despises" a child should fear God. It is better for a potential tempter to radically deal with himself (cut off hand or foot) than to lay hands on "one of these little ones." Jesus emphasizes the warning by saying that "their angels always see the face of my Father who is in heaven."[27] In other words, nothing can be done stealthily, in secret. The angels see it and have direct access to God the Father. So, the child's temptation definitely comes to the attention of the Lord God and he will avenge the damaged child.

What else does this "child" have to do with the church and Christian disciplinary procedure? Jesus is not saying a child molester must be patiently visited and admonished. Implicitly, this may be what is meant, but that is not what the Lord is concerned with. Rather, the child whom Jesus places in the midst of

---

[26] For an extensive discussion and justification, see Henk Bakker, *'Familia Dei': de Mattheaanse gemeente geprofileerd in een synoptische vergelijking van Matthëus 18* (Master thesis Rijksuniversiteit Utrecht, 1990), and Ulrich Luz, *Das Evangelium nach Matthäus, 3. Teilband: Mt 18–25*, EKK (Zürich: Benziger Verlag, 1997), 5–86. See also Nigel Wright, *Free Church, Free State: The Positive Baptist Vision* (Carlisle: Paternoster Press, 2005), 10, 63-64.
[27] Matthew 18:6, 10.

the circle of his disciples is a model of the believer Jesus desires. These children are characterized as the "little ones who believe in Me." They represent the true followers of Jesus.

The church of Christ, then, is a community of people who believe in Jesus and, as spiritual children, know themselves to be "little." By smallness, Jesus does not mean thinking low of yourself in the pathetic sense of thinking you cannot do, know or be anything. On the contrary, a Christian may stand up for what he can do and for who he is. Rather, by smallness Jesus means *insignificant* and *powerless* in the concrete sense of the word.

Jesus is concerned with a mental attitude of *humility*, but even more concerned that his people lead a life of compassion and are *willing to take the lowest place*. Think of hospitality (such as taking in children in foster care), boundless forgivingness (being able to step over yourself), not hanging on to possessions but giving them away out of charity, not caring about power and position.[28] In this way, Christians should consider themselves small and insignificant. They do not, so to speak, "stand on their rights or on their stripes" to be weighty, rich and prosperous.

How the focus in Jesus' speech shifts from the child to the Christian, and then to the conflict between Christians, is clearly shown by the repetition of the words, "one of these little ones." These words occur three times and clearly place the shift in focus.

> but whoever causes *one of these little ones* who believe in me to sin, it would be better for him to have a great millstone fastened around his neck and to be drowned in the depth of the sea.... See that you do not despise *one of these little ones*. For I tell you that in heaven their angels always see the face of my Father who is in heaven.
>
> If a man has a hundred sheep, and one of them has gone astray, does he not leave the ninety-nine on the mountains and go in search of the one that went astray?... So it is not the will of my Father who is in heaven that *one of these little ones* should perish.[29]

---

[28] Luz, *Das Evangelium nach Matthäus, 3. Teilband*, 15.
[29] Matthew 18:6, 10, 12, 14. Author's italics.

The first "little one" is the child Jesus placed in the middle, then the "little one" is more than this concrete child. No one should despise believing children of God, that is, Christians, and take advantage of them. Finally, the "little one" is the sheep that got lost. The shepherd leaves ninety-nine sheep and goes to find the lost one, Jesus says.

If these statements are related, and we assume they are, then the text means to say that a Christian, a "little one," can deviate from the right track of God in a time of temptation and trial. However, he should not be despised and shunned by others for this. On the contrary, those who are touched by the sin of this "little one," like the shepherd, "go" to "win" this brother or sister and help them back to the straight path of God.[30] The shepherd's love for the little sheep is great, and it is precisely in this spirit that the other "little ones" of Christ's community also look out for the lost. Driven by pastoral care, they are instructed to seek out the sinful "little one" and lead it back to the way of God.[31] Discipline, so to speak, is all about the love and care of Christians among themselves.[32]

If the sinful "little one" does not listen, the pressure is increased by lovingly, and with good intentions, bringing one or two witnesses. The path of compassion and reconciliation requires care, and is therefore walked with multiple witnesses. The "little one" has the right to be heard. But if it should turn out that the "little one" is on the wrong track and, in spite of all attempts at redress, continues to hold to the error, then the community of Christ has no choice but to observe this and expressly question the faith of this "little one." But this is only an ultimate and painful possibility. Anabaptists, however, took this ultimate possibility seriously, and enshrined this arrangement in their principles of faith and "rules of procedure."[33]

---

30 The word *go* is also repeated, though with other Greek words (18:12 and 15, Gr. *kai poreutheis dzētei to planōmenon...hupage elenxon auton*). The word *gain* or *win* in this context is unique, see Luz, *Das Evangelium nach Matthäus, 3. Teilband*, 43.
31 Luz, *Das Evangelium nach Matthäus, 3. Teilband*, 36.
32 Luz, *Das Evangelium nach Matthäus, 3. Teilband*, 58.
33 See Walter Klaassen, ed., *Anabaptism in Outline: Selected Primary Sources*, Classics of the Radical Reformation 3 (Waterloo: Herald Press, 1981), 211–231. See also Luz, *Das Evangelium nach Matthäus, 3. Teilband*, 50.

The remainder of Jesus' speech has the goal that every effort should be made to continue to walk the way of reconciliation and forgiveness after Christ (as qualified by him). The command of responsibility and discipline gives the congregation the right to forbid or approve of a particular attitude, action or lifestyle. The emphatic pronouncement of forgiveness also follows from this, for if a "little one" repents, the congregation can affirm forgiveness and welcome the lost sheep back into its midst. Again, Jesus emphasizes that the congregation must be intent on this. He also indicates that he is there, when the "two or three witnesses" go and visit the "little one": "if two of you agree on earth about anything they ask, it will be done for them.... For where two or three are gathered in my name, there am I among them."[34] The Good Shepherd himself is there when the two or three witnesses go to seek the lost. Together with the great Shepherd, they are concerned, and when they pray and ask for restoration and reconciliation, Christ promises his full grace.[35] When we attempt reconciliation, Christ is "more strongly present" than at other times. Thus, the Anabaptist community counted on the powerful and gracious presence of Christ in its midst, especially when someone had strayed from the spiritual fold, so to speak.

The disciplinary procedure really does involve the "angelic patience" of God and the church, and this is confirmed by the parable which concludes Matthew 18. A king is settling accounts with his staff and hits a servant who is heavily in debt to him. The amount is so high that he can never pay off the debt. The king then orders that the man, along with his family and possessions, be sold and the money accepted as repayment. The servant kneels down before his master and begs him for a reprieve. The master is touched by the servant's grief and actually takes pity on him. This compassion radically changes the master's plan. He cancels the servant's debt and lets him go home a free man.

The remarkable change, however, is not the point of the parable, for that lies with what happens once the servant has been released. He sees someone who owes him a small amount of

---

[34] Matthew 18:19–20.
[35] According to Luz, verse 20 is the Christological centre of the whole passage; Luz, *Das Evangelium nach Matthäus, 3. Teilband*, 52.

money, grabs the man by the throat and immediately demands the amount owed. When the man throws himself on the ground, begs for mercy and cannot pay, the king's servant has the debtor imprisoned.

The servant's ruthless harshness does not go unnoticed, however. His fellow servants see everything and bring the sad message to their lord. The latter summons the heartless servant and hands him over to the court. Jesus concludes the parable with the words: "So also my heavenly Father will do to every one of you, if you do not forgive your brother from your heart."[36]

Jesus' insistent warning is self-evident: those who know how much they have been forgiven cannot help but look with compassion at others who owe them. This is the beating heart of God's intervention in church disciplinary procedure. This is also how Anabaptists sought to work it out, although sometimes serious differences of interpretation (ironically) led to fruitless removals and splits.

3.3 The confessions of Smyth and the Waterlanders

Menno Simons, and with him many other Anabaptist Christians, considered Matthew 18 an essential characteristic of the church of Christ; so they consistently applied the sayings of Jesus to practical church life. Initially this worked well, but gradually there was disagreement within the Anabaptist ranks about the *rigour* with which they regularly proceeded to exclude the "little ones." During Simons' life, their perspective shifted from "care for the transgressor" to "care for a holy congregation." The grace character of the disciplinary measure was thus moved from the forefront to the background. After Simons' death, this difference of opinion grew into a divisive issue, driving Dutch Anabaptists apart.[37]

The spiritual focus of most Anabaptists shifted toward being and remaining "a pure congregation," a one-sidedness that in retrospect may be regretted. A sizeable group, who were less

---

[36] Matthew 18:35.
[37] Van der Zijpp, "Early Dutch Anabaptism," 80–82. See also Samme Zijlstra, *Om de ware gemeente en oude gronden. Geschiedenis van de dopersen in de Nederlanden 1531–1675* (Hilversum: Uitg. Verloren, 2000), 271–283, and Visser, "Mennonites and Baptists in the Netherlands, 1535–1700," 306.

rigorous and stepped out of the larger context of the Anabaptist community in 1555, was the so-called Waterlander congregation.[38] This is when the name "Anabaptists" arose, because they wished to distinguish themselves explicitly from the Mennonites.

Because of their moderate views on exclusion, the Waterlander community was called by their opponents "de drekwagen" (literally, the manure cart).[39] Indeed, various outcasts, who had been excluded elsewhere, were hospitably welcomed by the Waterlanders. Surely, Christ himself received sinners and ate with them, the Dutch Baptists argued.

The Waterlanders (from the water-rich province of North Holland) were more flexible when it came to the application of church discipline. They were also more spiritualistic and therefore freer in their religious thinking than the others.[40] Emphasis was placed on the "inner Word," the inner light. Knowing Christ inwardly was more important than knowing the letter of Scripture. For some, therefore, baptism and preaching in the service were superfluous. It was sufficient for them to gather in silence and merely meditate. "The letter kills but the Spirit gives life" were words that often sounded in this context.[41]

This spiritualistic tendency meant they wanted to do justice in a way that saw the union of Spirit and Scripture. By "inner Word," we should not think of the caricature of an "inner voice." After all, the "inner voice" was the echo of God's speaking in Scripture. The "inner Word" was derivative of the written Word, so to speak, and in principle it was not really separate from it.[42]

The Waterlanders also developed a congregationalist structure, entirely in line with their vision for the church community. In the view of the Waterlander Anabaptists, a pure church on earth was an illusion. The claim that Anabaptists were the true congregation of God was abandoned by the Waterlanders at the beginning of the seventeenth century. They were not in favour of keeping themselves completely aloof from the world. As

---

[38] Visser, "Mennonites and Baptists in the Netherlands, 1535–1700," 313.
[39] Zijlstra, *Om de ware gemeente en oude gronden*, 272. See Visser, "Mennonites and Baptists in the Netherlands, 1535–1700," 324: "The Waterlanders were a wild shoot from Menno's trunk."
[40] See Williams, *The Radical Reformation*, 1190.
[41] 2 Corinthians 3:6.
[42] Zijlstra, *Om de ware gemeente en oude gronden*, 267.

mentioned, God's kingdom, according to the Anabaptists, also had everything to do with the sensory reality of the here and now. In retrospect, we can say that these Waterlanders, who allowed themselves to be called Anabaptists and distanced themselves from the name Mennonite, coloured and shaped Anabaptist thinking and faith in the Netherlands for centuries to come.[43]

At the turn of the century (toward the seventeenth century), Waterlander Anabaptists constituted only a small minority of Dutch Anabaptists (about twenty per cent),[44] so they were not very influential in John Smyth's time. Moreover, as mentioned, the Waterlander community became deeply divided from within during the seventeenth century, and its collective potential evaporated.[45] By about 1600, the Anabaptist movement in the Low Countries was already so fragmented that people spoke of Waterlanders, High Germans, Frisians and Flemings, named after their geographical origins.[46] Attempts to restore unity failed. In Amsterdam, there were two Anabaptist communities: a community of strict Flemings and free Waterlanders. It was the less strict Anabaptist variant, the Waterlanders, that John Smyth came to know in Amsterdam and who attracted him.

Meanwhile, Anabaptist confessions were drawn up here and there. The confession drawn up by Hans de Ries (1553–1638), spiritual leader of the Waterlanders and elder at Alkmaar, was one of the best known of the time. De Ries was originally a Calvinist minister at Antwerp, while he practiced as a physician in the vicinity of Amsterdam. De Ries had probably left the Reformed church because he found it too belligerent: violence was too easily preached and condoned in Reformed circles.[47] Yet, de Ries always remained sympathetic to the Reformed liturgy.[48]

---

[43] Estep, *The Anabaptist Story*, 175–176.
[44] Zijlstra, *Om de ware gemeente en oude gronden*, 276, and Visser, "Mennonites and Baptists in the Netherlands, 1535–1700," 313.
[45] Zijlstra, *Om de ware gemeente en oude gronden*, 280.
[46] Selderhuis, *Handboek*, 398–404. See also *Documenta Reformatoria: Texts from the History of Church and Theology in the Netherlands since the Reformation*, part 1, ed. J.N. Bakhuizen van den Brink, W.F. Dankbaar, W.J. Kooiman, D. Nauta, N. van der Zijpp (Kampen: Kok, 1960), 70–71.
[47] James Robert Coggins, *John Smyth's Congregation: English Separatism, Mennonite Influence, and the Elect Nation*, Studies in Anabaptist and Mennonite History 32 (Waterloo: Herald Press, 1991), 72–73.
[48] Visser, "Mennonites and Baptists in the Netherlands, 1535–1700," 322–323.

When John Smyth wanted to join the Waterlander Anabaptists with his congregation in 1609, a shortened and edited confession of Hans de Ries and Lubbert Gerritsz from 1580 was given to him: *A Short Confession of Faith* (1610). The confession had forty articles. Smyth was also expected to put his views on paper and compare them with those of the Waterlanders. Thomas Helwys and John Murton could not follow Smyth's approach to the Waterlanders and excommunicated their former friend.[49] Smyth, in their opinion, would prove to be an unreliable spiritual leader. Helwys was left with only ten men and could not refrain from protesting to the Waterlanders on behalf of the entire congregation. Smyth was said to have become apostate, even committing sin against the Holy Spirit.

In the few years that Smyth's English congregation stayed in Amsterdam, it had adopted more and more Anabaptist ideas.[50] It was now high time the refugee church came under one spiritual roof with the Waterlanders, for the cacophony of views among them threatened to tear the community apart. At first, unification was rejected because it met with resistance from the Anabaptist Frisians (with whom the Waterlanders were in a kind of union). Only after Smyth's death in August 1612, did the chances for inclusion grow. It was not until January 20, 1615, that the merger of the two churches came about.[51] Helwys' protests were declared inadmissible.

---

[49] Helwys distanced himself from Smyth's views, and repudiated several Waterlander doctrines, as he clearly addressed these in 1611 in his treatise *An Advertisement or Admonition to the Congregations, Which Men Call the New Fryelers, in the Low Countries, Written in Dutch and published in English*. See Joe Early, *The Life and Writings of Thomas Helwys*, Early English Baptist Texts (Macon: Mercer University Press, 2009), 93–154. See also John Briggs, "The Origins of the People Called Baptists" (2009), 5.

[50] Opinions differ as to exactly when, and precisely how, Smyth changed from Puritan-separatist confessions to more Anabaptist-Arminian ones. See Erik Wickman, "General Baptist Origins and Original Sin," *Baptist Quarterly* 51/2 (2020): 47–55, and Stephen Holmes, "When Did John Smith Embrace Arminianism—And Was the First Baptist Congregation 'Particular'?", *Baptist Quarterly* 52/4 (2021): 146–157, at 157: "the Mennonites had a profound effect on Baptist beginnings, being the cause of the Smyth-Helwys church abandoning its Calvinism." Holmes nuances the findings of Brachlow and Wickman. The first Baptist church started as a particular Baptist church, and quickly changed, and split.

[51] De Ries and Gerritsz approved of the baptisms of the English, except Smyth's. After all, his *self-baptism* (*se-baptism*) was unscriptural.

The confession that Smyth drafted on behalf of thirty-two fellow believers in 1609 was clearly Anabaptist and Arminian in scope ("Short Confession of Faith in XX Articles").[52] A few excerpts from it clearly demonstrate this. The confession had been edited and expanded after Smyth's death. The expansion was used to expedite merger talks with the Waterlanders. The edited confession read "Propositions and Conclusions Concerning True Christian Religion" (1612–1614).[53]

We now want to compare some parts from both confessions (from "Short Confession of Faith in XX Articles" and "Propositions and Conclusions") with "A Short Confession of Faith" by Hans de Ries (1610),[54] and finally also with the confession of the group of stragglers by Thomas Helwys, "A Declaration of Faith of English People Remaining at Amsterdam in Holland" (1611).[55]

Hans de Ries, as an Anabaptist teacher, was well aware of the discussion on predestination about which we started this book. When John Smyth drafted his "Short Confession of Faith in XX Articles" in 1609, and a year later Hans de Ries came out with his "Short Confession of Faith" of the same name, the northern Netherlands were in the throes of debate over the doctrine of predestination. Jacobus Arminius had died in 1609, but it was only after his death that the knives about the conflict were really sharpened. As mentioned, the Netherlands was balancing on the edge of civil war in the ensuing years. The theological contradictions seemed insurmountable. In Alkmaar, Amsterdam and other places, incidents occurred regularly; sometimes these seemed to end in widespread social uproar. At times, the Remonstrants were called "baboons" while Counter-Remonstrants were put in the corner of the "mud-paupers" (*slijkgeuzen*).[56]

In 1610, Arminius' followers, including Johan van Oldenbarnevelt, issued a "Remonstrance," calling for a revision of the

---

[52] William Lumpkin, *Baptist Confessions of Faith*, rev. ed. (Valley Forge: Judson Press, 1969), 100–101.
[53] Lumpkin, *Baptist Confessions of Faith*, 124–142.
[54] Lumpkin, *Baptist Confessions of Faith*, 102–113. This confession is an abridged version of the Waterlander Confession: 'A Brief Confession of the Principal Articles of the Christian Faith' (1580/1581), Lumpkin, *Baptist Confessions of Faith*, 44–66.
[55] Lumpkin, *Baptist Confessions of Faith*, 116–123.
[56] See A. Th. van Deursen, *Bavianen en slijkgeuzen. Kerk en kerkvolk ten tijde van Maurits en Oldenbarnevelt* (Franeker: Van Wijnen, 1998), 320–345.

Dutch Creed and the Heidelberg Catechism.[57] In five points, the Remonstrants explained why Gomarism went against Scripture and tradition, and what the Remonstrant alternative was.

The Remonstrants taught that Christ's sacrifice was meant for all men, none excepted. No one was damned to hell by God's eternal decree before the foundation of the world. Christ died for all, and all men were called to believe in the Son of God. But no man had this faith by himself. No one could believe by himself with the faith needed to come to forgiveness and redemption of sins. The Remonstrants stood more or less side by side with the Counter-Remonstrants in regard to this article of the confession. God himself worked faith in the hearts of people, but according to the Remonstrants, he did not do that because certain people were chosen for grace. God worked faith through the Word, the preaching and the working of the Spirit. If there could be talk of a certain election, then God chose from eternity people for salvation whom he *foresaw* would believe in Christ. For Remonstrants, the free possibility of not accepting God's offer of grace was essential to both a pure image of man and a pure image of God. Anyone could oppose God's grace.

As soon as a person did open his heart to grace, it was grace that carried the Christian from beginning to end of his life, and allowed him to share in God's goodness. The Christian's perseverance to the end was also a fruit of God's grace. No Christian anywhere in the world could boast of his own merits. Here we see Remonstrants and Counter-Remonstrants in agreement again.[58]

The opponents of the Remonstrants submitted a "Counter-Remonstrance" in 1611 in which they tried to refute the arguments of the Remonstrants point by point,[59] and also called for religious disputes not to be brought before the government, but to be discussed in a church meeting and conference. The Counter-Remonstrants did not want government intervention in church

---

[57] Selderhuis, *Handboek*, 421–425.
[58] See *Canons of Dort* I.1-5.
[59] See the *Canons of Dort*: "The Dordtse Leerregels (Canons of Dort) being the five articles against the Remonstrants or judgment of the National Synod of the Reformed Churches of the United Netherlands, held within Dordrecht in the years 1618 and 1619, on the well-known five chapters of doctrine, about which there has been a difference in the Reformed Churches of the United Netherlands." Most Remonstrants were able to agree on the text of the Heidelberg Catechism and the Belgic Confession.

conflicts and disagreements. The Remonstrants were called the "political ones" (*politieken*) and advocated the position that the government did have certain authority to decide on church order, ministers and worship services.

Hans de Ries' Anabaptist confession, like the Remonstrance, came out in the year 1610. Both confessions expressed an aversion to the idea that God was the author of evil because in his eternal plan he would have predestined people for hell.[60] Both the Anabaptists and the Remonstrants were thus opposed to the views of the Counter-Remonstrants. This similarity, incidentally, did not lead to a degree of affiliation, in fact the opposite was the case: the Anabaptists kept the Remonstrants at a distance. In de Ries's eyes, the Arminians were far too dogmatic, rationalistic and not experiential enough.[61]

De Ries also denied original sin. God had made man "good" and in Adam he had intended all men for good. When Adam fell into sin, God's promise of salvation and redemption had immediately restored him to glory,[62] and God had relieved all of Adam's posterity of original guilt. Therefore, people were still born "good" and were truly free to choose for or against evil. God's thoughts and intentions for all people were thoughts of peace, freedom and grace. According to de Ries, no one was predestined for hell and damnation. Only a man's unbelief plunged him into judgement:

> But those who disdain and scorn the offered grace of God... and persist in unrepentance and unbelief, they make themselves unworthy of the blessed state and are rejected.[63]

Whoever despised God's grace and remained unbelieving and unrepentant was not worthy of the blessed life with God, and was

---

60 The *Canons of Dort* clearly distanced themselves from the idea that predestination would make God the author of sin (I.15): "And this is the decree of rejection, that God by no means makes God an author of sin (which is blasphemous to think)."
61 Zijlstra, *Om de ware gemeente en oude gronden*, 278.
62 Genesis 3:15.
63 "But they which despise and condemn this proferred grace of God...persevere in impenitence and unbelief, they make themselves unworthy of blessedness, and are rejected," Hans de Ries, "A Short Confession of Faith" (1610), paragraphs 4–5 and 7.

rejected by God, according to de Ries. But this was ultimately his choice, not God's choice.

For Anabaptists, Christ was in every respect the fulfilment of God's promise in the Old Testament. The promise to Adam, in which the first man and all his descendants received restoration, was more than fulfilled with the coming of the Son of God. What the old covenant did not bring and where it fell short, was brought with Christ, and became a reality with his death and resurrection. For de Ries, Jesus Christ was in every respect the fulfilment of the law of Moses. Like Menno Simons did, de Ries explained the Old Testament Christocentrically and typologically.[64]

Born-again Christians were baptized on the basis of their faith.[65] Baptism was a visible breaking point with the old life. As born-again people, Christians were a new creation of God,[66] and therefore they no longer had the "burden" of the law to bear; Christ had fulfilled the law. According to De Ries, Jesus was the fulfilment of all Old Testament *shadow* symbols, such as the *temple*, the *altar*, the *sacrifices*, the *priesthood*, the *kingship* and the *kingdom*, the *sword*, the *war* and the right to *vengeance*.[67] Indeed, war and sword disappeared with the completion of Christ's work on earth. The Spirit of Christ no longer taught war. Believers had been reconciled to God and had a "living and working" faith, and had turned their earthly swords and spears into peaceful plowshares and scythes. Thus, they no longer took up the sword.[68]

Christians did not have to obey the government if it went against the Word of God.[69] According to de Ries, because government functions were strongly intertwined with worldly law, and therefore with decisions of violence and war, Christians could not perform governmental functions.[70] It was clear that de Ries and other Anabaptists were outpacing the Remonstrants with this position. The Remonstrants thought differently and diversely

---

[64] Visser, "Mennonites and Baptists in the Netherlands, 1535–1700," 305–306. On Menno Simons, see especially Werner O. Packull, "Enkele aspecten van de hermeneutiek van Menno Simons," Doopsgezinde bijdragen, *Nieuwe Reeks* 22 (1996): 143–157.
[65] de Ries, "A Short Confession of Faith" (1610), paragraphs 29–30.
[66] de Ries, "A Short Confession of Faith" (1610), paragraph 20.
[67] de Ries, "A Short Confession of Faith" (1610), paragraph 10.
[68] de Ries, "A Short Confession of Faith" (1610), paragraphs 13, 18.
[69] de Ries, "A Short Confession of Faith" (1610), paragraph 35.
[70] de Ries, "A Short Confession of Faith" (1610), paragraph 35.

about war and peace. The Waterlanders were un-Reformed[71] and also non-violent, elastic and spiritualistic at the same time, and in this they were unique.

When Hans de Ries presented this confession to Smyth, he and forty-one others signed it. By signing it, they indicated that they were ready to join the Waterlander community. They also now endorsed the Anabaptist attitude toward the sword, government and the oath. In August 1612, Smyth died.

About a year before the signing, Smyth had drafted his own creed of twenty short articles. Its contents made it clear that the Calvinist Puritan (that Smyth had been just a few years before) had turned into a sort of Anabaptist. In Amsterdam, the pastor from Scrooby had come to the conviction that no man was compelled to sin because God would have devised it in his plan. Those who sinned chose to do so themselves, Smyth said. With that, he threw out the idea of original sin and original guilt. Human beings were not born sinners. Therefore, children were not to be blamed for their sins.[72]

The gospel, according to Smyth, was meant for all people and whoever repented and became a believer was justified by the righteousness of Christ, which he received, and by the righteousness that he himself, by his new inner nature, would produce. Justification and sanctification by faith was explained by Smyth as spiritually receiving and producing at the same time.[73] In this reasoning, we hear the typical Anabaptist view that "faith alone" was not enough. Faith must be proved by works. Faith worked together with good works,[74] and these did not come forth out of the sinful "flesh." Christian works were the spiritual fruit of a born-again heart. Therefore, a Christian could only be baptized if he could demonstrate those fruits. Therefore, according to Smyth, children could not be baptized.[75]

---

[71] Strictly speaking, Anabaptists could not be called Arminian. Long before Arminus, they had their own views on free will that are very similar to later Arminianism.
[72] John Smyth, "A Short Confession of Faith in XX Articles" (1609), paragraphs 3–5.
[73] Smyth, "A Short Confession of Faith in XX Articles" (1609), paragraph 10: "That man's justification…consists in part in the imputation of the righteousness of Christ, assumed by faith, and in part in one's own righteousness, in the saint himself, by the working of the Holy Spirit, which is called regeneration and sanctification."
[74] James 2:20–26.
[75] Smyth, "A Short Confession of Faith in XX Articles" (1609), paragraphs 11–14.

Finally, with Smyth we also recognize the Anabaptist emphasis on the discipline of faith. Clear sympathy for the less strict views of the Waterlander variant is evident from Smyth's preference to exclude an offender only after he had been admonished three times. The latter was to be shunned in the church yard, but not outside it, such as at work.[76]

3.4 "Propositions and Conclusions"

As mentioned, after the death of their spiritual leader, believers from Smyth's circle produced a confession that contained elements of both Smyth's "Short Confession" and de Ries' "Short Confession" (both are called "Short Confession" for short). We infer that Smyth's group had developed a mature English Anabaptist *mindset* within just a few years. Smyth's congregation completely dissolved into the Waterlander congregation.

The "Propositions and Conclusions Concerning True Christian Religion" came about in the years 1612 to 1614. Like de Ries' confession, this document opened with the position that God was not the author or creator of sin or the sinner. God had not predestined anyone to eternal damnation.[77] He had intended people to glory and salvation and had equipped them with a free will. Even after the fall into sin, man retained his freedom of will and his capacity to seek God. The Fall, by the way, was entirely Adam's own choice, not God's.[78] Insofar as original guilt and original sin arose as a result of the Fall, Christ's death had already stopped the inheritance of sinfulness and guilt before the birth of Cain and Abel. Indeed, Christ was said to be the Lamb who was "known before the foundation of the world."[79] Christ's death on the cross, according to the Christians of Smyth's congregation, thus brought retroactive salvation.[80] This idea was necessary in

---

[76] Smyth, "A Short Confession of Faith in XX Articles" (1609), paragraphs 17–18.

[77] "Propositions and Conclusions Concerning True Christian Religion," paragraph 25: "God doth not create or predestinate any man to destruction," in Lumpkin, *Baptist Confessions of Faith*, 128.

[78] "Propositions and Conclusions Concerning True Christian Religion," paragraphs 10–17.

[79] 1 Peter 1:19–20.

[80] "Propositions and Conclusions Concerning True Christian Religion," paragraph 19 and 27.

order to hold *both* to the seriousness of sin *and* the free will of man, and was entirely consistent with the view of Hans de Ries.

What was remarkable was how explicitly this first Baptist-Anabaptist confession brought up God's love in paragraphs 21 through 32. Making God's love a theme was rare in confessions of those days, and the suspicion is justified that a discussion was taking place in the background. Possibly these texts from the "Propositions and Conclusions" were to be understood polemically, and were intended to correct the one-sided image of humanity portrayed in Reformed confessions. Anabaptists certainly took sin and its destructive effects seriously, but also brought balance to the dark picture by explicitly pointing to God's great love for people. Some excerpts are as follows:

[21] (We believe) That all actual sinners are image bearers of the first Adam, in his innocent state, in his fall and in his restoration through the sacrifice of grace (1 Cor 15:49)....

[22] That when Adam had fallen, God did not hate him, but still loved him and sought good for him (Gen 3:8–15).[81] Nor does He hate any man who falls into sin with Adam. For God loves humankind and out of His love sent His only begotten Son into the world to save the lost and to seek the sheep that have gone astray (John 3:16).

[23] God never forsakes his creatures unless there is no more possible solution. Nor is there an eternal rejection of what He has created in innocence. God rejects only when people remain unrepentant in sin....

[24] Just as in all people there is a natural tendency to do good to their young, the same is seen in God with regard to man. Indeed, every glimpse of goodness in creatures is infinitely good in God....

[27] Just as God made all men in His image, so He also redeemed all who fall by the doing of sins. But God, in order to redeem, did not deviate from the way of grace He intended to show in His creation....

---

[81] We find a similar thought in the Belgic Confession, Article 17: "We believe that our merciful God, when He saw that man had thus plunged himself into bodily and spiritual death and made himself utterly unhappy, in His wonderful wisdom and goodness Himself began to seek it." See also article 26, and *Canons of Dort* I.2 and II.9.

[28] (We believe) That Jesus Christ came into the world to save sinners, and that God sent Him because He loves His enemies.... Christ died for His enemies (Rom 5:10). He bought free those who rejected Him...and thus teaches us to love our enemies....

[32] Although the sacrifice of Christ's body and blood, offered to God the Father on the cross, is a fragrant aroma and sacrifice, and God therefore delights in Christ, this sacrifice does not reconcile God to us, because God never hated us nor was He our enemy. Christ's sacrifice reconciles *us* to God (2 Cor 5:19), and strikes down *our* enmity and hatred towards God (Eph 1:14, 17; Rom 1:30).[82]

The English Anabaptist separatists in Amsterdam emphasized in their confession that God did not dislike people even when they sinned. God loved his enemies, just as Jesus did, and he was out for their good. God did not seek to take revenge on people who were rebellious. God did not even need to be reconciled with man. It was the other way around; Christ's death on the cross reconciled humankind to God. God paid the price of redemption for all people, but that did not automatically save everyone. Reconciliation was offered, but it could not be imposed. Before God, so to speak, the way to reconciliation was open. Every person could come to him and count on his grace and forgiveness. God would not reject anyone. But people struggled with their wants and desires. They had to let themselves be reconciled.[83] They were angry and rebellious. Not God.

It could indeed be doubted whether God had to be characterized as an *avenger* so emphatically, as for example was done in the *Canons of Dort*. There it was stated that God was the "awesome, blameless and just judge and avenger of sin."[84] The combination "Judge and Avenger" was not in itself unjustified, since God actually was both.[85] But this was one side of the gospel of God, a

---

[82] For the original text, see Lumpkin, *Baptist Confessions of Faith*, 127–129.
[83] See 2 Corinthians 5:18–21.
[84] *Canons of Dort* I,15.
[85] See Nahum 1:2 (Hebr. *noqem*, cf. Jer. 51:56) and 1 Thessalonians 4:6 (Gr. *ekdikos*, cf. Rom 12:19). See H.G.L. Peels, "Wraak, vergelding," in *Woordenboek voor bijbellezers*, ed. A. Noordegraaf, G. Kwakkel, S. Paas, H.G.L. Peels, A.W. Zwiep (Zoetermeer:

side that was not to be emphasized unilaterally. The other side (two sides of the same coin) was God's gracious side. Could it be that Smyth and his friends felt that the gracious side of the gospel was underemphasized in Reformed circles? Had this been part of the reason for Smyth's shift toward Anabaptist thinking? Were the Dutch Calvinists too strict, too judgemental and too much occupied with speculative predestination theology?[86]

God's vengeance and judgement, according to Smyth, came to be seen in a false light if his grace and love were not also spoken of. Grace and justice described one and the same face of God. The Reformed probably felt that the "dark side" of God was not sufficiently expressed by the Anabaptists. The Anabaptists believed that the Reformed thought too small of God's gracious side.

Since God knew no hatred, according to Smyth and his congregation, a Christian was also not allowed to hate or kill.[87] No pressure was to be put on the conscience of other people, nor was the government to interfere in matters of faith of an ecclesiastical or individual nature. Smyth's congregation was one of the first churches to openly advocate religious freedom.

> (We believe) That the magistrate is not by virtue of his office to meddle with religion, or matters of conscience, to force or compel men to this or that form of religion, or doctrine: but to leave Christian religion free, to every man's conscience....[88]

One of the duties of a public servant was to use force for the common good. But if he converted to the Christian faith, he could do no more than take up his *cross*, renounce violence and resign his social function, according to Smyth's circle.[89]

The spiritualistic character of Smyth's congregation (he was guided by the "inner word")—which bore resemblance to that of the Waterlanders, and in some respects to that of the Zwickau

---

Boekencentrum, 2005), 725–728.
[86] Both Arminius and Gomarus were speculative in their thinking. Theorizing about predestination provokes this. The spirit of the Heidelberg Catechism and the Dutch Confession of Faith is different.
[87] "Propositions and Conclusions Concerning True Christian Religion," paragraph 63.
[88] "Propositions and Conclusions Concerning True Christian Religion," paragraph 84.
[89] "Propositions and Conclusions Concerning True Christian Religion," paragraph 85.

prophets—was expressed in the words that those who were God's "new creation" no longer needed any external aids to faith.

> Brothers and Sisters, the sacraments, the institutions of the church, yes even the written letter of Scripture, were but simple outward aids, which a true Christian had better do without, since he had enough of the inward testimony of God, namely: the Father, the Word, and the Holy Spirit.[90]

These three were sufficient for Smyth to trust blindly. Did 1 John not say:

> But you have been anointed by the Holy One, and you all have knowledge…but the anointing that you received from him abides in you, and you have no need that anyone should teach you. But as his anointing teaches you about everything, and is true, and is no lie—just as it has taught you, abide in him.[91]

Christians who lived spiritually needed no teaching or any kind of spiritual guidance from outside. The so-called "believing inner self" was sufficient, they believed. The Waterlanders and Smyth, meanwhile, with their spiritualist leanings, deviated far from the course of Menno Simons. Yet, they were no exception within the broad spectrum of the Anabaptist movement, especially in the Netherlands.

So far it has become clear that the confession of Smyth ("Short Confession of Faith") and the confession of the circle of Smyth ("Propositions and Conclusions") and the confession of Hans de Ries ("A Short Confession") were close in content.[92] Barring

---

[90] "Propositions and Conclusions Concerning True Christian Religion," paragraph 61. See 1 John 5:7, a verse which is of later date and translated in brackets or already omitted in recent translations (see the text-critical apparatus).
[91] 1 John 2:20, 26–27.
[92] Lee concludes his book on Smyth's theology with emphasizing de Ries' direct influence, without there being significant theological keystones which may have smoothened Smyth's turn to Anabaptism, see Jason K. Lee, *The Theology of John Smyth: Puritan, Separatist, Baptist, Mennonite* (Macon: Mercer University Press, 2003), 292: "There were certain facts of Smyth's theology before he became a Mennonite that might have made him more susceptible to accepting their views. However, his

minor differences, the tone, tenor and theological outline spoke of the same basic ideas. The doctrine of predestination was firmly rejected, as was the idea of original sin and original guilt. God could not be held responsible for the fall of the first man, nor for the fall of all men thereafter.

God had made man according to his good pleasure and each person was therefore the object of God's care and love. The Anabaptist idea of the restoration of capacity to choose was ingenious. Because the sacrifice of Christ was in view, Adam, and in him all men, received back their own free will and retained responsibility for the direction of their lives. Thus, people could still choose for or against grace. Furthermore, we see similarities in the way Smyth and the Waterlanders thought about the issue of non-violence, government and freedom of conscience. And, naturally, there was great unity on the principle of baptism by faith.

Things were different, however, between the confessions of Smyth and Helwys. While both spiritual leaders were united in doctrine and life before their stay in Amsterdam, not long after their arrival in the Dutch refugee city their friendship and unity were over. Helwys was able to follow Smyth in his view on the baptism of faith—this had already been discussed in England. But Smyth's decision to knock on the Waterlanders' door was a bridge too far for Helwys. Thomas Helwys and John Murton believed that Smyth had relapsed into ecclesiastical thinking. They had been baptized in Amsterdam as they should have been, so why did they still need the approval of the Waterlanders?

Helwys rejected this spiritual control of the Anabaptists as officious and successionist; the whole evoked associations with hierarchy and high church institutionalism to him. A number of Anabaptist views he could not adopt. Over the years, Helwys had become more Arminian in his thinking,[93] but he certainly thought differently about the so-called "crown jewels" of the Anabaptists,

---

agreement with them was not caused by any existing aspect of his theology. He came to believe these views from the direct influence of Hans de Ries and the Waterlander Mennonites of Amsterdam. The influence of Hans de Ries on Smyth's theology has not been fully appreciated." See also 83–95, 126, 164–165, 207–208, 242–243, 287–288.
[93] See Wright, *Free Church, Free State*, 37–39: "Generally, opinion points to Baptists being a development from within English Puritans and Separatists. But it is impossible to exclude the possibility that there were Anabaptist influences upon them" (38).

3.5 The confession of Helwys

Thomas Helwys had drafted his own confession in 1611, "A Declaration of Faith of English People Remaining at Amsterdam in Holland," in which he took a position on discussions, which divided the Smyth congregation. This confession was remarkable in its anti-Arminian and at the same time anti-Calvinist tenor.

Helwys was clearly not detached from his Puritan-Calvinist background, yet he also held on to some newly acquired insights about the gracious scope of the atonement. Helwys' salvation views were even strikingly Anabaptist in nature.[94]

It was this mixture of Reformed and Anabaptist thought that Helwys and a handful of others brought to England in 1611, and which served as the basis for the first Baptist congregation in England (Spitalfield, London). With his confession, Helwys laid the foundation for a denomination that from the beginning would be called *General Baptists*.[95] The name expressed that the redemption Christ had accomplished was intended for *all* people (*general atonement*, therefore *General* Baptists).

Helwys surprisingly opened his "Declaration" with the imputation of Adam's sin to all men, and the obedience of Christ, which made it possible for all men to be restored to the original state of righteousness. Yet this sacrifice of Christ did not take away the fact that every human being was by nature a "child of wrath."[96] Helwys viewed man as utterly lost in sin. People were inclined to all evil, but could nevertheless (by God's grace) open or close their inner being to the gospel.

---

[94] The manuscript can be found at: https://archive.org/details/shortdeclaration00helw/page/n7/mode/2up
[95] See, in particular, Helwys's letters on church, church order and confession in Early, *The Life and Writings of Thomas Helwys*, 53–73, and the comparison between Smyth and Helwys on 26–36.
[96] Thomas Helwys, "A Declaration of Faith of English People Remaining at Amsterdam in Holland" (1611), paragraphs 2–4.

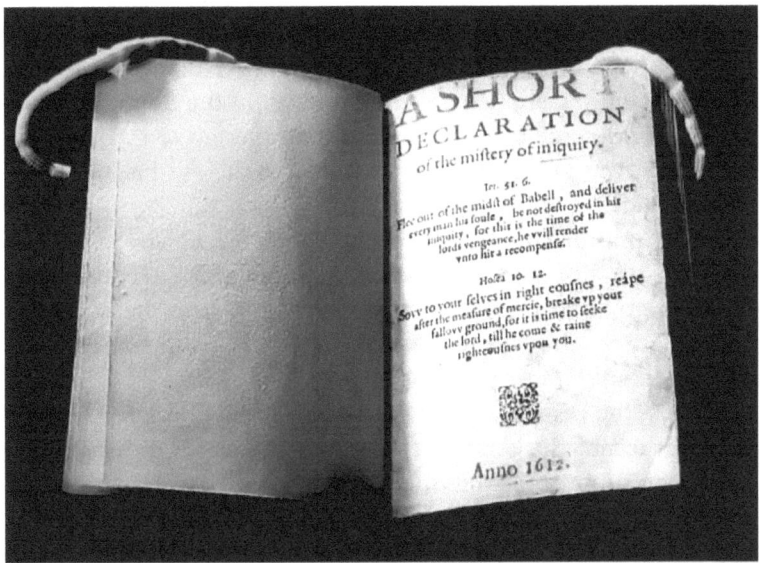

The Confession of Helwys

All people, through Christ's death and resurrection, were objects of God's grace and love, and yet they had an evil disposition, and the judgement of God rested upon them as long as they did not repent. According to Helwys, there was no "double predestination" with God (electing some people to salvation and some to damnation), but God had decided from eternity that only those who would believe would be saved.[97] Therefore, anyone who did not believe would be lost because of his unbelief.[98] Thus, Helwys also emphatically emphasized that God was not the source of people's condemnation. God had not devised and decided who would and who would not enter eternal glory and

---

[97] See Helwys's treatise published in Amsterdam on June 2, 1611: "A Short an Plaine Proof by the Word and Works of God that God's Decree is not the Cause of Any Man's Sins or Condemnation," in Early, *The Life and Writings of Thomas Helwys*, 74–92.

[98] Helwys, "A Declaration of Faith of English People Remaining at Amsterdam in Holland" (1611), paragraph 5: "That GOD before the Foundatiō off the World hath Predestinated that all that beleeve in him shall-be saved…and al that beleeve not shalbee damned."

eternal hell. God did ordain that faith and unbelief would determine the direction a person's life and final destination would take.[99]

God sought the salvation and restoration of every person. Therefore, all people had to come to faith in the Son of God. A person could come to faith but could also let go of it. By falling away from the grace of God, he could even lose his salvation, Helwys said.[100]

Furthermore, Helwys spoke out about the congregationalist church form, discipline, Christian assembly and the community "really getting to know" each other ("That the members off everie Church...ought to knowe one another"), and emphatically rejected infant baptism.[101]

Finally, the Broxtowe Hall gentleman openly declared himself in favour of the Christian duty not only to honour governments, but also to support them in the use of the sword. Christians could serve in government service, Helwys believed. After all, governments were institutions of God, and therefore could not be denied access to Christ's church.

> They beare the sword off GOD,—which sword in all Lawful administracions is to be defended and supported by the servants off GOD....[102]

It could therefore be necessary for Christians to take the oath for a just cause, Helwys said.[103]

The separation between Smyth and Helwys is of great significance for the perception of the genesis of the first Baptist congregations in Europe. Smyth's congregation can rightly be called the very first Baptist congregation, but which side of that congregation are we talking about? Do we mean the group around

---

[99] Helwys, "A Declaration of Faith of English People Remaining at Amsterdam in Holland" (1611), paragraph 6.
[100] Helwys, "A Declaration of Faith of English People Remaining at Amsterdam in Holland" (1611), paragraph 7.
[101] Helwys, "A Declaration of Faith of English People Remaining at Amsterdam in Holland" (1611), paragraphs 11–12.
[102] Helwys, "A Declaration of Faith of English People Remaining at Amsterdam in Holland" (1611), paragraph 24. Lumpkin, *Baptist Confessions of Faith*, 123.
[103] Helwys, "A Declaration of Faith of English People Remaining at Amsterdam in Holland" (1611), paragraph 25.

Smyth that moved into the Waterlander community? Or do we mean the small group around Helwys that continued as General Baptists in England? Or can we perhaps say that the schism is to be regretted, and that the first Baptist congregation was on Amsterdam soil and was an amalgam of Calvinist and Anabaptist (Arminian in appearance) thought? We argue for the latter, because both groups mutually influenced and repelled each other. Helwys was definitely shaped by Anabaptist thought, even though he rejected the Anabaptist "crown jewels" as mentioned. Smyth, too, as an Anabaptist Arminian, still held to a number of Puritan-Calvinist principles (which he had come to know in England), such as the rejection of government interference in church affairs, and resistance to empty forms of outward religion. The cradle of the first Baptist congregation was thus the Amsterdam of 1609, in the accommodations that the Waterlander community so generously offered Smyth and the English dissenters.

One of the discussions that ran high in the young Baptist congregation was about the typically Anabaptist view of Christ's bodily existence on earth. We do not have time to go deeply into this issue, but in the Dutch Anabaptist movement, in the wake of Menno Simons, Dirk Philipsz and Melchior Hoffman, the view was defended that the body of Jesus did not come from Mary.[104] This would have been too much honour for Mary; moreover, with an earthly body, Jesus could easily be suspected of sinning. With a body from his mother Mary, Jesus stood in the lineage of Adam, and was just as lost as any other human being. But apart from Adam, without a sinful body, Jesus could make every Christian partake of the original, sinless nature of Adam in a process of sanctification.[105] Christians were rooted in the sinless state of the new Adam, according to Hoffman.

To prevent Jesus from being declared a man from "below," with an unclean body, Menno Simons assumed that Jesus was entirely from "above."[106] He had to be completely from heaven,

---

[104] See especially Sjouke Voolstra, *Het Woord is vlees geworden. De Melchioritisch-mennniste incarnatieleer* (Kampen: Kok, 1982).

[105] Voolstra, *Het Woord is vlees geworden*, 125–128.

[106] See Marten Mikron, *Een waerachtigh verhaal der t'zamensprekinghen tusschen Menno Simons ende Martinus Mikron van der menschwerdinghe Iesu Christi* (1556), in *Documenta Anabaptistica Neerlandica*, Vol. 3, ed. W.F. Dankbaar (Leiden: Brill, 1981), 74

in spirit and body. Therefore, it is sometimes taught that Menno Simons believed that the body of Jesus was "heavenly flesh."[107]

Menno read John 1:14 differently than the orthodoxy views of the time. It is written, "the Word became flesh."[108] In other words, the eternal Word of God himself came to man in a body, and only then became Son. These words, according to Menno, could not be understood as though God's eternal Son came to the world and took up residence in a body prepared by Mary (for Menno there was no eternal, pre-existent Son, because there was no Son without a Father and without a body).[109] Jesus would thus have become too much a person of two worlds.[110] For Menno, it was a dark thought, for Jesus would then have had to have had a soul from below and from above, from the Father and from Mary.

According to Dirk Philipsz and Menno Simons, there was only one Son of God who became flesh by receiving heavenly flesh "out of the Spirit" (from the Father) and taking on this flesh in the womb of Mary.[111] Simons' argument was always: since there is no Son without a Father, Jesus could only be Son as a human

---

(§110). Menno denied that Jesus was of Mary's flesh. Mikron's "story" recounts the debate he had with Menno Simons on February 6 and 15, 1554.

[107] See Mikron, *Een waerachtigh verhaal*, §196: "Ick bekenn oock wel, dat Iesus Christus waere God ende waere mensch zy...auer zeg, dat hy zyner menschlicker natuere oorspronk heeft niet van onzen vleesche, auer wt der substancy des hemelschen Vaders" (115), and §110: "Wy hebben eenen hemelschen, ende niet eenen aerdischen Christum, gehelijck ghy doet" (74).

[108] See Menno's argument on John 1:14 in Mikron, *Een waerachtigh verhaal*, 51–52 (§60-63). See also Voolstra, *Het Woord is vlees geworden*, 128–133.

[109] Menno said: "Dar is gheen zoon zonder vader ende moeder, daerom kann oock Christus Godes Zoon niet zijn, dan na zyner menscheit…. Ick holde dat de gheheele Christus Iesus, Godes Zoon zy oock na zyner menschlicker natuere." Mikron, *Een waerachtigh verhaal*, 40 (§37–38).

[110] Mikron, *A waerachtigh verhaal*, §41, 153, 174: "After this thy confession share ghy Christum, and now put two persons in him" (105). Mikron, who follows the confession of the church, is accused by Menno of a kind of Nestorianism. The Anabaptists were apprehensive of a Nestorian dichotomy of the Son of God. See how the church responded to Nestorianism in the fifth century in Karl Suzo Frank, *Lehrbuch der Geschichte der Alten Kirche* (Paderborn: Ferdinand Schöningh, 2002), 276–281, and Reinhold Seeberg, *Lehrbuch der Dogmengeschichte*, 2. Band (Graz: Akademische Druck- und Verlagsanstalt, 1953), 214–220.

[111] Mikron, *A waerachtigh verhaal*, 43–45 (§44-47). Menno argues that the fruit in Mary's womb was entirely of the seed of the heavenly Father. Women had no seed, according to Menno. Mary merely passed on food to her fruit in her body (55–56, §69–70).

being if he came from the same Father in spirit and in body. Simons felt that the existing theology divided Christ too much. Christ was and is undividedly One, according to Menno Simons.¹¹²

However, the Waterlander community did not share Simons' view. The Waterlander community was the first Anabaptist group that dared to turn against the Melchiorite-Mennonite doctrine.¹¹³ Thomas Helwys also subtly contradicted Simons' views in his "Declaration." The eighth paragraph explicitly stated:

> (We believe and confess) That Jesus Christ is the Son of God, the second Person…and that in the fullness of time He appeared in the flesh, as the seed of David…, as the Son of the virgin Mary, made of her human material…by the power of the Holy Spirit who overshadowed her.¹¹⁴

According to Helwys, Jesus received his body in its entirety from his mother Mary. The Holy Spirit overshadowed her, and she became pregnant, by the power of God. Most Anabaptists did not think this way, and eliminated the contribution of Mary. In doing so, however, they did not seek salvation in a docetic form of Christianity, for Jesus certainly did not just *appear* to suffer, and his body was *truly* a body. They were seeking to secure the absolute holiness of Christ in spirit and body, as one Person who came from "above." Salvation could not expect, and did not need, input from "below." Salvation from God had to come entirely from heaven.¹¹⁵

---

112 Mikron, *A waerachtigh verhaal*, 76 (§113). Menno suggested to Mikron: "Wat ghy oock on mynen inconuenienten antwordet, altijd zult ghy moeten Christum deelen en onreyn maken." Trans. "He who divides our Christ, he is Anathema. He who makes an unclean Christ, he is Anathema. He who makes Christ into two persons, that one also is Anathema," and §177: "I allow that there is a difference between person and nature: but I say that the whole Christ is God and man, mortal and sufferable: you put one part mortal, and the other sufferable" (106).
113 Zijlstra, *Om de ware gemeente en oude gronden*, 273.
114 "(Wee beleeve and confesse) That IESUS CHRIST, the Sonne of GOD the second Person…in the Fulness off time was manifested in the Flesh, being the seed off David …the Sonne of Marie the Virgine, made of hir substance…. By the power off the HOLIE GHOST overshadowing hir," Lumpkin, *Baptist Confessions of Faith*, 119.
115 See William Echard Keeney, *The Development of Dutch Anabaptist Thought and Practice from 1539–1564* (Nieuwkoop: B. de Graaf, 1968).

This thinking was closely aligned with the Anabaptist view of a holy Christian life. To live a holy life, a Christian had to focus primarily on what came from above, not on what came from below.[116] The apostle Paul said:

> If then you have been raised with Christ, seek the things that are above, where Christ is, seated at the right hand of God. Set your minds on things that are above, not on things that are on earth.[117]

3.6 Anabaptism and openness

Anabaptism never remained entirely on the sidelines of Dutch society. After the predominantly aggressive early days had blown over, the non-violent variant remained and Anabaptists in the Netherlands were soon a tolerated minority.[118] This minority consisted largely of people from the lower classes of society. Most had received little or no education. However, being able to read Scripture independently was an incentive to learn to read and receive an education. A need for independence developed powerfully in Anabaptist thought.[119] Although initially they did not really participate in the growing and flourishing Dutch culture during the Golden Age, this began to change during the seventeenth century. The individualistic attitude, which manifested itself in cultural and social isolation, transformed into progressive thinking about freedom of conscience and human will, and proved to connect well with the emerging humanism of post-Reformation

---

[116] See Wright, *The Early English Baptists, 1603–1649*, 9–10 ("the boundaries between the godly and the profane"), and Briggs, "The Origins of the People Called Baptists," 8.
[117] Colossians 3:1–2.
[118] Cornelius Krahn, "Anabaptism and the Culture of the Netherlands," in *The Recovery of the Anabaptist Vision*, ed. F. Hershberger, 219–220. See also Mary Sprunger, "Waterlanders and the Dutch Golden Age: A Case Study on Mennonite Involvement in Seventeenth-Century Trade and Industry As One of the Earliest Examples of Socio-Economic Assimilation," in *From Martyr to Muppy (Mennonite Urban Professionals): A Historical Introduction to Cultural Assimilation Processes of a Religious Minority in the Netherlands: the Mennonites*, ed. Alistair Hamilton, Sjouke Voolstra, Piet Visser (Amsterdam: Amsterdam University Press, 1994), 133–148.
[119] See, for example, for the Flemish Anabaptist denomination, Marjan Blok, "Het Vlaamse doperdom en de gedrukte tekst: over de paradigmatische verschuiving van oraliteit naar tekstualiteit," *Nederland Theologisch Tijdschrift* 60 (2006): 149–163.

times. Incidentally, Dutch Anabaptism never had a purely individualistic and politically impassive character.[120]

The Waterlanders were more willing than other Anabaptist groups to adapt to the prevailing culture where desirable and possible. Their humane attitude translated into social interest and helpfulness, honesty and diligence, idealism and cultural vision. The Mennonites of Europe have therefore been called the "honeybees of the land."[121] They gladly devoted themselves to the development of their fellow citizens, especially since the threat of persecution had all but disappeared, and the cultural winds were in their favour.

Around 1650, the Anabaptists in Amsterdam and in the provinces of Friesland and Groningen made up about 20 per cent of the population. The Calvinists (no more than 25 per cent of the population) and Catholics had to learn to live with Anabaptists as their neighbours.

A well-known Amsterdam Anabaptist, as we have seen, was Joost van den Vondel, the author and poet with whom we began this book. His parents were Anabaptist Christians, expelled from the Southern Netherlands to the northern provinces. Van den Vondel even served for some time as a deacon in the Anabaptist community of Amsterdam. Other well-known names from Anabaptist circles were Adriaensz Leeghwater and Pieter Teyler, whose free spirit still lives on in the Teyler Institute in Haarlem. It is also said of Rembrandt van Rijn that he was an Anabaptist, but this assumption cannot be proven. What is certain is that he maintained friendly ties with the Amsterdam Anabaptist community.

In the past four centuries the Mennonite community in the Netherlands has been able to contribute significantly to cultural and social developments that have made the country what it is: an open democracy, which protects the rights of citizens and also of religious dissenters. In the twenty-first century, the Anabaptist spirit touches Holland because of its mild and tolerant attitude toward "deviant" believers and thinkers. Now, when we think of this Anabaptist tolerance, we should definitely not think of the endless "who cares?" tolerance that characterizes our time. That

---

[120] Krahn, "Anabaptism and the Culture of the Netherlands," 226.
[121] Krahn, "Anabaptism and the Culture of the Netherlands," 227.

form of tolerance generally stems from indifference: "Everyone should do whatever they feel like."[122] This is called *indifferentism*.

Anabaptist tolerance of the sixteenth and seventeenth centuries was a conviction for which there was an explanation and a clear spiritual story. It was a lived and convinced tolerance. Tolerance simply because it had to be done, or because what someone else thought and did was none of my business, was far removed from the Anabaptist vision of humanity and social responsibility. What touched people in the Anabaptist community was heartfelt attention and interest, without the intention of wagging the finger or touching the soul of the other. It was possibly a combination of warmth and space, stemming from strong spiritual convictions about God, Christ and the eternal value of the human soul.

3.7 Excursus 4: The Overtons

The story of Richard Overton (*fl.* 1640–1664) speaks to the imagination of this theme, and we want to dwell briefly on his life. Overton was from Thomas Lambe's General Baptist congregation in Bell Alley in London, near St. Paul's Cathedral, which likely had continuity with the congregation founded by Thomas Helwys, and succeeded by John Murton.[123] His life is somewhat symbolic of the (Ana)Baptistic movement, which is addressed in this book. He belonged to a community that had undergone influences from both Baptist and Anabaptist sources.[124]

Concerning Richard Overton, there is but scant information available about the greatest part of his life. We know only something about the beginning of his stay in Amsterdam and about the last twenty years of his life, when he was back in England.

---

[122] See Stephan van Erp, "Vrijheid in verdeeldheid. Geschiedenis en actualiteit van religieuze tolerantie," in *Vrijheid in verdeeldheid. Geschiedenis en actualiteit van religieuze tolerantie*, ed. Stephan van Erp (Nijmegen: Valkhof Pers, 2008), 7–24.

[123] Murray Tolmie, *Triumph of the Saints: Separate Churches of London, 1616–1649* (Cambridge: Cambridge University Press, 1977), 47, 151. On the continuity of Thomas Lambe's congregation with the Helwys/Murton church see Stephen R. Holmes, "The Church of Helwys, Murton, and Lambe: An Argument for Continuity," *Baptist Quarterly* (2023). See also Glen H. Stassen, *Just Peacemaking: Transforming Initiatives for Justice and Peace* (Louisville: Westminster/John Knox Press, 1992), 137–155.

[124] See Coggins, *John Smyth's Congregation*, 157: "It was demonstrated that the Mennonites were the source of the 'Arminianism' of both Smyth and Helwys."

Overton had fled with John Robinson and John Smyth to the "free Holland" in 1608. Overton is known to have joined the Waterlander congregation in 1615, and shortly before that had been baptized into Smyth's congregation. Holland was for him a model for the spirit of tolerance and freedom of conscience that God, in principle, demanded from every national government.

In 1615 Overton drafted his own confession,[125] which showed both Baptist and Anabaptist sympathies and incorporated themes that would form the raw material for his later struggle for human freedom. The four fundamental ideas were:

1. Man was made in the image of God, and therefore Christ died for all men, no one excepted.
2. Christ was the only true norm for the church (the *norma normans*), not the tradition handed down (which had invalidated Christ's words on non-violence).
3. Hierarchy and power structures stood in the way of the spiritual life of the church and were to be firmly rejected.
4. The principle of freedom of conscience was to be followed, and church and state were therefore to be kept apart.

Furthermore, Overton addressed issues of non-violence and peace, care of the poor, loving your enemies and several themes clearly drawn from the Sermon on the Mount.

Then we hear nothing from Richard Overton for more than twenty-five years, until he suddenly turns up in London in 1642, as a writer and publicist of pamphlets and brochures. In the 1640s Overton was writing satirical and humorous tracts, which sensitively denounced all sorts of abuses around the issue of religious freedom. They were sharply spiced and left nothing out in terms of clarity. Usually the existing hierarchy was taken to task with the inconsistencies and decadence of English bourgeois morality either unfavourably or painfully exposed. Overton's implicit theme in each case was the autocratic rule of Christ versus all human thoughts of power.

---

[125] To join the Waterlander congregation, Overton had to be able to compose and submit his own confession.

For his use of science and insights that were modern for the time, Richard Overton has frequently been portrayed as an apostate or liberal Christian, but it is questionable whether this is a fair assessment of this "defender of the faith." In addition to the Bible, Overton often used scientific insights that were making national news in his day. In any case, he cannot be characterized as a seventeenth-century secularist.[126] Like the apologists in the first centuries of our era, Overton sought to convince his readers of the unreasonableness of religious persecution by letting them fall onto their own sword on their own turf.

A highlight of Overton's stormy œuvre was the publication of the satire *The Arraignment of Mr. Persecution* (1645). In this short story, a certain Mr. Persecution is on trial for high treason against Christ, for causing divisions among nations, churches, families and friends. Mr. Persecution turns out to be a danger to humanity and is found guilty. Overton wanted this story to indicate how disruptive and sickening was the "right" to violate human freedom. This Anabaptist pamphleteer was one of the first who openly advocated for the rights and freedoms of every human being across the globe (not unlike universal human rights), and also went to jail in London for it.

In February 1547, Overton published a farce about his own arrest and that of his wife (*A Commoner's Complaint*). The state had not granted permission for its publication and had Overton arrested. As he was dragged down the street, he held a copy of the Magna Carta firmly under his arm. The Magna Carta was a precursor to the English Act, which limited the rights of the king and defined the rights of the free citizen.

From prison, this warrior for human freedom continued unbroken and tirelessly to write, while his wife kept the printing press rolling at pace—until she too was discovered and arrested. Her attitude of passive resistance when the court officers came to arrest her was known.[127] Outside of this, however, we know virtually nothing about Mrs. Overton; we do not even know her first name. We also do not know how long the Overtons had been

---

[126] Stassen, *Just Peacemaking*, 144.
[127] See Michael L. Westmoreland-White, "The Story of Mrs Overton: A Random Chapter in the History of Nonviolence" (Sunday, Sept. 1, 2002); https://levellers.wordpress.com.

together, whether Mrs. Overton had fled from England to Amsterdam, whether Richard Overton had met his wife in Amsterdam or only when he had returned to England. What we do know is that, like her husband, she was an advocate for Christian freedom of conscience and human rights,[128] which concerned all people of all faiths. Together they wrote critical pamphlets, and together they were part of a General Baptist congregation and devotedly served the Lord Jesus. However, it is not certain and actually not probable that an ethic of non-violence was then a standard part of the General Baptists' faith. Baptists did opt for a separation of church and state, but they did not have to be opposed to violence on principle to do so; "Government did not carry the sword of God in vain." Possibly, the Overtons were an exception within their church community in England.

On principle, Mrs. Overton did not want to assist in her own arrest, so she refused any cooperation. The police chief ordered her to get up and come with him, but she did not move. She behaved passively and without resistance, so she could not be pushed or pulled along. When she was threatened that she would be dragged away by horse and cart, Mrs. Overton replied with something like, "Do what you think you should do, but I stand by my position." The police chief then flew into a rage and ordered his officers to lift her, and the baby she was holding in her arms and carry them away to Bridewell Prison. The officers, however, were so impressed by the woman's determination and argument that they refused to carry out the order. The police chief hastily summoned a new group of officers but they also refused to participate in this and left.

As a last resort, the police chief summoned some servants to do the executioner's work. They broke down Mrs. Overton's barricaded door and jumped on her to snatch the baby from her arms, which failed. Finally, the woman was dragged across the street by her legs, through the mud, while she held her screaming baby in her arms as safely as possible. At this scene, the police

---

[128] Of course, in the seventeenth century we cannot yet speak of human rights being about inalienable subjective rights. Equal rights (the principle of equality) are only just beginning to be discovered in Europe, and are pushing forward during the Age of Enlightenment.

chief and his entourage openly called Mrs. Overton a whore and a slut, so as not to give the stunned bystanders the impression that an innocent woman was being led to jail.

From prison, Richard Overton and his wife continued their work as usual. Behind bars, the Overtons were often barely fed, except for the little food that could be smuggled in by family and friends. Overton then began to look into the rights of prisoners, including those sentenced to death. Hardly anyone heard from him for a long time. Who ever heard of a Mr. or Mrs. Overton? Perhaps, Richard Overton was still a familiar name to some, but who knows what his wife's name was, and who can tell what she did?

Mrs. Overton's spiritual strength is reminiscent of another strong woman in Anabaptist history. We refer to Margret Hottinger (we do know her name), and she lived over a hundred years before the Overtons.[129]

3.8 Excursus 5: Margret Hottinger

Margret Hottinger (c. 1500–1530) was the daughter of Jakob Hottinger, the farmer of Zollikon, who was sentenced to a heavy fine in June 1523 for daring to contradict a clergyman in public.[130] Two years later Jakob Hottinger was baptized, and in 1530 arrested and put to death. Hottinger had learned to read, and he had a German New Testament at his disposal. With Scripture in hand, he took on his superiors when, in his opinion, they deviated from the Word of God. Thus, boldness, some would say insolence, cost the farmer of Zollikon dearly.

Margret was born into this simple peasant family at the turn of the century.[131] Despite that simplicity, or perhaps because of it,

---

[129] C. Arnold Snyder and Linda A. Huebert Hecht, ed., *Profiles of Anabaptist Women: Sixteenth Century Reforming Pioneers*, Studies in Women and Religion 3 (Waterloo: Wilfed Laurier University Press, 1996), 43–53. See also the chapters on Hille Feicken of Sneek (288–297), Divara of Haarlem (298–304), Fenneke van Geelen of Deventer (305–315), Anna Jansz of Rotterdam (336–351), Elisabeth en Hadewijk of Friesland (359–64), Anna Hendriks of Amsterdam (378–383), Soetjen Gerrits of Rotterdam and Vrou Gerrits of Medemblik (384–405).

[130] See C. Arnold Snyder, *Anabaptist History and Theology*, rev. student ed. (Kitchener: Pandora Press, 1997), 13–14, 18, 20, 24.

[131] Snyder, *Anabaptist History and Theology*, 97–99, 116–117.

the Hottinger family was known as pious (in the good sense of the word) and reformist. In 1524, Margret's uncle had been beheaded as a heretic at Lüzern. Two of her brothers and also some cousins were active in the Reformation of Zollikon, and the radical student Conrad Grebel was a friend of the Hottingers. Margret's father was one of the first to be baptized at Zollikon, and it is no surprise that shortly thereafter Margret and two of her brothers also followed their father's example.

The Hottinger family was thus on a collision course with the authorities of Zürich, who in 1525 arrested Sattler, Blaurock, Mantz, Grebel and Margret Hottinger, among others, and forcibly revoked their religious beliefs. It is typical of Margret that she stood her ground (not Sattler at the time), and ended up in the infamous Wellenberg Prison, a cold and damp tower bunker in the middle of the Limmat river. After locking her up for four months in cold and misery, the authorities still did not succeed in breaking Margret's will. Even at a second interrogation, she stood by her conviction. She still considered her baptism right and good. Two months later, the young woman finally did break. By now she was exhausted and easily influenced, but once recovered, Margret did not appear to have changed her mind.

In 1526, Margret was described by a certain Johannes Kessler of St. Gall in the following words:

> Among the Anabaptist women, a wild and presumptuous error reared its head, especially at the hands of a young woman, from Zollikon in the canton of Zürich, by the name of Margret Hottinger.... (She) led a disciplined life, was much loved, and was held in honor by the Anabaptists.[132]

Subsequently, this Kessler accused Margret of blasphemy and religious madness, but he could not deny that she lived an exemplary and sober life, and that the Anabaptists believed that she was (in their words) "devoted to and immersed in God." These words speak for themselves. Margret Hottinger must have had an influence on the spiritual course that the Anabaptist movement

---

[132] Snyder, *Anabaptist History and Theology*, 98.

took in the early years of its genesis in Switzerland. She was a woman who was listened to and looked up to.

A radical spirit worked vigorously among the Swiss Anabaptists between 1525 and 1526, also pushing forward women with leadership talents. It is clear that this fact both united and divided the Anabaptists, noting the comment in the *Schleitheim Confession* about "false brethren" who lived in "spiritual debauchery." The practice to which this confession was referring was probably the belief in "prophetic utterances" parallel to the revelation of Scripture, as an accompanying voice of God. Margret Hottinger possessed prophetic gifts and used them within the Anabaptist community. Even though she was therefore hindered or shunned by other Anabaptists, she apparently did not allow herself to be silenced.

By 1527, the Zürich authorities had already managed to intimidate and scandalize most of the city's Anabaptists to such an extent that most of them revoked their "Anabaptist baptism." Margret did not agree with this and so she had to flee. She hid over the following years, but in 1530, together with her father and younger brother Felix, she was spotted and arrested just north of the Sea of Constance while they were on their way to Moravia. The younger Felix was released because of his age, but Jakob Hottinger was killed, as was his daughter.

Margret was sentenced to death by drowning. According to tradition, she was launched into the water and pulled up just before death occurred, to give her a chance to recant. Short-tempered as the woman was, she replied, "Why did you pull me out? The flesh was already almost defeated!" Thereupon, Margret Hottinger was held under water until death.

3.9 General Baptists

With the examples of Margret Hottinger and the Overtons, we have entered the Christian sphere of gracious freedom of conscience, non-violence and equal rights for all people, including women, which the first "Baptist community" on Dutch and English soil advocated.

We cannot expect that in this young community there was no inequality or that innocent people were never hurt. In church circles, there is always a difference between ideal and reality. We should not expect more from Anabaptist congregations, simply because they are Anabaptists. It is to be commended that at least there, the rights of people in matters of faith and conscience were considered early on, and the first steps were taken toward the separation of church and state and the freedom of religion regulated by law.

In 1612, the world had certainly not yet reached that point. Sometime that year, Thomas Helwys and some like-minded Baptists from Amsterdam left for England. We have noted that their confession showed Calvinistic and Arminian Baptist traits.[133] "Planting" congregations with these convictions in England was certainly not without risk at the time. Dissenters were persecuted under James I.

In 1612, Helwys published the first English petition on the thorny topic of freedom of belief: *A Short Declaration of The Mystery of Iniquity*.[134] In his own hand, Helwys wrote these famous words in the copy of the book sent to James I:

> Listen king, do not despise the advice of the poor. Let their complaints come to you. The king is a mortal man, he is not God, and therefore he has no power over the immortal souls of his subjects, to promulgate laws and regulations for them and to appoint spiritual lords over them. If the king would have authority to appoint spiritual lords and to promulgate laws, then he would be the immortal God, rather than a mortal man. O king, do not let deceivers deceive you into sinning against God. You have to obey Him. Do not sin against your poor subjects either, who should and will obey you in all things with body, life and property. Otherwise let their lives be taken from the earth. God be with the king.[135]

---

[133] Coggins, *John Smyth's Congregation*, 104–107.
[134] Helwys wrote his "most famous and influential work" in 1612, while living in Amsterdam, see Early, *The Life and Writings of Thomas Helwys*, 155–310.
[135] "Hear, O King, and despise not the counsel of the poor, and let their complaints come before thee. The king is a mortal man and not God, therefore has no power over the immortal souls of his subjects, to make laws and ordinances for them, and to set spiritual lords over them. If the king has authority to make spiritual lords and laws, then he is an immortal God and not a mortal man. O King, be not seduced by deceivers to sin against God whom you ought to obey, nor against your poor subjects who ought

Thomas Helwys would die in captivity in England in 1616. John Murton (1585–c. 1626) then took over the leadership of the English Baptist community. After their return to England, Helwys and other members of the Helwys-Murton church were involved in the struggle for freedom of belief. Leonard Busher wrote a treatise called *Religious Peace*, which was published in 1614 (and unfortunately lost), and may have been financed by the Waterlander Mennonites in Amsterdam.[136]

By 1626, despite oppressions and persecutions, five General Baptist congregations had already arisen in England (adding up to about 150 members), and they had negotiations with the Dutch Waterlanders about a possible union. Because of a difference of opinion, however, these negotiations were broken off. Although it is certain that the General Baptists maintained contact from England with the Waterlander Anabaptists in Holland for decades, the English request to be admitted to the brotherhood of the Dutch Anabaptists was rejected.

The English Baptists did not refuse to swear an oath, nor did they forbid their members from holding government positions. The General Baptists also thought differently than the Dutch Anabaptists on the issue of using the sword. There was also fundamental disagreement about the nature of the Body of Christ.

We have noted that Thomas Helwys' confession differed substantially in content from that of John Smyth in a number of respects. It is likely that Helwys simply edited and recast Smyth's twenty articles, and touched them up with his own nuances.[137] In summary, Helwys' thoughts came down to this:

1. The coming of Jesus was at hand and God's kingdom of peace would soon come.
2. A group of believers who met biblically was a church, and

---

and will obey you in all things with body, life and goods, or else let their lives be taken from the earth. God save the king." Brian Haymes, "On Religious Liberty: Re-Reading A Short Declaration of the Mystery of Iniquity," *Baptist Quarterly* 42 (2007): 198.

[136] Leonard Busher, *Religious Peace; or, a Plea for Liberty of Conscience, long since presented to King James and the High Court of Parliament then sitting, by L. B., Citizen of London, and printed in the year 1614.* See Stephen Wright, "Leonard Busher: Life and Ideas," *Baptist Quarterly* 39/4 (2001): 175–192, and "Leonard Busher: An Additional Note," *Baptist Quarterly* 39/7 (2002): 360.

[137] Bakker, *John Smyth*, 84–85.

The character of the early Baptist church

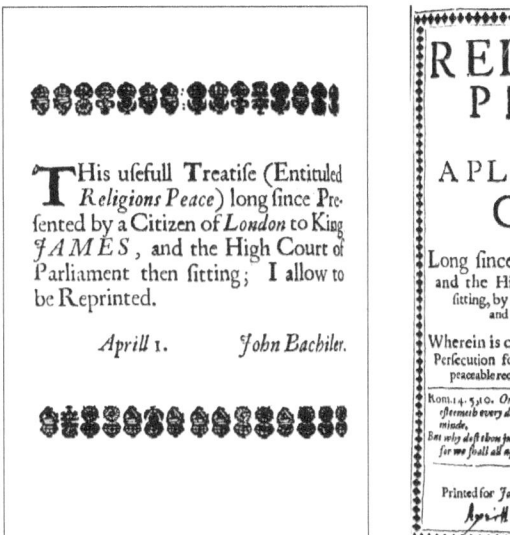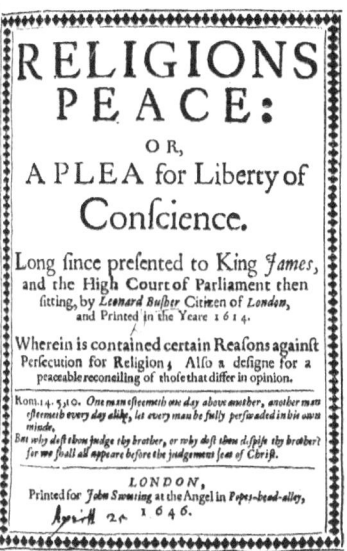

Title pages from Leonard Busher's *Religious Peace* (1614) in its 1646 reprinting

was allowed to minister the sacraments independently of ordained ministers.
3. The foundation of the church was not the covenant with God, but believer's baptism.
4. Children were not baptized, because original sin did not exist. (Shortly after crossing over to England Helwys would teach original sin; at this time Helwys' theology was clearly still developing.)
5. The doctrine of election conflicted with the universality of God's grace and love.
6. Man had no free will and needed the intervention of grace to believe; this grace he could resist.
7. A Christian was permitted to hold government office.

Helwys was actually the main interpreter of Smyth's ideas and can therefore be seen as one of the spiritual fathers of the Baptist churches. The changes Helwys made to Smyth's confession mainly concerned the points that Smyth adapted to the teachings of the

Waterlanders, such as on the oath, government office, free will and inherited debt.[138] Helwys was more Calvinistic on these points, although he certainly did not compromise on the position of religious freedom and freedom of conscience.

In order to distinguish themselves from the evangelical mysticism of George Fox and the Quakers, the English Baptists soon came to draw up their own confession. They did not want to be lumped in with groups that placed a so-called "inner light" *above* the authority of Scripture. In 1651, therefore, under the reign of Oliver Cromwell, the *Midland Confession* was drawn up on behalf of thirty congregations and signed by sixty-one delegates at Leicester. In this confession, baptism by "immersion" was confessed for the first time: "That the way and manner of baptizing… was to go into the water, and to be baptized" (article 48).[139]

For the rest, the content was almost identical to the confession of 1611 (Helwys' "Declaration of Faith"). The important article on the "general atonement," that the atonement in Christ is sufficient for all men, was confessed in article 17: "That Jesus Christ, through (or by) the grace of God, suffered death for all mankind, or every man."[140]

In 1654, a second confession was added by the General Baptists, again with the intention of distancing themselves from the Quakers and other free circles. *The True Gospel-Faith Declared According to the Scriptures* consisted of thirty articles. Six years later (in March 1660), a general assembly of General Baptists in London adopted the *Standard Confession* (encompassing 25 articles). From 1663 onward, this confession was subscribed to by all General Baptists of England and Wales. More than 300 Baptists, including the famous John Bunyan, were imprisoned at that time, and often because they were mistakenly held to be "anabaptists" or Quakers. The *Standard Confession* therefore, began (understandably) with the words:

---

[138] Bakker, *John Smyth*, 86–87.
[139] "The Faith and Practise of Thirty Congregations, Gathered According to the Primitive Pattern," article 48, in Lumpkin, *Baptist Confessions of Faith*, 182.
[140] "The Faith and Practise of Thirty Congregations, Gathered According to the Primitive Pattern," article 48, 178.

A Brief Confession or Statement of Faith, drawn up by many of us who are erroneously called Anabaptists, to inform all in these days of slander and blame of our innocent convictions and walk of life.

The distance between Smyth's Anabaptist beliefs and Helwys' more Calvinist Baptist beliefs had grown considerably in half a century.[141] The General Baptists now emphatically declared they had nothing to do with Anabaptists. This also applied to the Anabaptist view of non-violence. In general, the principle of non-violence (not the idea of separation of church and state) was alien to English Baptists.

In the *Standard Confession* we do find the clearest formulation up to that time of the idea of freedom of belief and thought:

It is God's will and God's judgment (since the gospel), that all men, without any pressure or persecution as to godliness or religion, may act freely and according to their own conscience.[142]

Baptists of various kinds shared this conviction. The notions of religious freedom and freedom of conscience were always deeply embedded in Baptists' historical consciousness. They were linked to Puritan and Anabaptist principles, which had had a founding and formative effect on the first Baptist congregations in Europe.

3.10 Particular Baptists

The latter was also true of the development of the so-called *Particular Baptist* congregations, from 1638 onward. Alongside the General Baptist congregations, another Baptist denomination sprang up in London, where they adhered more strictly to the

---

[141] See L. Russ Bush and Tom J. Nettles, *Baptists and the Bible: The Baptist Doctrines of Biblical Inspiration and Religious Authority in Historical Perspective* (Chicago: Moody Press, 1980), 26–45.

[142] "Standard Confession," Article 24: 'That it is the will, and mind of God (in these Gospel times) that all men should have the free liberty of their own consciences in matters of Religion, or Worship, without the least oppression, or persecution, as simply upon that account," Lumpkin, *Baptist Confessions of Faith*, 232.

Reformed principles of Puritanism. These *Particular Baptists* were originally Puritan separatists who started their own congregationalist congregation in 1616, known as the Jacob Lathrop Jessey Church.[143]

After a lapse of fourteen years, during the reign of terror of Charles I, the idea of believer's baptism came up strongly within these circles. A certain man with the surname Dupper withdrew from the church because he held that infant baptism was invalid. Three years later, Samuel Eaton did the same. He sought, what he called, a "farther Baptism."[144] In 1638, a group that rejected infant baptism finally split from this congregation, and introduced believer's baptism. This group, led by John Spilsbury (1593–c.1668), is generally considered the first Particular Baptist congregation. This was nearly thirty years after the first Baptist congregation was formed in Amsterdam.[145]

In a short time, during the confusing years of the tug of war between Charles I and the English Parliament, as many as four to five different Particular Baptist churches arose from Spilsbury's congregation. In 1640 it was Richard Blunt, a member of the Particular Baptist congregation at Eaton, who first began to propagate baptism by immersion. One was to be baptized "by dipping the body into the water, resembling burial and rising again."[146] A year later he was sent to Holland to orient himself on the proper way of baptism (by immersion). Apparently, Holland was a model country for the English in this respect, so, Blunt was baptized here at the so-called Rijnsburg Collegiants.[147] After returning, Blunt baptized Mr. Blacklock, the congregation's

---

[143] After Henry Jacob (1601–1663), John Lathrop (1583–1654) and Henry Jessey (1603–1663) directed the congregation successively.
[144] Bush and Nettles, *Baptists and the Bible*, 47.
[145] For more about the Particular Baptists, see Michael A.G. Haykin, *Rediscovering Our Engelish Baptist Heritage* (Leeds: Reformation Today Trust, 1996), Paul Clarke, Don Garlington, Erroll Hulse, David Kingdon and Bill Payne, *Our Baptist Heritage* (Pensacola: Chapel Library, 1993).
[146] Baptisms "were to be done by immersing the body in water to express burial and resurrection," Bush and Nettles, *Baptists and the Bible*, 48.
[147] The Rijnsburg Collegiants was a free group of Remonstrant believers, although they did not join any group. They were averse to any church organization and practiced adult baptism. Holiness, community spirit and inner life were the most important notions of the Collegiants' thinking and faith. Later they were influenced by Socinianism (anti-trinitarianism).

spiritual teacher, and the two baptized no fewer than fifty-one other believers. So, by 1641, the Particular Baptists had also developed their own baptismal tradition.

In 1644, the Particular Baptists drafted their own confession, the *London Confession*, which uses moderate Calvinist wording. Experts often draw connections between the *London Confession* and the confession of Henry Ainsworth, a member of the "Ancient Church" of Francis Johnson (the Amsterdam Brownists).[148] We have seen that Smyth sought to join this community in Amsterdam thirty-five years earlier, and how that attempt ended in failure.

The *Second London Confession* came out in 1689, and it is this confession that has set the tone for Reformed Baptists' beliefs and practices for centuries.[149] The well-known Puritan-influenced *Westminster Confession* (1646) was the model for the drafting of the *Second London Confession*.[150] The Calvinist spirit is therefore more emphatically present in this confession.

By 1660, some 131 Particular Baptist congregations (and 115 General Baptist congregations) were in existence. Well-known Reformed Baptists included William Kiffin (1616–1701), Hanserd Knollys (1599–1691) and Benjamin Keach (1640–1704).[151]

The Particular or Reformed Baptists had a strong missionary focus and founded many churches in North America, from which, in turn, many missions sprang. William Carey (1761–1834), considered the father of the modern missionary movement, left England to pursue missions in India. Adoniram Judson (1788–1850) left America, also to preach the gospel in India and Burma.[152]

---

[148] Thomas J. Nettles, *By His Grace and For His Glory: A Historical, Theological, and Practical Study of the Doctrines of Grace in Baptist Life* (Grand Rapids: Baker, 1986), 57–58.
[149] See Samuel E. Waldron, *A Modern Exposition of the 1689 Baptist Confession of Faith* (Darlington: Evangelical Press, 1989). See also Clarke, et al, *Our Baptist Heritage* and Peter Masters, *The Baptist Confession of Faith 1689, With Scripture Proofs* (London: The Wakeman Trust, 1989).
[150] *Westminster Confession of Faith* (Glasgow: Bell and Bain Ltd., 1997).
[151] Michael A.G. Haykin, *Kiffin, Knollys and Keach: Rediscovering Our English Baptist Heritage* (Leeds: Reformation Today Trust, 1996).
[152] Erroll Hulse, *Adoniram Judson and the Missionary Call* (Leeds: Reformation Today Trust, 1996).

William Carey
(1761–1834)

Charles Haddon Spurgeon
(1834–1892)

One name that should not be missed here is that of Charles Haddon Spurgeon (1834–1892). Spurgeon is one of the most famous Reformed Baptists and has been called the "prince of preachers." He served for a long time in London at the Metropolitan Tabernacle, where 6,000 visitors came weekly (5,000 seats; 1,000 standing places). Spurgeon founded, so to speak, the first "megachurch" in England. Today, Reformed Baptists number in the millions worldwide.

There are, in summary, significant differences to be noted both between Smyth's Anabaptists and Helwys' General Baptists, and between General and Particular Baptists.[153] The spiritual distance between the Particular Baptists and Smyth's congregation is obviously the greatest. The estrangement between Smyth and Johnson, Smyth's own mentor in his student years is, as it were, symbolic of this.

---

[153] Poh Boon Sing, *What Is a Reformed Baptist Church?* (Malaysia: Good News Enterprise, 2017).

In addition to significant differences, substantial similarities between these faith traditions can be identified. The most important are: (1) the baptismal view; (2) the congregational view; and (3) the view of church and state (especially freedom of conscience, not governmental responsibility).

These similarities have historically proven to be sufficiently distinctive to speak of a *Baptistic* vision of faith. Perhaps it would be better to speak of an entirely distinctive *congregational* vision and doctrine,[154] around which the congregation's own notions of baptism and religious freedom circle. Congregation, baptism and freedom are the core values, then, that have shaped the history, development and structure of Baptist churches today.

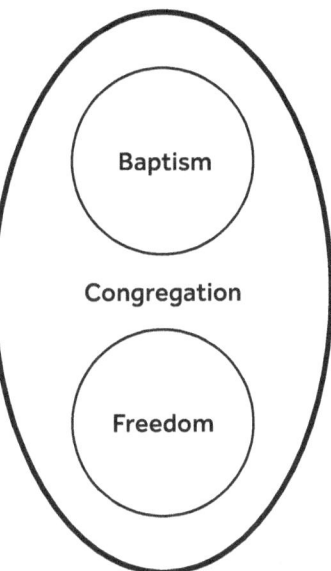

Core values of the Baptistic tradition

---

[154] See Gordon L. Belyea, "Origins of the Particular Baptists," *Themelios* 32 (3, 2007): 40–67.

4

Church and government

We now want to briefly consider some views of government at the time of the Reformation.[1] To understand the thoughts of the peaceful Anabaptists on the position of church and government, the spirit of the Sermon on the Mount and the early church must be juxtaposed with the views of the Reformers.

4.1 Luther and the state

We would first like to consider the ideas of the reformer Martin Luther. Some things have already been said about him in this context, which we will now elaborate on. In the early years of the Reformation, Luther owed much to Frederick the Wise, Elector of Saxony, who was kind to him and gave him needed protection. The reformer, therefore, developed a different conception of the role of government than radical Anabaptists.

---

[1] The appendices on "Peace-loving and tolerant" and "No military service" are also relevant to this discussion.

Following the medieval tradition, Luther still saw the world as the *corpus Christianum*, Christendom, where church and government powers are intertwined. Within this corpus, however, he made a distinction between *spiritual* and *temporal* power. Both powers were in the hand of God and acted distinctly in the *corpus Christianum*. The church was the spiritual power standing in the freedom of Christ, proclaiming the Word of God that conquered human hearts. The government represented secular power, assailing the devil's stronghold, maintaining order, guarding peace and punishing disobedience. The first power covered the dimension of the inner and often invisible freedom and peace, the second power applied to the area of visible peace. And precisely in this area, ethical freedom did not always have to be pursued—sometimes outright coercion had to be applied. Luther was thinking of Anabaptists who had gone astray.

The European Christian, according to Luther, thus belonged to two regiments. On the one hand, he owed obedience to Christ; on the other, he had to obey the government. As a result, the Christian sometimes had to deal with two kinds of morality: a personal morality, summarized in the ethics of the Sermon on the Mount, and a state morality, derived from general natural law and the Ten Commandments.[2] Both worlds could collide in the mind and heart of the Christian.

God's direct guidance was given in the ethical way, which he revealed in the Scriptures. The Christian could study the Bible and find out from it what the will of God was. Did he want to know if it was lawful to take revenge on his enemy? Killing was forbidden, as were lying and hating. But in the end, the Christian could also be confronted with the duties of the authorities because, according to Luther, the hand of the Lord was visible in this as well. God's will for the individual was therefore also reflected in the government's program. God's providence guaranteed this. A Christian may not kill, but it could be God's will that a Christian was called to defend his country with the sword.

From this ethical perspective, Luther could even claim that God's hand was—through the government—providing the

---

[2] See G.J. Heering, *De Zondeval van het Christendom. Een studie over christendom, staat en oorlog* (Arnhem: Van Loghum Slaterus, 1928), 69.

Christian with the sword. And therefore, it was not the Christian man who treats the attacker with "hanging, torture, decapitation, and general warfare." This God himself did: "Here it is not I who strikes, stabs and kills but God and my sovereign, of whom my hand and body are now a servant."[3] For Luther, the soldier was a living tool of God, and he had to realize God was acting through him and bringing order by force. Therefore, he need not hesitate to use the sword or the club. He could calmly combine piety and violence. Luther taught the soldiers to say a prayer before battle and then to attack with passion: "So, commend your Life and Soul into his Hands, and pull off, and strike out in God's Name."[4]

With regard to the advancing Muslims on mainland Europe, Luther initially believed that the Muslims were God's judgement on Europe. For Luther, their arrival was a reason for Christendom to humble itself and do penance. Taking up arms against the Muslims was initially interpreted by the reformer as fighting against God.[5] Toward the end of Luther's life, when the Muslims invaded Hungary in 1541, this conviction began to change. Emphasis was then no longer on penance and suffering, but on actively taking up arms against the anti-Christian danger.

The Muslims were eventually compared to the papacy. In both cases, the arrows were aimed at the heart of the Christian faith and Christians were allowed to oppose and resist. The idea that the Muslims were disposed by God to force Christians to repentance was nuanced and soon dropped. Christians were allowed, indeed required, to take up arms against the Muslims now, and any Christian killed in this holy struggle was, in Luther's eyes, a glorious martyr. After all, the survival of Christianity itself was now at stake; the very existence of *corpus Christianum* was now being threatened.[6]

---

[3] Martin Luther, *Ob Kriegsleute auch in seligen Stande sein können* (1526) in *Martin Luther: ausgewählte Werke*, Band 4, ed. K. Bornkamm and Gerhard Ebeling (Frankfurt am Main: Insel Verlag, 1982) 177, 213. See Heering, *De Zondeval van het Christendom*, 72–73.

[4] "Und befiehl damit Leib und Seele in seine Hände und zieh' dann vom Leder und schlag' drein in Gottes Namen!" *Martin Luther: ausgewählte Werke*, 4. Band, ed. Bornkamm and Ebiling, 221.

[5] See from Luther: *Vom Kriege wider die Türken* (1529) and *Heerpredigt wider den Türken* (1530).

[6] Luther, *Vermahnung zum Gebet wider den Türken* (1541). See in particular *Martin*

It is sad that behind the Roman and Islamic attack on Protestant lands, Luther now also saw Jewish "magic arts" at work. Papists and Muslims were not in fact the source of the evil that had come upon Europe—Jews were identified by the reformer as the perverted culprit. Jews were, so to speak, the megabrain behind this attempt to destroy true Christianity.[7]

4.2 Calvin and the state

Calvin was more cautious and restrained than Luther in his judgement of the Muslims. He also disapproved of the methods of coercion used to convert captured Muslims to the Christian faith. If a Muslim was captured, a terrible time awaited him in a Christian prison. Exhausted by hunger, thirst and cold, he was forced to convert to Christianity. Calvin considered this practice to be inhumane treatment, unworthy of humankind. Calvin had an eye for the general humanity that connected all people across the round of the earth. For him, Muslims were first and foremost humans.[8] Calvin was also not at all keen on persecuting heretics. The law in Geneva, where Calvin lived for a long time, was more tolerant and humane than in most other European cities.[9]

Yet, even for Calvin, government was an ally of both the grace and judgement of God. In his view, the state was called to be a servant of God. For Calvin, secular government and ecclesiastical authority did not, in principle, clash. In fact, the task of civil government was to "support and protect the external religion, defend the sound doctrine of piety and the state of the church."[10] This "government support" would only be set aside when the kingdom of God came, and it was not yet that time.

The Anabaptists believed the church could be a community where the power of the kingdom—through the living presence of

---

Luther: *ausgewählte Werke*, 4. Band, ed. Bornkamm and Ebiling, 275–300; (297: "Darum führen wir einen gottseligen Krieg gegen die Türken und sind heilige Christen und sterben selig").

[7] Humbert Fink, *Martin Luther. The Widersprüchliche Reformator* (Munich: Verlag Molden, 1994), 273–279. See also Henry Smith, "Luther and Islam," *The American Journal of Semitic Languages and Literatures*, Vol. 39 (No 3, April 1923): 218–220.

[8] J. van Eck, *God, mens, medemens. Humanitas in de theologie van Calvijn* (Franeker: Van Wijnen, 1992), 204, 235–236.

[9] W. Balke, *Calvijn en de Bijbel* (Kampen: Kok, 2003), 26–28.

[10] Calvin, *Institutes* 4.20.2–3.

Jesus—changed people and morals, and even made the civil law unnecessary. This was true for the church of Christ but also for true Christianity in civil society. For Calvin, this Anabaptist ideal was nothing more than a foolish imagination. Humans would never reach this state of perfection, he believed.[11]

As long as there were people on earth and Christ had not yet returned to earth, the government code and the Ten Commandments remained in full force. In this, Calvin was driven by the theocratic ideal he found in the Old Testament and wanted to give form to in Reformed Geneva.

For Calvin, the ideal of theocracy (the direct government of God) meant that two seemingly opposite dimensions of daily reality, the *regnum spirituale* (the spiritual realm) and the *regnum politicum* (the political realm), flowed together because they served the glory of God.[12] The merging of the two realms meant that a government could no longer be secular. Biblical beliefs and inherently secular government had to be able to produce one Christian society.

John Calvin
(1509–1564)

In a theocracy, beliefs were turned into strategic political goals and, where possible, implemented with government power.[13] In effect, for Calvin, this meant that government had to listen to the

---

11 Calvin, *Institutes* 4.20.2: "Such perfection they foolishly imagine, since it can never be found in the community of men." Johannes Calvijn, *Institutie, of onderwijzing in den christelijke godsdienst*, Vol. 2–3 (book 3–4), ed. A. Sizoo (Delft: Meinema, 1931), 558. See Balke, *Calvijn en de Bijbel*, 275. See also Calvin's, *Briève Instruction, pour armer tous bons fideles contre les erreurs de la secte commune des Anabaptistes* (1544). In the *Briève Instruction*, Calvin sought to refute Schleitheim's seven articles. See Wulfert de Greef, *Calvijn, zijn Werk en Geschriften* (Kampen: Kok, 2006), 217–219.
12 Balke, *Calvijn en de Bijbel*, 288–308.
13 S. Paas, Jr., *Vrede stichten. Politieke meditaties* (Zoetermeer: Boekencentrum, 2007), 247, 265.

church and make its political power available as an extension of the church. Although the arm of the church was short—after all, it could not by itself exercise worldly authority—it could be extended by the strong arm of government. Government power thus became a kind of prosthesis for spiritual power.

This mutual involvement made it possible, for example, for the church to impose punishments from God that only the government could carry out "in the name of the law." Calvin by no means opted for an entanglement of the two powers in the performance of their duties, but their interests could overlap in many respects (think, for example, of diaconal aid from the church and social services from the government). For him, both powers, the worldly and the spiritual, were deeply oriented toward the future kingdom of Christ.[14] By this kingdom, Calvin did not mean the millennium, the millennial kingdom of peace, but the eternal state with God. He found the chiliasm (the expectation of a millennial kingdom) of the Anabaptists dangerous and too childish for words.[15]

While Luther saw war primarily as a weapon of defense, Calvin could agree to war as a weapon of attack under certain conditions. A war could be lawful and necessary to exercise God's "public vengeance."[16] The government was allowed to resort to arms if the purpose was justified, and good morals were respected even in times of war.[17] This included teaching the Christian soldier to fight with reluctance and restraint. But war, in itself, was not wrong.[18] For a right cause, war could be used.

Man was not allowed to act as his own judge. After all, practicing vengeance over personal enemies had been forbidden by the Lord of the Sermon on the Mount. For Calvin, however, the punishment imposed by the government was not merely a human

---

[14] Balke, *Calvijn en de Bijbel*, 277–278.
[15] Calvin, *Institutes* 3.25.5: "the Chiliasts...but their fabrication is too childish than it would need refutation or be worthy of it," Calvijn, *Institutie*, ed. Sizoo, 555. See Balke, *Calvijn en de Bijbel*, 308, 311. For Calvin, the grossly absurd interpretation of Revelation 20 and the messianic kingdom in the Old Testament rested on faulty exegesis. The texts should be interpreted metaphorically and spiritually.
[16] Calvin, *Institutes* 4.20.11–12.
[17] Heering, *De Zondeval van het Christendom*, 80–81.
[18] War can be a tool to maintain the state, Balke, *Calvijn en de Bijbel*, 295, no.175.

judgement for government was appointed by God.[19] He writes,

> We are to consider that the vengeance of the magistrate is the vengeance not of man, but of God, which, as Paul says, he exercises by the ministry of man for our good (Rom 13:8)."[20]

Calvin almost sounds like Luther here. The striking hand of government was, so to speak, the hand of God.[21] And because God and the government exercised justice (and vengeance) together in this way, it was possible for the individual Christian to continue to love their enemy. It was possible for Calvin to bring in justice while practicing kindness.[22] A Christian could continue to be kind to someone he brought to justice. The heavy hand he was not allowed to use, he outsourced to the government and to God.

4.3 Michael Servetus

John Calvin soon found himself on shaky ground when he advocated for capital punishment in times of war (and beyond) and also wanted to hold to the commandment that "all Christians are forbidden to kill."[23] How could a godly government that carried out the death penalty be considered pious? Calvin's response to the question was clear and complex at the same time:

> If all Christians are forbidden to kill, and the prophet predicts concerning the holy mountain of the Lord, that is, the Church, "They shall not hurt or destroy," how can magistrates be at once pious and yet shedders of blood? But if we understand that the magistrate, in inflicting punishment, acts not of himself, but executes the very judgments of God, we shall be disencumbered of every doubt. The law of the Lord forbids to kill; but, that murder may not go unpunished, the Lawgiver himself puts the sword into the hands of

---

[19] Romans 13:1–7.
[20] Calvin, *Institutes* 4.20.19.
[21] With an appeal to Romans 13:1–4.
[22] Calvin, *Institutes* 4.20.20–21.
[23] Calvin, *Institutes* 4.20.10.

his ministers, that they may employ it against all murderers. It belongs not to the pious to afflict and hurt; but to avenge the afflictions of the pious, at the command of God, is neither to afflict nor hurt. I wish it could always be present to our mind, that nothing is done here by the rashness of man, but all in obedience to the authority of God. When it is the guide, we never stray from the right path... unless, indeed, divine justice is to be placed under restraint, and not allowed to take punishment on crimes.[24]

The questions that arise from reading this passage are: Why can it not be considered "inflicting suffering" if one "at God's command avenges the afflictions of the pious"? Is so-called divine vengeance, carried out by ordinary human hands, suddenly no longer "inflicting harm"? Is there such a thing as a "clean execution" or a "clean war"? Because an execution is carried out by order of God, is this death suddenly no longer gruesome and reprehensible? Is the death of a bad person a different kind of death than the death of a righteous one? Is the death of the former accompanied by less sorrow? Is it a lesser death?

Calvin justified putting to death enemies of God and of the state in times of war provided they posed a real danger to the church and society if they continued to live. There were, according to the reformer, so-called "lawful causes to start a war" (*legitima causa belli, the ius belli*) and on this basis, of course, also a right to the sword (*ius gladii*). But this right of the sword also applied outside of times of war, when the peace in society was endangered, for example, by seditious citizens.

Calvin agreed, for example, that on October 27, 1553, the arch-heretic Michael Servetus (1511–1553) was tried and condemned to the stake in Geneva.[25] Servetus was a Spanish physician and theologian. He rejected the doctrine of the Trinity and compared the holy Trinity to the Greek three-headed hell monster Cerberus. Servetus also rejected infant baptism and the Reformation's *sola fide*. In 1553, he published his *Restitutio*

---

[24] Calvin, *Institutes* 4.20.10.
[25] See T.H.L. Parker, *John Calvin: A Biography* (Philadelphia: The Westminster Press, 1975), 117–123.

Christianisme (Restoring Christianity), which led to him being burned at the stake within the same year.[26]

On Sunday, August 13, 1553, when Servetus attended a service in Geneva at the Madeleine Church at which John Calvin himself presided, the Spaniard was recognized and immediately imprisoned. He was then tried and found guilty, declared a heretic and sent to the stake. Although Calvin attempted to commute this verdict to a more lenient death (beheading), it was without result.

Michael Servetus
(1511–1553)

Servetus' life ended at the stake. As terrible as Calvin thought this was, he had brought something into existence that he himself could no longer properly control.

We can certainly characterize this episode in Reformed history as a theocratic derailment.[27] Of course, Geneva's theocracy was a new and unique experiment, but then again, you do not experiment with heretical lives. Servetus can possibly be seen in retrospect as a

> type of free, individualistic man, who will not acknowledge any obligation outside his own perspective or self-made speculative mindset, thus showing complete indifference, even toward God's revelation in the Scriptures.[28]

---

26 On the life and death of Michael Servetus, see especially Guus Kuijer, *The Killing of a Man* (Amsterdam: Athenaeum-Polak & Van Gennep, 2007). See also S. van der Woude, *Verguisd geloof. De lotgevallen van Michaël Servet, martelaar van protestantse onverdraagzaamheid en Sebastiaan Castellio, apostel der godsdienstvrijheid* (Delft: W. Gaade, 1954).
27 Paas, Jr., *Vrede stichten*, 265: "I think Christians today must accept that not only is the time of theocracy...over, but that theocracy was also a theological error."
28 L. Praamsma, *Calvijn* (Wageningen: Zomer en Keunings, z.j.), 180.

This can be said of Servetus, and possibly it is true, but should he die because he was a self-willed individualist, had influence and violated the honour of God? Did he have to die because he was out to disrupt the Reformation and undermine the position of Calvin? The biblical scholar Sebastian Castellio (1515–1563) took a straightforward stand against Calvin and Geneva in the Servetus case.[29]

Calvin's successor in Geneva, Theodore Beza (1519–1605), wrote an essay on the killing of heretics and heartily agreed with the government's heretical inquisition (*De haereticis a civili magistratu puniendis*, 1554?).[30] Johannes Bogerman (1576-1637), later the well-known president of the Synod of Dort, translated part of Beza's tract into Dutch to substantiate persecution of dissenters in and around Sneek in Friesland in 1601. In the northern provinces, it was mainly the Anabaptists (Baptists) who were a thorn in Bogerman's side. For the sake of local peace, a "legitimate" way had to be found to get at the Anabaptists.[31]

---

[29] See Diarmaid Macculloch, *Reformatie: het Europese Huis gedeeld, 1490–1700*, trans. Huub Stegeman (Spectrum/Standaard Uitgeverij, 2005), 34–36, and Balke, *Calvijn en de Bijbel*, 27–28.

[30] Dirk Volkertsz Coornhert (1522–1590) reacted in 1590 with a letter against the threat to religious freedom that he heard from Beza and from Justus Lipsius (1589, *Politicorum seu civilis doctrinae libri sex*): *Proces vant ketterdoden ende dwang der conscientien. Tusschen Iustum Lipsium, schryver van de Poilitien anno 1589 daarvoor ende Dirick Coornhert daarteghen sprekende*, part 1, and *Trial of heresy and the coercion of conscience. Tusschen Wolf-aardt Bisschop, advocaet van Theodore de Beza metten daarvoor ende Dirick Volkartsz. Coornhert daarteghen sprekende*, part 2 (against Beza's *De haereticis a civili magistratu puniendis*).

[31] See the site of Tresoar (http://www.tresoar.nl/vanderaa/index.php?sub=Sneek) and therein the *Geographical Dictionary of Abraham Jacob van der Aa (1792–1857)* which appeared in 13 volumes between 1839 and 1851. A remark from this: "The Mennonites in Sneek have long been the object of persecution. In the spring of the year 1600 the pastors Gosuinus Geldrop and Johannes Bogerman, supported by the government of the city, went three times to the meeting of the Mennonites, to teach the simple people, as they said. However, they received no response. Shortly thereafter the Baptist Teachers, on certain punishment, were forbidden to preach their doctrine, so they abstained from the meeting, although the congregation continued to come together. Both of the above-mentioned preachers thought they had a good opportunity to convince the congregation, which was in a certain sense shepherdless, to follow their sentiments, and for this purpose they often went to the place where they were meeting, but their efforts were fruitless. It appeared that Pieter van Ceulen, who had settled in Sneek, did not strengthen their faithfulness to the Mennonite faith that much. They now began to discuss religious issues with this man, of which the unfavorable outcome could have been expected. The members of the government who were present declared

We find more often in situations like this that the privileged church wants to use the law for itself, demand government protection of the true faith and insist on action. This church-political alignment could be called a error in judgement in that many times it was used to anticipate the judgement of God—wanting to help determine the course of history and read God's agenda. People saw themselves as an advance post of God, sent down from heaven to earth. This meant not always waiting for the final judgement of God. In addition, there was a firm belief that it was blasphemous to allow heretics to live, and a country that allowed heretics to go unpunished was asking for trouble.

If the theocrats felt that Paul's words "let him be accursed" applied to a dissident, they could carry out the curse with the support of the powerful arm of government.[32] The accursed was threatened, banished, mutilated or killed, and the authorities "knew" they had God's support. For Anabaptists, this was precisely where the resistance lay. How could God want the death of one for whom Christ had died? Why not exercise patience? Had

---

Van Ceulen's words to be null and void, but this did not help to convert the man. What they added, however, 'that they, as Government, would not tolerate any other doctrine than Christ's pure teaching, not considering the childish reasons of the example of others or neighboring cities,' indicated that more evil was brewing. It did not take long for the storm to break out. In 1601 Geldrop and Bogerman translated a piece by Beza, about the punishment of heretics, from Latin into Dutch, in which even the killing of heretics was defended, and dedicated it with a preface to the Council of Sneek. In this preface they declared that, for political reasons and to keep peace between the inhabitants of the country and the citizens of a city, one should not excuse the heretics; this was keeping peace with Satan. One should only tolerate one religion in the state. Thus they did not want to rule over consciences themselves, but let God rule over them by His command. Concerning the loss of trade and commerce in the city: 'It was better to have a wild and uninhabited city than a rich one full of heretics; for it was better to possess a little with a good and sound conscience than to have countries and cities full of trade, with a gnawing worm and a trembling heart.' It was soon seen, what an impression this work made on the government of the city, because they soon had a decree proclaimed, in which all meetings and preaching were forbidden to the Mennonites, on penalty of money. There was, however, one among the Mennonites, Barend Jacobsz, who, in spite of this edict, allowed sermons to be preached in his house, and refused to pay the demanded fine, so that some of his household goods were openly sold."

[32] See Paul in Galatians 1:8–9 (Gr. *anathema estō*), and eg. the text of the Nicaenum against Arius: *tous de legontas 'ēn pote hote ouk ēn' kai 'prin gennēthēnai ouk ēn'...anathematizei hē katholikē ekklēsia*, H. Denzinger, A. Schönmetzer, *Enchiridion symbolorum, definitionum et declarationum de rebus fidei et morum* (Rome: Herder, 1976), 53. The statement *anathematizei hē katholikē ekklēsia* ("(him) curses the Catholic Church") occurs frequently throughout dogma history.

not God had infinite patience with the apostle Paul, for example? The apostle himself wrote of this:

> I thank him who has given me strength, Christ Jesus our Lord, because he judged me faithful, appointing me to his service, though formerly I was a blasphemer, persecutor, and insolent opponent. But I received mercy because I had acted ignorantly in unbelief, and the grace of our Lord overflowed for me with the faith and love that are in Christ Jesus. The saying is trustworthy and deserving of full acceptance, that Christ Jesus came into the world to save sinners, of whom I am the foremost. But I received mercy for this reason, that in me, as the foremost, Jesus Christ might display his perfect patience as an example to those who were to believe in him for eternal life.[33]

Should we not expect patience rather than military impatience from a church that imitates and proclaims Christ?

4.4 Calvin and the Anabaptists

It is remarkable that some Calvinists believe that Calvin and the Anabaptists hardly differed in a number of areas of Christian thought and life. Willem Balke therefore speaks of a "critical kinship" between Calvinism and Anabaptism.[34]

Oepke Noordmans (1871–1956) even saw in the Reformed Christian the twin brother of the Anabaptist:

> I have always been convinced and have also expressed this conviction several times, that the Reformed is the twin brother of the Anabaptist.... He has made compromises that the Anabaptists rejected. But never did he resign himself so unreservedly to existing institutions and conditions as the Lutherans.[35]

---

[33] 1 Timothy 1:12–16.
[34] Balke, *Calvijn en de Bijbel*, 154, 345.
[35] O. Noordmans, *Verzamelde werken, deel 2: Dogmatische peilingen rondom Schrift en Belijdenis* (Kampen: Kok, 1979), 464. See also W. van't Spijker, *Gereformeerden en dopers. Gesprek onderweg*, Reformatie Reeks (Kampen: Kok, 1986), 119–120.

Like Anabaptists, Calvinists do not resign themselves to what exists. The state is only a temporary emergency measure, in view of sin; the state is not eternal. Balke himself pointed out a gulf between Reformed and Anabaptist Christians regarding their views of the state.[36]

Anabaptist theology, with its vision of man, church, ethics and the future, in many respects reached back to the first centuries of church history and chose a more radical path to church renewal than Calvin and Luther did. Humanists such as Erasmus also reached back to the ideas of the primitive church, especially to the Sermon on the Mount.[37] Anabaptists and humanists therefore have a certain kinship; in both movements the sources of Christian thought were opened up. In addition, secular thinkers were also studied, such as the Stoic philosopher Seneca (c. 4 BC–AD 65), who had the same reverence for human life. Had not this Roman written, "man be sacred to man"?[38] Every human life was to be valued and treated with respect, even the life of a great criminal.

This reverence for life explains not only why Anabaptists had a different conception of the state than Calvin, but also why they had idiosyncratic thoughts about an ideal society. Balke rightly notes that Anabaptists *materialized*, as it were, the expectation of the heavenly kingdom.[39] Eschatological renewal was filled in a concrete material way, and they coloured their future expectations with (sometimes naive) representations that strongly reflect early church chiliastic movements.

The kingdom of God was not constructed as a spiritual abstraction from alien, otherworldly elements. The Anabaptists were concerned with this broken world (with broken governments), which would change and where God's power and renewal would lead to visible results. God loved this world so much that he sent his Son to the cross for it. Christians could not and should not ignore the world. Believing the gospel was not an escape from the world. Anabaptists never wanted to send the signal with their

---

[36] Balke, *Calvijn en de Bijbel*, 268, 273, 346.
[37] Erasmus, *Lof der zotheid* (*In Praise of Folly*) (1509; Utrecht: Het Spectrum, 1977), 130–131, 145–147.
[38] Seneca, *Epistulae* 95.33 (*homo sacra res homini*). See Heering, *De Zondeval van het Christendom*, 83.
[39] Balke, *Calvijn en de Bijbel*, 311.

worldly avoidance that the world *itself* was unimportant in God's eyes.[40] Anabaptist contempt for the world (*contemptus mundi*), like Calvinism, did not mean a disqualification of creation. It expressed that the Christian participated in the history of Jesus and as such led a new life. Life with Christ was not an ahistorical event. Salvation was historical and took place in *this* world.[41] Anabaptist doctrine did not deny or ignore this fact.

4.5 "Radical Christian materialism"

Anabaptist radicality is perhaps best summarized in the words of Baptist theologian James McClendon. In his discussion of the fundamental morality of the human body, the body ethic given by it and the difficulty we have with the idea that God is interested in matter and substance, he writes, "Yet this radical Christian materialism is the very fiber that…forms our ethics."[42] The supporting vision behind the powerful apocalyptic vistas of the Anabaptist movement could not be better put into words. The notion of "radical Christian materialism" is a powerful one and, in the good sense of the word, has an observable orientation. In short, the things of God's kingdom are also to be seen, smelled and touched, and this expectation can therefore be translated politically. The Sermon on the Mount is also concrete and earthly in scope. Christianity is grace that becomes *visible* and *audible* and *tangible*. This was and still is the Anabaptist view.

Since the late Middle Ages and the Reformation, times have changed dramatically, and the apocalyptically focused Christian is now rarely hounded. He can now simply read his newspaper, cast his vote, and even walk in demonstrations if he wants to. As a minority, he can even be protected. The twenty-first century Anabaptist Christian can engage politically without risk, without losing his loyalty to the kingdom of God. But the Anabaptists, in

---

[40] Wim Rietkerk oversimplifies the anabaptists in *Vreemdelingschap en regeringsdeelname*, Mr. G. Groen van Prinsterer lecture (Amersfoort: Wetenschappelijk Instituut van de ChristenUnie, 2007), 18.

[41] Olof de Vries, *Leer en praxis van de vroege dopers uitgelegd als een theologie van de geschiedenis* (Utrecht: Rijksuniversiteit, 1982), 137–156.

[42] "Yet this radical Christian materialism is the very raw material that (along with a few others) makes our ethics." James William McClendon, *Systematic Theology, Vol. 1: Ethics* (Nashville: Abingdon Press, 2002), 1:97.

the first two centuries of their existence, thought differently about this.

If we refer to the basic form of Anabaptist thinking as "radical Christian materialism," we understand why there was little understanding among Anabaptists of the Reformed notion of an "invisible church." After all, an invisible church is not a church. If the raw material for being church has to do with "following," in the sense of obedience to the faith, then by definition the church cannot be invisible. This is true, because even a peacemaker does not remain hidden.

In Reformed theology it has become common to speak of the *visible* and the *invisible* church. The purpose of this was to enable distinction between the congregation and the true church, for those who looked at the actual church congregation could never know exactly who were true believers and who were hypocrites. After all, the visible church and the *true* church did not coincide, thought Augustine, for example, and later various Reformers. In Augustine's view, the church was a mixed collective, a *corpus permixtum*, within which there were true and false Christians who were strongly intertwined.[43] God alone knew who were saved and who were not.

Reformers (Calvin to a lesser extent) concluded from this that the (extent of) the true church was invisible;[44] it consisted of all true believers in all times and all places. This included, for example, Moses and David, Martha and Perpetua. The blessed in heaven were part of that invisible and universal church. However, it could be said that the universal church expressed itself visibly and noticeably in the local congregation (thus the church is both invisible and visible).

Reformed doctrine made this distinction primarily to distance itself from the Catholic view of the church. For the Catholic, the visible church certainly *did* coincide with the true church. Christ was *literally* present at the celebration of the Eucharist, and also the deceased saints were literally present. After all, their images were displayed there. They were looking on, as it were. The living Christians were also seen as true Christians. After all, they had

---

[43] Matthew 13:27–30.
[44] See Balke, *Calvijn en de Bijbel*, 211–229.

been baptized, had received confirmation, celebrated the Eucharist and received forgiveness in confession. How could they not be true believers?

For the Anabaptist Christian, too, the visible church coincided with the true church,[45] only in a completely different way than in Roman Catholicism. To him, images and buildings, confession and saints, the Eucharist and vestments had nothing to say; he was not concerned with this form of visibility. If the visible and the invisible church coincided, it was because Christ asked for a radically different visibility.

The church was to be a holy church, and holiness was obviously *visible holiness*, concrete fruit of the Holy Spirit.[46] After all, it was about visible "love, joy, peace, patience, kindness, goodness, faithfulness, gentleness, self-control."[47] Had not Jesus himself said that one recognizes a tree by its fruit?[48] The fruit of the Spirit thus provided clear "identity markers" for the true church of God. The church of Christ, in all its veracity, was where the fruit of Christ grew and flourished. Therefore, the church could not be invisible. An invisible church was a ghost church, a docetic church.

Docetism was an early church error which the apostle John already opposed at the end of the first century. Docetism denied Jesus had a true human body and could really suffer. If Jesus was sent from God, then he had to be an angelic figure or a purely spiritual apparition. The body he had, while *appearing* to be simply human, was not. It was a kind of "make-believe body." John vehemently denied this and therefore began his first letter with the words:

> That which was from the beginning, which we have heard, which we have seen with our eyes, which we looked upon and have touched with our hands, concerning the word of life—the life was made manifest, and we have seen it, and testify to it....[49]

---

[45] See Paas, Jr., *Vrede stichten*, 260–261.
[46] The church is built with "visible saints." James E. Tull, *Shapers of Baptist Thought*, Reprints of Scholarly Excellence (Macon: Mercer University Press, 1972), 12.
[47] Galatians 5:22–23.
[48] Matthew 7:16, 20; 12:33.
[49] 1 John 1:1–2.

Jesus was not a transparent spirit, he was fully human: audible, visible and tangible. According to Anabaptists, the congregation of the Lord should be as visible and tangible as the Lord Jesus was. No endless theorizing and debating, but concrete walking after Christ, that is what it was all about. Wherever a few came together to actually follow Christ, there was already a congregation. In short, this was the Anabaptist "church minimum" (the ecclesiological minimum).[50] Of course, there were all kinds of invisible aspects to this. For example, Jesus taught his disciples to pray, fast and give without wanting to be seen.[51] There was such a thing as a "hidden relationship with God." A Christian was not to *show off* his spirituality. In addition to this vital, invisible rooting in Christ, there were the lifestyle and good works that *could* be seen.

In addition to perceptible spiritual fruit as the legitimization of radical Anabaptist faith, we must also think of political concreteness when we talk about "radical Christian materialism." The community of Christians could also be seen as a political counterculture, pointing ways to new forms of citizenship and Christian responsibility.

The community of disciples of Christ was the "light of the world"; it was a "city on the hill," Jesus said, a city that could be seen from a great distance. A lamp was not to be placed under a bowl but rather on a stand, in plain sight for all to see. Good works done by Christians had to be seen, because only then could light shine in the darkness.[52] God's people were "shining lights in the world."[53] By being a follower of Christ, a Christian was a ray of light. He only had to be who he was in Christ, as a visible and tangible man or woman of God. The Anabaptist community was therefore sometimes called a *restitution movement*[54] because it was a restoration movement and wished to fully live like the early church.

---

[50] See Nigel Wright, *Free Church, Free State: The Positive Baptist Vision* (Carlisle: Paternoster Press, 2005), 18–20, and Teun van der Leer, "De kerk op haar smalst. Op zoek naar een ecclesiologisch minimum voor de kerk aan het begin van de eenentwintigste eeuw" (Masters thesis, Vrije Universiteit, Evangelical and Reformation Theology, 2006).
[51] Matthew 6:3–4, 6, 17–18.
[52] Matthew 5:15–16.
[53] Philippians 2:15.
[54] Balke, *Calvijn en de Bijbel*, 274.

Anabaptists were builders and proclaimers of the kingdom and saw the local congregation as a testing ground for the kingdom.[55] But the kingdom of God in the church could not be celebrated if the community was tied hand and foot to the "Constantinian compromise." That is, only if the Christian congregation could develop free from political interference and without political compromise could it be the place where God's kingdom took visible shape. Essential to this shape was (again) the contours of the Sermon on the Mount.

The kingship of Jesus was visible and noticeable when the church was the place where Christ could assert his compassion without political compromise. The kingdom of God was all about compassion. That was the hard and yet so sweet lesson of Jesus for his disciples. No compassion? no church! And conversely, no church without compassion. The true Christian community was above all a community of peacemakers, full of the forgiveness of Christ. The visible and true stature of the church was pre-eminently that of reconciliation. Paul wrote:

> All this is from God, who through Christ reconciled us to himself and gave us the ministry of reconciliation; that is, in Christ God was reconciling the world to himself, not counting their trespasses against them, and entrusting to us the message of reconciliation. Therefore, we are ambassadors for Christ, God making his appeal through us. We implore you on behalf of Christ, be reconciled to God.[56]

A church that wanted to be a true apostolic church was a church that could reconcile visibly and tangibly. She reconciled herself (as Christians to each other) and reconciled others (to each other, and to God). She had been entrusted by God with the "ministry of reconciliation." This implied that reconciliation was her most appropriate service to God, and not only that, reconciliation was also the most urgent, the most necessary service.[57]

---

[55] See Paas, Jr., *Vrede stichten*, 252.
[56] 2 Corinthians 5:18–20.
[57] Philip E. Hughes, *Paul's Second Epistle to the Corinthians*, NICNT (Grand Rapids: Eerdmans, 1962), 206.

Within its ranks, judgement was supposed to be delayed as long as possible. The disciplinary rule also called for extreme care and caution. Exclusion was a very last measure, which could only be taken with great pain in the heart. In principle, the church was supposed to be a sanctuary where people's judgement was suspended, as Paul wrote. The apostle did not even judge himself, nor was he impressed by others who did judge him. He knew that judging should be left to God. Therefore, his maxim was, "Do not pronounce judgment before the time, before the Lord comes."[58]

In the light of the eschaton, for Anabaptists, a powerful reservation fell over every human judgement. That is why the use of the sword was so wrong. Discipline sufficed, and was not done without anticipation of the final judgement.

---

[58] 1 Corinthians 4:5.

5

Congregation, baptism and freedom

The Dutch soul, which produced the free Dutch Golden Age—of which the colonial side is covered in dark shades of loss, pain and guilt[1]—and with it the typical Dutch urge for freedom and tolerance, is not conceivable without the contribution of the Anabaptist and Baptist names we have already touched upon. The Anabaptists and English Separatists, with their divergent ideas and tenacious propheticism, helped shape the Dutch nation into what it is today. The Dutch ideal of freedom, as exemplified in the writing and life of Joost van den Vondel, stems at least in part from the Anabaptist spirit.

The questions now are: What we can learn from this today? What does our Anabaptist and Baptist history have to say to us

---

[1] See Willie James Jennings, *The Christian Imagination: Theology and the Origins of Race* (New Haven: Yale University Press, 2010), in particular "The Architecture of Loss," 38–60.

now? Does this history have any current value, and if so, does this value go beyond the nice reference of a late medieval statue to a long forgotten past? I believe that in the history of the Baptistic movement there is much to learn for Dutch churches, and for churches throughout Europe and North America. Indeed, Anabaptist history is perhaps more relevant for the Western church than ever before.

5.1 Relevance of Baptist and Anabaptist history today

Let us briefly review the three crown jewels of the Baptistic tradition and question them on their relevance and topicality:

1. The congregational vision.
2. The doctrine of baptism.
3. The principle of freedom of faith and conscience, and the duty to refrain from violence.

1. The congregational vision

It is no exaggeration to say the church in the Western world finds itself in turbulent and exciting times. There is talk, as far as Europe is concerned, of a post-Christendom era.[2] Many churches are reconsidering their position, calling, missionary heart and structure. After decades of erosion, secularization may have reached its peak in the late 2020s, and we can but hope and pray for better times for the Western church in the decades to come.

In any case, spirituality and religion are popular again (especially so-called unbound spirituality), and invitations from the public sector to churches to join the national debate on meaning, values and norms, volunteering, religion and tolerance, can be quite explicit. From all directions, Christian believers are being invited to participate in social and academic dialog, particularly after the Covid-19 pandemic. Churches themselves are looking for ways of being church that are appealing and missionary in character, and yet continue to embrace the core values of the

---

[2] See Stuart Murray, *Post-Christendom. Church and Mission In a Strange New World* (Bletchley: Paternoster Press, 2004) and *Church After Christendom* (Bletchley: Paternoster Press, 2004).

gospel. For that, new forms of being church are needed, especially a church structure that is both closed and open. The congregationalist type of church offers useful alternatives in this regard.[3]

In the Congregationalist tradition, one does not merely *belong to* the congregation, but one also *embodies* the congregation. The importance of the church as an institution is much less important in the Baptistic view than coming together as a living community. For (Ana)baptists, the *organism* of the congregation is more important than the *organization* of the church. Church structures are not placed over the Christians but offer support under them (so-called "Spirit over structure"). Visions are developed and controlled from the bottom up, and not unilaterally imposed from above.

Every Baptist should feel responsible for the spiritual life of the local congregation to which he or she belongs. He knows himself to be addressed as a "priest of God,"[4] and set over the "holy things" of God. The history of Baptistic churches makes it clear that Anabaptist Christians, with their congregationalist church form, took the Reformation adage of the "priesthood of all believers" more seriously than the reformers themselves when it came to church restructuring. Thus, the radical group around Zwingli consistently drew the lines of church renewal further than the reformers themselves did.[5]

Every Christian—old or young, woman or man—is a vital part of the body of Christ and should therefore be able to participate in matters of faith that concern the church. Strictly hierarchical forms of organization in the church are not in accord with Scripture and prevent the necessary involvement and input of the members; in fact, these tend to spawn a passive attitude. The congregation of Christ is all about the fellowship of the Lord. The congregation is a living community and should learn to

---

[3] See Teun van der Leer, *Looking in the Other Direction: The Story of the Believers Church Conferences*, Amsterdam Series in Baptist and Mennonite Theologies (Eugene: Pickwick, 2023), and Teun van der Leer, Henk Bakker, Steven R. Harmon and Elizabeth Newman, eds., *Seeds of the Church: Towards an Ecumenical Baptist Ecclesiology*, FCCT (Eugene: Wipf and Stock, 2022)

[4] 1 Peter 2:5, 9 and Revelation1:6.

[5] See Henk Bakker, "'We are all equal' (*Omnes sumus aequales*): A Critical Assessment of Early Protestant Ministerial Thinking," *Perspectives in Religious Studies* 44/3 (2017): 353–376.

think and decide from common ground and reciprocity. We can rightly call this a "communal turn" (a paradigm shift toward community thinking), because the natural tendency of churches and church leaders is to concentrate power.

"Top-down" churches, which are usually run like companies, do not have a future, especially in Europe. People are looking for honest and warm involvement in their churches and communities, a new sense of belonging, and from that involvement they want to fully participate, cooperate and bear responsibility.[6] Thinking in terms of power stands in the way of authentic love and cooperation.

The church of Christ reflects in its midst the loving and gracious community of the Father, the Son and the Spirit. The Trinity is present in all its glory in the church. More than that, Christians learn precisely what communion is by coming to know God as Trinity and, through Christ, to enter into communion with God himself. The very doctrine of the Trinity then turns out not to be an irrelevant and meaningless theory, but fundamental to our thinking about what true community can be.[7]

The mystery of the Trinity is this: Father, Son and Spirit are one and yet different and distinct. They merge into each other and yet they are distinct from each other.[8] One Person of the Trinity is not more or better or greater than the other, and yet they do not coincide. It is precisely because Father, Son and Spirit are different that they can be one. One can only be united with another when he offers his uniqueness for the sake of unity. In this way, Christians also learn to give themselves without losing themselves. In this, Christianity in its creed and experience of faith has something completely unique to offer humanity and society. A church or society can be more than the sum of its parts. The added value lies in the fact that in order to speak of true unity, people must be able (and dare) to be truly different. In a

---

[6] To be sure, this is a mark of the Baptist church's positive inclination toward catholicity, see Henk Bakker, "Towards a Catholic Understanding of Baptist Congregationalism: Conciliar Power and Authority," *Journal of Reformed Theology* 5 (2011): 159–183.

[7] On this topic see especially Miroslav Volf, *After Our Likeness: The Church as the Image of the Trinity*, Sacra Doctrina (Grand Rapids: Eerdmans, 1998).

[8] See Henk Bakker, "Spirituality and Ethnicity in Holland," *Journal of European Baptist Studies* 7 (January 2007): 38–49. See also Nigel Wright, *Free Church, Free State: The Positive Baptist Vision* (Carlisle: Paternoster Press, 2005), 115–116, 232–234.

tide of massive polarization in Europe and North America, even among Christians, this message from the heart of the church seems so urgent.

When applied to congregationalism, we find that this church form has everything in it to shape the Trinitarian community. At the ground level of the congregation, everyone is taken seriously and can speak their mind, even if their visions are opposing. The word of one who volunteers in Sunday school is not inferior to that of an elder. Indeed, one sees that the other's unique gifts and contributions are necessary for the congregation to be united in its complementary parts.[9] This is how the church may overcome the present days' culture of polarization, and can be biblically inclusive, freed from social, ethnic and gender biases (Galatians 3:28).[10]

The church of the future is the congregation that wants to learn to practice this Trinitarian communion and to make space on the ground level to listen to God's voice and to each (and every) other. The congregation of tomorrow can no longer hide behind formalities and hierarchies, which often turn the church into an impenetrable forest of regulations and tend to extinguish rather than reinvigorate spiritual inspiration. Twenty-first century humans seek authentic community and involvement in the church, rather than eternal, timeless truth.[11] For them, the principle of "truth" is largely a function of their social life. Truth is what people share, think and experience together. Truth is not removed from people's experience and critical perception.[12] Nor

---

[9] See Henk Bakker, "A Learning Community in Progress," *Journal of European Baptist Studies* 21/2 (2021): 1–24, and "Discerning Churches," in Teun van der Leer, *et al, Seeds of the Church*, 44–54.

[10] See on Paul's perspective on slavery in his time in particular Robin G. Thompson, *Paul's Declaration of Freedom from a Freed Slave's Perspective*, Biblical Interpretation Series 210 (Leiden: Brill, 2023).

[11] See especially Robert E. Webber, *The Younger Evangelicals: Facing the Challenges of the New World* (Grand Rapids: Baker Books, 2002). See also Henk Bakker, "Towards an Evangelical Hermeneutic of Authority," in *Evangelicals and Sources of Authority: Essays Under the Auspices of the Center of Evangelical and Reformation Theology* (CERT), ed. M. Klaver, S. Paas, E. van Staalduine-Sulman, Amsterdam Studies in Theology and Religion, Vol. 6 (Amsterdam: VU University Press, 2016), 25–43.

[12] I do not mean by this to defend the "relational concept of truth," T. Baarda, J. Davidse and J. Firet, *God met ons. Over de aard van het Schriftgezag*, Speciale kerkinformatie 113 (Utrecht: Libertas, 1981), but I believe that "connectedness" always

is Christian truth separate from communal service to God, communal prayer, mutual conversation about Scripture and communal worship. On the contrary, it is precisely there that theology *happens*.

Theology does not consist merely of some abstract wisdom. Theology is the living reflection on spiritual convictions that God is revealing to his congregation. It is only afterward that theology becomes a systematized reflection on faith, entering colleges, seminaries and universities. The practice of theology is—in the first instance—an essential part of church community life, where prayers, singing and meditation on the Scriptures are offered. The studied theologian should therefore be a "teacher of the church" (*doctor ecclesiae*) rather than a "teacher of the academy" (*doctor academiae*). Living theology is a grassroots event that is part of congregational processes that consist primarily of liturgical moments and spontaneous, creative spiritual impulses. Theological identity, therefore, cannot be determined by academics, church governors or lead pastors. To examine the theology of a church, its ecclesial *life* must be studied. Theological identity can thus be mapped[13] but not "designed at the drawing board."

Baptists feel at home in this way of being church and practicing theology. This is rightfully "doing theology the Baptist way." Theology is not above church life, but is the reflection on life with God in the midst of the congregation. How does God speak among his people? How does he make himself known? How is he honoured and served? How do Christians speak about this together? (Ana)aptists believe in a *communal hermeneutic*, that is, by listening to one another, they understand more about life with God and with one another. By praying together and opening the Scriptures, they gain new light on themselves and their spiritual lives. In shared conversations about the Bible text, they listen to each other, and Baptists come to a new understanding of

---

entails a hermeneutical lens that colours our understanding of truth, see Nicholas Wolterstorff, *Reason Within the Bounds of Religion* (Grand Rapids: Eerdmans, 1984), 71–75.

[13] See eg. Rollin G. Grams, Parush R. Parushev, ed., *Towards an Understanding of European Baptist Identity: Listening to the Churches in Armenia, Bulgaria, Central Asia, Moldova, North Caucasus, Omsk and Poland*, A Research Publication of the International Baptist Theological Seminary (Praha: IBTS, 2006).

themselves with the help of each other. In reading Scripture, biblical history provides a fixed background that gives meaning and significance to the unpredictable life in the foreground (our daily lives). Our capricious and fleeting lives take place against the background of God's long history of faithfulness and grace. A communal hermeneutic keeps this framework of shared interpretation alive in mutual conversation. We discover and share how the biblical narrative is linked to our Christian experience, and say: "This is that." In other words, what we are experiencing today, is essentially what Joseph, Ruth or Paul also went through.

Here the Baptist theologian James McClendon recognizes the typical "Baptist vision" of faith and life. Baptists, as a rule, have proved to be childlike biblical Christians, who laid the Scriptures on the table and said "this is that."[14] They recognized their stories matched those of biblical times, and that God spoke through them. In the same way, the Sermon on the Mount was read, and it was recognized by the first Anabaptists that it was in this speech of Jesus that the essential shape of the Christian life is given. The profile of the Christian in the Sermon on the Mount is a *sine qua non* (absolute condition) for the church of all times. Without these basic Christian traits, there is not even a Christianity.

If churches and communities in their specific regions and cultures want to make a spiritual *difference* for their country, and be truly *different* from so many other people and organizations,[15] they will have to start studying the Sermon on the Mount again, and consciously serve the Lord of the Sermon on the Mount. The aim should be to develop a communal hermeneutic of the Sermon on the Mount for this century, to build a new way of thinking about community. The difference then will not be directly in the quality of the worship service or the number of visitors one attracts, but in the unique, different way Christians treat their fellow humans and how they deal with their money, how they think

---

[14] James William McClendon, "The Baptist Vision," graduation address at the Baptist Theological Seminary, Rüschlikon (Switzerland) on April 25, 1985 (unpublished presentation), and McClendon, *Systematic Theology, Vol. 1: Ethics* (Nashville: Abingdon Press, 2002), 26–34.

[15] Ephesians 4:20–23, "But that is not the way you learned Christ!—assuming that you have heard about him and were taught in him, as the truth is in Jesus, to put off your old self...and to be renewed in the spirit of your minds."

differently about peace and violence, wealth and greed, intimacy and infidelity.[16] Christians in the early church stood out—in part—because they dealt with wealth and violence differently than their non-Christian peers. These are the two fixed hinges of the Sermon on the Mount on which the door of God's kingdom has been turning for centuries.

2. The doctrine of baptism

The Anabaptist variant is also of interest to people of our time in terms of the vision of baptism. We have explained that baptism is a rite of passage. It is a farewell rite and an initiation rite, based on a voluntary choice. Baptism is the external symbolization and presentation (reenactment) of existential union with Christ. Baptists therefore cannot go along with the idea of Catholic sacramentalism, nor with the conviction of reformed covenantal thinking. Baptism does not communicate grace, nor does it automatically lead the baptized person into the covenant with the patriarchs of Israel. Only life with Christ from forgiveness communicates grace. Baptism is the pure expression of that unification, and as a ritual it is part of the firstfruits of that unification. Grace and fruit belong together, and that is why Anabaptists are eager to see someone baptized on the grounds of personal faith.

Here we come again to the visible imitation that should characterize a disciple of Jesus. The Anabaptists considered the *sola fide* to be too minimally deployed.[17] That *faith alone* meant, in the first instance, an extremely salutary reduction of the Catholic faith (as in: "faith *and* works" or "Scripture *and* tradition") was not regrettable in the sixteenth century. Yet there was a danger during the Reformation that the notion of *faith* could become a cerebral abstraction and become disconnected from the *evidence* and *fruit* of such faith.[18] True faith cannot remain idle, argued

---

16 See Jacques Ellul, *Money & Power* (Basingstoke: Marshall Pickering, 1984).
17 Piet Visser, "Mennonites and Baptists in the Netherlands, 1535–1700," in *A Companion to Anabaptism and Spiritualism, 1521-1700*, Brill's Companions to the Christian Tradition 6, ed. John D. Roth, James M. Stayer (Leiden: Brill, 2007), 305.
18 Although it was certainly never intended, see Heidelberg Catechism Q&A 64: "But does not this doctrine make men careless and profane? No, for it is impossible that those who are implanted into Christ by true faith, should not bring forth fruits of thankfulness."

Balthasar Hubmaier. We cannot deny the importance of penitently following the Lord of the Sermon on the Mount. After all, grace must not degenerate into "cheap grace."

Hopefully the church of the future will once again be a church that knows and serves the Lord of the Sermon on the Mount. No distinction should be made between faith and works, because faith *must* work through love;[19] without works of love there is no faith. In a time when religion and spirituality are once again popular and are participating fully in the public square, the question of whether a Christian really wants to carry his cross will again become relevant. Baptism is the first sign of this, and confirms the baptized person in his desire to be part of the community of the redeemed.

We have already pointed out that it was always important for Anabaptists and Baptists alike that the visible and invisible church coincide as much as possible. Those who are, so to speak, members of a church should also be true followers and disciples of Christ; there should be no ambiguity about this. Church members should not be "vague" Christians, and if they are, this should be pointed out to them and they should be helped to see their need to live more in surrender to Christ.

3. The principle of freedom of faith and conscience, and the duty to refrain from violence

How relevant are the Anabaptist and Baptist views on the question of freedom of faith and conscience? After more than 400 years, the relevance of this issue has not diminished. In most Western countries, the issue of "how far should tolerance go?" is part of national debate.

Tolerance should never put itself at risk or endanger itself. This also applies to the core value of tolerance in a democracy like ours (speaking of Holland where tolerance and democracy are strongly related). People's freedom stops where freedom puts itself at risk. A free country cannot be so free that the majority allows itself to be bullied by a minority in some religious way. But, by the same token, a minority need not automatically

---

[19] See Galatians 5:6, "For in Christ Jesus neither circumcision nor uncircumcision counts for anything, but only faith working through love."

submit to the majority. Nor is that the essence of a democracy. Democracy means that minorities are at least heard, and taken into consideration: that is democracy, and that is a blessing.[20] Democracy is not that "the majority is right," or that the will of the majority must be automatically done. Nor does democracy mean that the minority is automatically wrong.[21]

How can the history of Anabaptism and Baptism help us in our discussion of freedom, and restriction of freedom? In each case, Baptists and Anabaptists emphasized *freedom of belief and thought*, and *the ability of various faiths to coexist peacefully*.[22] A faith should always be able to be lived and experienced. So, by tolerance we mean the willingness to accept (and respect) others in their otherness, even if we dislike their views.[23] This means that people of a different faith should be able to practice their faith within the bounds of fairness and acceptability. Conscience is sacred ground and governments have no business interfering with it; the area of conscience is not governmental territory. Too often, worldly authorities have encroached on this dimension of the inner self and put pressure on people. Conversely, the established church has often used the strong arm of government to impose its will on dissenters. Not infrequently has this led to deadly collaboration that claimed innocent lives.

---

[20] The value of Western democracy (and the principle of equality) is in many ways a blessing from God. See Henk Bakker, "De ziel van Europa en de Geest van God" in *De werking van de Heilige Geest in de Europese cultuur en traditie*, ed. Erik Borgman, Kees van der Kooi, Akke van der Kooi and Govert Buijs (Kampen: Kok, 2008), 73–85; David Gushee, "Defending Democracy from its Christian Enemies: A Central Task for Christian Social Ethics Today," inaugural address, Vrije Universiteit, Faculty of Religion and Theology, May 4, 2022.

[21] On the roots of democracy in ancient Greek culture, see Plato, *Protagoras* 309d-338a. The main idea is that with respect to governing the city, each has his say. Each is blessed by the gods with knowledge of the subject of citizenship (*hè politikè technè*). Protagoras was friends with Pericles, the great Athenian statesman. The father of Greek democracy was definitely Solon, see Diogenes Laërtius, *De vitis philosophorum* I,45–67 (45, 52, 59, 66b–67). Plato himself was opposed to the democratic state form, see *Politeia* 555b-565d. From democracy, according to Plato, arises tyranny.

[22] We have seen that the first to think about tolerance and dare to write about it were predominantly Anabaptists, such as Balthasar Hubmaier, Thomas Helwys and Richard Overton.

[23] Wright, *Free Church, Free State*, 217.

A church that is faithful to its calling cannot think and act against peace. Christ pronounces the peacemakers blessed,[24] and therefore it is fundamentally wrong for Christians to impose by force their beliefs and rules on dissenting Christians or non-Christian citizens. Baptists always emphasized voluntarism in the spiritual realm, as did Paul when he wrote, "where the Spirit of the Lord is, there is freedom."[25] By this the apostle is saying that God's Spirit delivers people by faith from evil, restricting powers. In Scripture, they were often referred to as "the world" or "spirits of the world" or "world powers."

In New Testament times, there was actually no distinction between the profane and sacred. Spiritual powers and political powers coincided, and in the eyes of Jesus' followers they were downright powers of chaos.[26] Powers, forces and spiritual dominions were cosmic systems, which attached themselves to visible authority and exerted a disintegrating and disruptive effect on people and society. The *world* and *spirits of the world* were therefore not neutral words. Behind them were always spiritual powers in which pagan forms of religion played a leading role. These forms of power were coercive and suffocating. The Spirit of God delivered people from this, by placing them outside the powers of chaos by the redemption of Christ. Paul wrote, "He has delivered us from the domain of darkness and transferred us to the kingdom of his beloved Son."[27]

According to the apostle Paul, the government was (and is) an "institution of God,"[28] but that did not prevent governments and incumbents from abusing their position. It is superfluous to give examples of this. We know them, whether from the Far East or South, from Europe, the Americas or across the globe. The state can become an ideological construct that devises dehumanizing systems, governments can be a *fabrica diabolica* (devil factory) that

---

[24] Matthew 5:9.
[25] 2 Corinthians 3:17.
[26] See Geurt Henk van Kooten, *Paulus en de kosmos. Het vroege christendom te midden van de andere Grieks-Romeinse filosofieën* (Zoetermeer: Boekencentrum, 2002), 19–126.
[27] Colossians 1:13.
[28] Romans 13:2. See Jakob van Bruggen, *Romeinen. Christenen tussen stad en synagoge*, CON (Kampen: Kok, 2006), 193–199. See also Wright, *Free Church, Free State*, 229–232.

turns society against itself and devises atmospheres of control, suspicion, humiliation and fear. When the right of the strongest rules or the most beautiful and wealthy become the divas of the day, then society can easily end up in the jungles of plutocracy and pornocracy. Big money and Barbie-doll bodies then call the shots.[29]

It is also conceivable that government structures can be placed in the service of God. A so-called "sanctification of structures" is possible, as in times of revival.[30] God can restore government powers to good order in submission to Christ.[31] Then social, societal and economic systems cooperate to develop a just society and create free space for science, faith and ideology. Anabaptists and Baptists pray for this and want to participate in the building of such a society, all too aware that sin is often more persistent than the strength of our spiritual ideals.

Throughout their history, Anabaptists and Baptists did not really turn away from governments. Most of the time, Anabaptists expressed their recognition of governments. They faithfully prayed for their superiors. Anabaptists did have problems with a government's command to "wield the sword." They themselves did not want to participate in this (generally, in contrast to the Baptists).[32] Furthermore, they felt governments were not to interfere with the interpretation of Scripture, the liturgy or the walks of life of believers. In such things church and state were to be separate entities.[33] In the area of faith, Scripture and piety, Christ was in charge, not the secular rulers. The government's duty was to create preconditions and parameters wherein both people and church could feel healthy and safe and could flourish. Governments were not there for themselves—they are "God's servants for your good," Paul wrote.[34]

---

[29] See A. van de Beek, *Ontmaskering. Christelijk geloof en cultuur* (Zoetermeer: Meinema, 2001).

[30] See H. Berkhof, *Christelijk geloof. Een inleiding tot de geloofsleer* (Nijkerk: Callenbach, 1993), 487–498; A. van de Beek, *De adem van God. De Heilige Geest in kerk en kosmos* (Nijkerk: Callenbach, 1987), 134–138.

[31] See H. Berkhof, *Christus en de machten* (Nijkerk: Callenbach, 1952), 52–60.

[32] Harold S. Bender, "The Anabaptist Vision" in *The Recovery of the Anabaptist Vision: A Sixteenth Anniversary Tribute To Harold S. Bender*, ed. F. Hershberger (Scottdale: Herald Press, 1962), 51–52.

[33] Hans J. Hillerbrand, "The Anabaptist View of the State," *The Mennonite Quarterly Review* 32 (2, 1958): 108. See also Wright, *Free Church, Free State*, 205–208, 213–215.

[34] Romans 13:4, Gr. *theou gar diakonos estin soi eis to agathon*. The government is, so to

5.2 The church's service to the government

What service can the church provide the government? Baptist ministers have their own view on this. For them, the church is definitely not an apolitical body.³⁵ She is made to bring about forgiveness and reconciliation; that is her spiritual nature and character. Therefore, in order to work toward this idea, we have paid special attention in this book to the meaning of Matthew 18, Jesus' forgiveness passage for the church, and to the "ministry of reconciliation" God has entrusted to his followers.³⁶ For 2,000 years, the church of Christ has been consciously or unconsciously engaged in a "politics of forgiveness"³⁷ that it must shape and offer to the world in God's name and in view of God's coming kingdom.

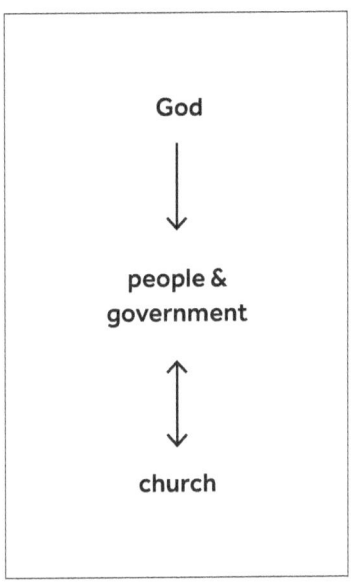

Relationships in the church

In this, the congregation's eye is also directly on the nations in a political sense. Jesus instructed his disciples to go out to all nations and make them disciples of God.³⁸ One of the main tasks of the church, therefore, is world missions—to tell the nations around the globe that the way to God's heart has been opened in Christ. In the gospel, God not only has the individual in mind,

---

speak, "deacon" of God.
35 See Elmer Neufeld, "Christian Responsibility in the Political Situation," *Mennonite Quarterly Review* 32 (2, 1958), 141–162: "The simple point of this paper is the conviction that when we are thoroughly motivated by the love of the Christ of the cross—when we all actually take our neighbor's interests as seriously as our own—our concerns will appropriately find expression in actions that do have political relevance" (161). The Mennonite Neufeld pronounced this as early as 1958!
36 2 Corinthians 5:18.
37 See McClendon, *Systematic Theology, Vol. 1: Ethics*, 234–236.
38 Matthew 28:19.

but also the countries with their various governments. It is a blessing when a country has politicians who know how to transform God's grace and compassion into social and societal policy. In this way, people are called to come to Christ and to enter into a gracious relationship with God. The churches have a missionary and mediating role in this, but they should not pull the political strings in the background like a "shadow government."

The church should not want to be above the authorities in a patronizing (and colonizing) way. For centuries, churches thought they had to stand "on behalf of God" far above the nations, like an outpost of heaven. But the place of the church is not above the people, or next to the people, but *under* the people; the church is servant in all things. The church may—and must—mediate from below, between God and people. The church comes forth from the world. It has been "called out" from among the peoples of the world and brought together by God. Yet, it has been "set apart" from the nations and called to serve God's kingdom.[39] The church is God's final gracious creation to bless Israel, the nations and the earth. We deliberately emphasize the words "final creation" and Christians do well to live, like the Anabaptists, fully conscious of the signs of "the end." God's kingdom on earth is coming and the church of Christ has a servant role to play in it.

God molded the earth to bring humanity into being. Then God blessed man in such a way that all kinds of people groups came forth from him. Then God shaped the nations in such a way that Israel was born from the nations. Then God blessed Israel to bring forth the Messiah. Finally, God molded his "Anointed One," Jesus, to bring forth and build the church; Christians (we, too) came forth from him. As such, the church has a final ministering function, and that function is dominated by the forgiveness and reconciliation of Christ. Its policy should in everything be directed to a "politics of forgiveness."

By a *politics of forgiveness* we think again of the centrality of the Sermon on the Mount. The quality of the local congregation, as reflected in the Sermon on the Mount, is a decisive factor in this

---

[39] See Guus Labooy, "De strijd van een christen," in *Wie het zwaard opneemt. Klassiek-theologisch licht over een vreeswekkend thema,* Utrechtse Cahiers, ed. Arjan Plaisier, Guus Labooy, Willem-Henri den Hartog and Nico den Bok (Zoetermeer: Boekencentrum, 2007), 45.

policy of reconciliation. It is there, at the local level, that one should be able to taste the full blessing of fellowship with God and with one another. We do not mean by this that there can never be problems, worries or conflicts in churches. What matters is whether or not the *politics of forgiveness* works in these moments. Is the church made up of followers of Jesus, as peacemakers? Is the Lord of the Sermon on the Mount really honoured and served? Is the congregation a safe place, where peace and love and security can be sought and found? Is there enough freedom to step on someone's toes and be lovingly rebuked? Does the right to discipline and restoration function without the blunt axe of rigour? Is there a group ethic of love and non-violence?[40] For how can a church that does not experience this within itself be an instrument of forgiveness and reconciliation for peoples and cities outside?

Churches should be model places of reconciliation and forgiveness for the world.[41] There, one should be able to see that forgiveness, reconciliation and trust can bring healing. There, one should see how humanely and heavenly problems are solved. Christians should be willing to do anything for reconciliation, even if it means taking risks. Sometimes they will have to take an uncompromising stand, taking sides with those who are damaged or forgotten. Christians should automatically be on the side of those who are deprived justice. By insisting on "law and justice," trust can be restored among people, and parties may be brought together. The shedding of innocent blood is never forgotten by God, and it is the task of the church to ceaselessly press for human rights with both God and people.[42]

Churches should intervene and make themselves heard when a culture of alienation and distrust, incomprehension and hatred, between citizens and population groups arises. Any society should be able to count on the commitment of churches in this respect. In Holland, the discussion about "identification with the Netherlands" has only just begun,[43] and what a good and

---

[40] James Leo Garrett, "The Nature of the Church According to the Radical Continental Reformation," *Mennonite Quarterly Review* 32 (2, 1958): 126.
[41] McClendon, *Systematic Theology, Vol. 1: Ethics*, 237.
[42] See Luke 18:1–8.
[43] See W.B.H.J. van de Donk, et al., ed., *Identificatie met Nederland*, WRR Rapporten

meaningful thing it would be if, in addition to concepts such as freedom and tolerance, terms like acceptance, forgiveness and reconciliation would also be discussed. In this respect, Christian politics is certainly not a simple addition to existing politics. Christian politics opens one's eyes to essential dimensions of life that would probably remain unnoticed or underexposed without Christian input. A reflection on the essence of Christian politics cannot escape the core idea of *peacemaking*.[44]

Making peace may mean that Christians must be *resilient*. Christian non-violence does not mean that Christians are happy to be abused without defending themselves. That is not how Jesus intended the Beatitudes to work.[45] Followers of Jesus are not characterless wimps or door mats. Each may defend himself against violence; self-defense is not wrong; it is our "good right." Jesus does call on us, however, if possible, to renounce the right of defense, because in the end violence solves nothing. We must choose wisely in this: violence and counter-violence always threatens to escalate and end in downward spirals. The choice and freedom to not engage in resistance, but, like Mrs. Overton for example, to resist passively, can have a de-escalating effect and take the weapons out of the enemy's hands. It is important for churches to know that Christ frees us from the need to resist.[46] Those who follow Christ lose the inner urge to always have to fight back. The hard duty of revenge releases the heart. Did Jesus not say "forgive, and you will be forgiven"?[47]

A church would do well to find a "peace path" (rather than a "war path") and bring this path communally as a vow before God. In this the church declares together to be "children of peace" before the Most High, and where possible to bring peace on behalf of God. Of course, these statements are not to be empty

---

(Amsterdam: Amsterdam University Press, 2007).
[44] See Klaas van der Zwaag, "Het smalle pad tussen theocratie en atheïsme. De spanning tussen Paas en Cliteur," *Zicht* 33 (2, June 2007): 24–28.
[45] Read D. Martyn Lloyd-Jones, *Studies in the Sermon On the Mount, Vol. 1: Matthew 5* (London: IVP, 1959).
[46] See Nico den Bok, "Geweld en het recht op zelfverdediging," in *Wie het zwaard opneemt. Klassiek-theologisch licht over een vreeswekkend thema*, Utrechtse Cahiers, ed. Arjan Plaisier, Guus Labooy, Willem-Henri den Hartog and Nico den Bok (Zoetermeer: Boekencentrum, 2007), 34–35.
[47] Luke 6:37.

words. Concrete plans and visions should be attached to such a path of peace.[48] It is a matter of standing between opposing parties, not writing people off or excluding them; and even in the most broken situations taking other people into your heart on behalf of Christ.[49] This last point is the most difficult. We can think of torn families, broken marriages and divided families. We can also think of divided neighbourhoods and various ethnic conflicts, as well as church splits and removals from Christian organizations. It is the priestly task of Christians to mediate, holding open attitudes and open minds toward one another. These are the true Catholic Christians, for they are only truly concerned with the "whole" and the "wholeness" of the Church.[50] They have a peace tactic, which is the way of Christ, the way of the cross and victory, the way of forgiveness. As well, each congregation should devise a "path of peace" for its own constituency. What path do you take when conflicts arise in your own congregation? Many churches have never thought about this procedurally.

As I stated earlier, those who forgive often suffer more than those who ask for forgiveness. A peace negotiator, therefore, often has more to do with those who have been hurt than with those who have hurt others. And so an attitude of understanding and patience is needed. Forgiveness is not settled in a moment. Churches that enter into the *politics of forgiveness* need to have stamina and perseverance and prayerfully pursue the way of (often silent) diplomacy.

---

[48] See Glen H. Stassen, *Just Peacemaking: Transforming Initiatives for Justice and Peace* (Louisville: Westminster/John Knox Press, 1992), and McClendon, *Systematic Theology, Vol. 1: Ethics*, 317–324.

[49] In particular, "the politics of the pure heart" and "the practice of forgiveness" in Miroslav Volf, *Exclusion and Embrace: A Theological Exploration of Identity, Otherness, and Reconciliation* (Nashville: Abingdon Press, 1996), 111–125.

[50] More attention should be given by Baptists to a forgotten side of the Body of Christ; i.e., its wholeness, its unity, and its propensity to remain whole (catholicity and ecumenism), see Henk Bakker, "Towards Free Church Ecumenical Theology: On the Pre-Given Vocation to Listen," *Internazionale Kirchliche Zeitschrift* 111 (2021): 5–23, and "The Changing Face of Unity or: Cutting the Right Edges in the Proper Way," in Dagmar Heller and Péter Szentpétery, ed., *Catholicity under Pressure: The Ambiguous Relationship between Diversity and Unity. Proceedings of the 18th Academic Consultation of the Societas Oecumenica*, Beihefte zur Ökumenischen Rundschau 105 (Leipzig: Evangelische Verlagsanstalt, 2016), 81–89. Congregationalism and catholicity go well together precisely because congregationalists are focused on the wholeness, the unbrokenness, of the community.

For example, there are churches that "make peace" by engaging in refugee issues (eg. asylum seekers) in a targeted way in certain city neighbourhoods. They help with reception or legal matters. In this way, they not only take away prejudices toward the receiving culture but also help to prevent polarization between various faiths. They are bearing faithful witness to Christ.

Active involvement in local politics can also be considered. Think of issues such as drug policy, prostitution, poverty, vandalism and so on. Why should churches not get involved and pray for these issues? Why not think about financially supporting local projects that have to do with addiction? Why not provide volunteers and have them undergo training at the church's expense? Why not set up volunteers to visit the lonely and the elderly (including the elderly beyond your church), to take care of their groceries, to keep up their gardens and to hear their life stories? In my opinion, this is all part of *peacemaking*, and there are many other ways to intervene and make peace. For example, a congregation can make targeted investments in relationship mediation, or in education about how to deal with conflicts in marriage, family, workplaces, in the street, between population groups. The need is great and those who never try anything always remain skeptical on the sidelines.

Even though Christianity is now far in the minority in Western Europe, as a royal priesthood it can, in all its smallness, still make a difference in society (see Jeremiah 29:4–7). Making peace, non-violence, promoting respect for those who think differently, "blessing the enemy," is like a powerful salt. This is how it was intended in the Sermon on the Mount. Salt is small, insignificant and unnoticeable to the eye, and yet a little salt in the food is enough to notice it is there. The genesis of the Anabaptist and Baptist faith in the sixteenth and seventeenth centuries is illustrative of this and proves extremely relevant to us today.

Final conclusion

As we close, we return to our original question: *Where did the first Baptists come from?* Our search has brought us to the Puritans in England, as well as to the Anabaptists in the Netherlands and surrounding areas. It was John Smyth, English separatist leader, refugee and *Amsterdammer* of multiple belonging, and Thomas Helwys, who laid the foundations for the earliest Baptistic church. Even though their paths diverged in Amsterdam, the leaders mutually influenced each other, and both were influenced by the Anabaptist doctrine of the Waterlanders. Smyth's congregation merged into the Waterlander community. Helwys founded the denomination of General Baptists in England.

The Anabaptist line within the original Baptistic movement is not strongly present. We have noted that Anabaptism was characterized by its own vision of salvation, baptism, congregation, non-violence and the relationship of church and state (the last two we called the Anabaptist "crown jewels"). Smyth adopted these, Helwys was critical and developed his own vision of congregation, freedom of conscience and the position of government. However, Helwys never lost the vague outlines of Anabaptism in his beliefs and confessions.

It is my wish that Baptist communities throughout the Western world may learn from this history that Baptists and Anabaptists are in many ways "birds of the same feather." We can learn from each other's tradition. Baptists might study the Sermon on the Mount more closely, and reflect on an ethic of violence and non-violence. How do we think about violence? Has not violence become very common even for Baptists? What is the place of the church in relation to the government? Are Baptists critical enough? As Christians, do we have a social role to play? Are Baptist congregations praying for their countries, for politicians and numerous interest groups?

Should we not also rethink radical Christianity? What is the place of congregational worship in it? Are we actually serving the Lord of the Sermon on the Mount? In short, our study raises many relevant questions for our time—sufficient to warrant a number of study evenings on this subject as a congregation.

Finally, this is not the place to provide a history with all kinds of theological commentary. I have chosen here to listen carefully to history, and to especially let persons who were rejected and persecuted speak out. In any case, we should listen better to each other, and this listening should begin with getting to know each other's history. I hope that this book will be an incentive to do so.

Appendices: The early church and non-violence

The Anabaptist ideal of forgiveness was not only closely aligned with the spirit of the Sermon on the Mount, but also with the heart of the early church. At numerous points in early church literature, we see that Christians who forgave those who threatened, oppressed or even executed them were models of Christianity for the church.

Appendix 1: Peace-loving and tolerant

We can safely say that during the first two centuries of its existence, the Christian church was mostly opposed to violence on principle. Christians rarely if ever interfered in the war policies of governments. As far as we know, only a few served in the army.[1] It

---

[1] The data provided by B.D. Eerdmans in his *Christendom en Ontwapening* (Den Haag: Haagsche Drukkerij, n.d.) by no means points to large numbers (see eg. Eusebius, *Historia ecclesiastica* 5.5.1–2).

seems that the number of Christian soldiers increased in the second half of the second century. In the third century this is certainly the case, although the voice of principled non-violence never died down during those centuries.[2]

Where the New Testament uses militaristic language here and there, its meaning must be understood in a spiritual sense.[3] The first generations of Christians generally believed God was against all forms of coercion and violence. For example, the letter of an unknown Christian author to a certain Diognetus stated that Christians blessed their accusers and loved their haters. In this way they were the soul of society and held the world together.[4]

A chapter further, the author noted, that from heaven God sent his Son, the Maker of the world, to men and that this coming was not accompanied by oppression and fear. It is a remarkable passage:

> Did He perhaps—as someone might think—send Him to oppress or to bring fear and dismay? Absolutely not, but in gentleness and humility He sent Him as a king who sends a son who is king, as He sends a man to men. He sent Him to save and convince and not to coerce because violence does not occur with God. He sent Him as one who invites and does not persecute. He sent Him as one who loves and does not judge. But He will send Him as one who judges. And who will stand against His coming?[5]

The words "violence does not occur with God" speak for themselves. We are talking about *coercion* or enforced obedience

---

[2] See Louis Praamsma, *De kerk van alle tijden. Verkenningen in het landschap van de kerkgeschiedenis*, Part 1 (Franeker: Wever, 1979), 32–33. Praamsma is correct in stating that the ancient church was not *pacifist* in the modern sense of this word. There may have always been Christian soldiers from the earliest times, but this does not mean the general view of the church was pro-militaristic.

[3] Adolf von Harnack, *Militia Christi: die christliche Religion und der Soldatenstand in den ersten drei Jahrhunderte* (Tübingen: J.C.B. Mohr, 1905), 1–46.

[4] *Ad Diognetum* 5.15 and 6.6–7. See also Henk Bakker, "Ze hebben lief, maar worden vervolgd," *Radicaal christendom in de tweede eeuw en nu* (Zoetermeer: Boekencentrum, 2007), 30-33; Henk Bakker, "'Helpers en bondgenoten voor de vrede.' Een peiling van vroege christelijke zelfinterpretatie," *Radix* 35/3 (2009): 190–205.

[5] *Ad Diognetum* 7.3–6.

through violent action.⁶ In other words, God did not use force to compel obedience from people. Violence did not belong and did not fit with God, the anonymous author believed.⁷

Possibly the *Epistle to Diognetus* was written at the beginning of the second half of the second century. In any case, this passage reflects the feelings of a large group of Christians at that time. If God had nothing to do with violence, coercion and imposed obedience, then his people also had to stay away from it. Even in times of ecclesiastical conflict, Christians were not to exert coercion on each other. In the event of church strife, the truly pious person would rather withdraw than further endanger unity.⁸

Christians had to let go of the right to retribution in this life, because retribution and violence were closely related. We see that persecuted Christians of the ancient church forgave their enemies and attackers and prayed for them. When Stephen was stoned and died, he cried out, "Lord, do not hold this sin against them."⁹ Similar words were also spoken by James, the Lord's brother, when he was thrown out of the temple and stoned to death: "Lord, do not hold this sin against them."¹⁰ Christian martyrs were tortured and killed with these words of forgiveness on their lips.

A certain Athenagoras (AD 133–190) wrote a speech of defense on behalf of persecuted Christians around AD 177, which he addressed to the emperor and his son, quoting Jesus' famous words from the Sermon on the Mount: "Now what are the words, which are the daily food for us? 'I say to you, love your enemies, bless those who curse you, pray for those who persecute you.'"¹¹ With these words, Athenagoras began his introduction to

---

6 *Ad Diognetum* 7.4. For the meaning of *bia*, see *A Greek-English Lexicon of the New Testament and Other Early Christian Literature*, Bauer–Danker–Arndt–Gingrich (BDAG) (Chicago: University of Chicago Press, 2003), 175, and for *proseimi*, BDAG, 877–878.
7 Violence, so to speak, was not *theoprepōs* for Christians (did not suit God, was not worthy of a god).
8 See Henk Bakker, *Exemplar Domini: Ignatius of Antioch and His Martyrological Self-Concept* (Diss., University of Groningen, 2003), 30.
9 Acts 7:60.
10 Eusebius, *Historia ecclesiastica* 2.23. The translation is from *Eusebius' Kerkgeschiedenis*, trans. C. Fahner (Zoetermeer: Boekencentrum, 2000), 106. Even though what Eusebius mentions about the martyrs is not all historical, the tradition he relies on speaks for itself and was dominant where it concerned the peacefulness of Christians.
11 Athenagoras, *Legatio (supplicatio) pro Christianis* 11.

Christian doctrine for Emperor Marcus Aurelius. The first thing he told him was that Jesus did not proclaim instantaneous judgement but forgiveness, non-violence and peace. Apparently, this attitude of Jesus was so surprising and unique that Athenagoras felt it necessary to lay the cards of Christianity immediately on the table. The principle of non-violence was, as it were, a unique selling-point of Christianity.

Athenagoras then pretended to be interrupted by virtual cheers and jeers from his listeners (for his words sounded quite extraordinary) and continued his argument with the words:

> Allow me here, since my speech is scarcely audible among the loud clamor, to appeal to the right of boldness in speech: for I am delivering my defense here before emperors who are also philosophers.... Who possess such inner purity that instead of hating their enemies, they love them and who—which testifies to very great self-restraint—instead of reacting with angry words to those who have begun with curses, bless them, and pray for those who threaten their lives? ... Among us you may find illiterates, craftsmen and old ladies: even if they are unable to explain by words the usefulness of their doctrine, they demonstrate by their actions the usefulness of their principles. Learned speeches they cannot memorize, but they can boast of good deeds: if they are beaten, they do not strike back; if they are robbed, they do not go to litigation; they give to those who ask and they love their neighbor as themselves.[12]

Athenagoras' rendering shows that non-violence and defenselessness sounded implausible and ridiculous to the ears of the average Roman citizen.

Yet, Christians adhered to the commandment of Christ. Jesus had commanded his followers to respect and love one's fellow man—just as every man loved himself—regardless of whether that person was kind to them.[13] At the time, the commandment of such sacrificial love sounded strange, unheard of and radically new.

---

[12] Athenagoras, *Legatio (supplicatio) pro Christianis* 112.
[13] Matthew 22:34–40; 19:19; Luke 10:27–28; John 15:12.

Justin Martyr (*c.* AD 100–*c.* 165) used more or less the same approach as Athenagoras. He wrote his first apology more than twenty-five years before Athenagoras' and referred to the particularity of Christ's teaching with an extensive summary of the Sermon on the Mount.[14] The written introduction to the Christian faith was intended for Emperor Antoninus Pius and his two adopted sons. Martyr obviously could not ignore Jesus' commandment of non-violence. On loving all men, he said Jesus taught the following:

> If you love those who love you, what groundbreaking thing are you doing? After all, so do those who commit fornication. But I say to you, pray for your enemies, and love those who hate you, bless those who curse you, and pray for those who abuse you.[15]

That one should be patient, helpful and gentle with everyone, Jesus expressed as follows:

> Whoever strikes you on one cheek, turn to him the other also, and if someone wants to rob you of your undergarment or cloak, do not prevent him from doing so. Whoever gets angry is condemned to the fire. Go with each one, who forces you to go one mile, two. Thus, one should not resist.[16]

Tertullian also believed that the patience and long-suffering that Christ taught was unseen and unheard of by the emperor.[17] Jesus' teaching on love and forbearance was unique, he believed. To Scapula, proconsul of Africa at the beginning of the third century, he wrote, "Each one loves only those who love him. It characterizes Christians that only they love those who hate them."[18] Even

---

14 Justin, *Apologia* 1:15–17.
15 Bartelink, *Twee apologeten*, 33–35. See Matthew 5.
16 Bartelink, *Twee apologeten*, 33–35. The last sentence is reminiscent of the curious verse, Matthew 5:39, "But I say to you, Do not resist the one who is evil. But if anyone slaps you on the right cheek, turn to him the other also." It is not so much about the devil as "the evil one" as it is about "who is evil" in a general sense.
17 Tertullian, *De patientia* 6.
18 Tertullian, *Ad Scapulam* 1.

though Tertullian's remark was not entirely accurate—defenselessness as an ideal was also prevalent in some other religions at the time—it did surprise those observing the lives of Christians.

The second writing of Clement of Rome, a recorded sermon from around the first half of the second century, confirmed this astonishment with the words that one "admired" the "excess of goodness" in Christians when they not only loved their own but also their haters and enemies.[19] Thus, loving enemies regularly garnered respect and admiration among non-Christians—Christians were known for it. In a sense, this distinctive element of Christian spirituality was also a missionary strength of the early church.

Justin Martyr himself, while still unconverted, had been deeply impressed by the way Christians endured martyrdom in deep peace and tranquility, patiently suffering their fate in times of severe vilification.[20] Seeing the fearlessness of Christians and their ability to remain pure in heart and focused on God until death came, led Martyr to the path of living faith in Christ. After his conversion to Christ, he would testify in his first apology that he, like other converted Christians, had changed dramatically. Previously, he despised people of divergent traditions and never thought of ever sharing his table with them. After his conversion, however, his resistance to dissenters was over, and Martyr even learned to love his enemies and pray for them.

> We who hated and killed each other, and who, because of their different traditions, did not open our house to those who did not belong to the same people group, now live as disciples after the coming of Christ, praying for our enemies and trying to convince those who wrongly hate us that those among them who arrange their lives according to the excellent guidelines of Christ can have good expectations that they will obtain, together with us, the same reward from God, the all-master.[21]

---

[19] *2 Clement* 13.4.
[20] Justin, *Apologia* 2.12.1.
[21] Justin, *Apologia* 1.14.3.

Apparently, it had been normal for Justin Martyr to shun and exclude people who had different customs and habits. After he became a Christian, however, that cold attitude began to change. Going the way of Christ meant he had to learn to love people who opposed him in his "old life." It is clear from the passage cited that this was the way Christians lived at that time and that prayer for sworn enemies was a powerful missionary force. Aristides' plea[22] stated that Christians comforted their oppressors and even "tried to make them their friends."[23] In this way, Christians sometimes managed to win their pursuers and opponents to Christ and the gospel.

Appendix 2: No military service

It has already been said that Christians in the first two centuries after Christ (with few exceptions) did not think of serving in the emperor's army. Followers of Christ should not bear arms was the general sentiment of most Christians at the time.[24] Christians were forbidden to kill, even if it was in self-defense. In addition, the life of soldiers was far too loose for Christians (a soldier could not be *pious* in the good sense of the word, a *miles pius*). Soldiers were required to take an oath of allegiance to the emperor, and as a soldier one could not avoid pagan celebrations and rituals on national feast and memorial days.

This apparent "disloyalty" to people and country meant that Christians were known to many as "bad citizens." They were, so to speak, not loyal to the emperor and the Roman ideal of conquest associated with him. For Christians, worship of the emperor and the state, and glorification of the army and of violence were clearly extensions of each other. After all, a government needed an army and an army used violence. Therefore, early Christians

---

[22] Aristides was a Christian apologist of the late first half of the second century. We know hardly anything about him.
[23] Aristides, *Apologia* 15.5.
[24] See von Harnack, *Militia Christi*, 48; John Helgeland, "Christians and the Roman Army: A.D. 173–337," *Church History* 43 (1974): 149–163; C. John Cadoux, *The Early Christian Attitude Toward War: A Contribution to the History of Christian Ethics* (New York: Seabury, 1982); Louis J. Swift, *Message of the Fathers of the Church*, Vol. 19: *The Early Fathers on War and Military Service* (Wilmington: Michael Glazier, 1983).

always had an ambivalent attitude toward governments. Their fellow citizens usually did not understand this and saw only subversive intentions behind the reserved attitude of Christians.

Reports of refusing military service by Christians are relatively late. The reason is that during the first 100 years of Christianity's existence, Christians hardly ever had to refuse service, because most Christians simply did not qualify for conscription. Generally speaking, they were too low on the social ladder to be allowed to defend the honour of Rome and the emperor. Emperors could generally get enough soldiers from affluent families who were willing to volunteer for service.

By the time we find reports of conscientious objection, the question, "Can a Christian enter the army?" had probably become a sensitive ethical issue in the Christian community. By the second half of the second century, there were many more Christians who were eligible for conscription given their age, standing and status. Even though the number of Christians who did not object to serving in the military was growing, the impression we get from some Christian authors of the time is that disapproval of military violence was still common among Christians. Martyrs, for example, were seen as Christian heroes, including the conscientious objectors, who were condemned for their principled stand.

We will now briefly discuss two late third-century testimonies of Christians who were convicted and executed for official conscientious objections. One was Maximilian and he died in AD 295; the other was Marcellus and he died in AD 298.

Maximilian was only a potential recruit for the imperial army when he indicated that he did not wish to enlist.[25] For this reason, he was subpoenaed before Governor Dion on March 12, AD 295, at the forum of Teveste in Namibia.[26] His lawyer was present, as was Vabius Victor, a landowner who had to provide his own son as a new recruit. When Dion asked Maximilian to confirm his name, the latter replied: "Why do you want to know my name? I am not

---

[25] In AD 293, Diocletian had established the system of tetrarchy. He himself was August of the eastern part of the empire in AD 295 and Galerius was Caesar there. Maximianus was August of the west and Constantius Chlorus (the father of Constantine, the first Christian emperor) was Caesar there.
[26] Ancient Namibia now covers Tunisia and part of Algeria.

allowed to enlist because I am a Christian."²⁷ When the governor had him measured with the yardstick, the young Christian again said, "I cannot serve as a soldier, I cannot do evil. I am a Christian."²⁸ When Maximilian turned out to be tall enough to be a soldier and they wanted to put the usual lead medallion on him as a seal, he again refused, saying, "I won't do it, I can't serve."²⁹

A brief discussion then ensued in which the governor kept trying to get Maximilian to change his mind. When they tried to force the military seal around his neck again, he declared firmly:

> I do not accept the seal of the world; if you put it on me, I will break it, because it means nothing. I am a Christian; I must not wear a piece of lead around my neck after having received the beatific sign from my Lord Jesus Christ.³⁰

When Dion continued to insist, Maximilian reaffirmed that he was a Christian. To this the governor brought up the argument that there were indeed Christian soldiers serving in the army. Maximilian did not deny this, but responded by saying, "They know themselves what is good for them. I am a Christian nevertheless, and I can do no wrong."³¹ Finally, Maximilian's name was struck off the list, and he was convicted of "wickedness" and "refusing the oath of war" and was beheaded with the sword. He lived to be only "21 years and 3 months and 18 days old."

Over three years later, the trial of a certain Marcellus, a Christian and centurion in the emperor's army, took place on July 28. Most likely Marcellus was already a centurion³² by profession when he came to faith in Christ. On July 21, AD 298, on the

---

27 *Acta Maximiliani* 1.2. The translation is from J.N. Bremmer, J. den Boeft, *Martelaren van de oude kerk. Bewaarde documenten van de christenvervolging tot circa 300 na Christus* (Kampen: Kok, n.d.), 107. See also Herbert Musurillo, *The Acts of the Christian Martyrs: Introduction, Texts and Translations*, Vol. 2 (Oxford: Clarendon Press, 1972), 244.
28 *Acta Maximiliani* 1.3; Musurillo, *The Acts of the Christian Martyrs*, 244.
29 *Acta Maximiliani* 1.5. The lead medallion is a military seal.
30 *Acta Maximiliani* 2.6.
31 *Acta Maximiliani* 2.9 Musurillo, *The Acts of the Christian Martyrs*, 246.
32 A centurion had about 80 soldiers under him. He was a well regarded figure and was well paid. Before becoming a centurion, a soldier had to have served for about 10 years.

festive anniversary of the emperor's assumption of office,[33] the centurion had already openly stated that he was a Christian and therefore no longer wished to serve in the army. Apparently, no reply to this statement was issued until Marcellus, the centurion of the pallbearers of the first cohort, openly took off his belt (*balteus*) and threw it on the ground together with his sword and staff in front of the holy banners of the legion. Marcellus was then imprisoned and tried for contempt of military rank. The centurion was allowed to be a Christian, but he was not allowed to defame the grandeur of the military order.

His first hearing at Tangier took place shortly after this incident on July 28. Governor Fortunatas asked Marcellus the pressing question, "How dare you strip yourself of your belt against military discipline and throw it on the ground with your sword and staff? The centurion's reply was, "I answered you openly in a loud voice on July 21 at the standards of this legion, when you were celebrating the anniversary of the emperor's assumption of office, that I am a Christian and cannot serve in this military service, but only for Jesus Christ, the son of God Almighty."[34] Fortunatas then declared that he could not condone this offense and would have Marcellus tried by the praetorian prefect Aurelius Agricolanus. This hearing did not take place until October 30.

Agricolanus questioned Marcellus and wanted to know if he had indeed thrown his weapons on the ground. Marcellus replied, "Yes; for it would not have been proper for a Christian, who fears Christ the Lord, to serve for the cares of this world."[35] Then Agricolanus pronounced the sentence: Marcellus was to be executed with the sword.

Both of these reports, which are historically almost certainly authentic, make it clear that even at the end of the third century, refusing to serve in war was considered by some to be a Christian ideal. By now there were many Christians who did serve, but

---

[33] Emperor Maximianus Herculeus.
[34] *Acta Marcelli* 2; Musurillo, *The Acts of the Christian Martyrs*, 251: "I could not serve under this military oath."
[35] *Acta Marcelli* 16; Musurillo, *The Acts of the Christian Martyrs*, 253: "For it is not fitting that a Christian, who fights for Christ his Lord, should fight for the armies of this world."

those who refused and risked it were, according to some, truly following in Christ's footsteps.

A century before the death of Marcellus and Maximilian, we see Tertullian (AD 160–240) in Carthage, North Africa, already struggling with the fact that there were Christians serving in the emperor's army at all.[36] A Christian conflict seemed to arise when, during military festivities, a soldier did not put on the laurel wreath because of his faith but held it stubbornly in his hand. He was questioned, found guilty and convicted. When asked why he acted differently from the other soldiers, he replied, "I am a Christian."[37] Tertullian praised the soldier, who he said showed himself to be more a soldier of Christ than of the world. A Christian had no business adorning himself with idolatrous wreaths and therefore was better off not joining the army at all.

The unrest that followed this incident came not from the side of the pagans, but from the side of the Christians. Tertullian immediately took the initiative to write a tract on the wearing of the wreath as a soldier, because there had been comments from the Christian community about the deviant behaviour of the soldier. Why did he so badly need to hold his laurel wreath in his hand, thereby putting other Christians—inside and outside the military—in a bad light? Why did he need to draw negative attention to himself and thus to the entire Christian community? As a result, the shaky peace Christians were enjoying in North Africa at the time was in jeopardy.[38] The condemned young Christian was seen by some of Carthaginian Christendom as a wayward troublemaker. His wilful refusal to wear the wreath on his head was to many an irresponsible and unnecessary provocation.

Tertullian took up his pen to defend the soldier and explain his choice to the general public. According to the Carthaginian teacher, Christians should *not* put pagan wreaths on their heads. Christians were not supposed to go into military service anyway. If someone was in military service at the time of their conversion,

---

36 Adolf von Harnack, *Die Mission und Ausbreitung des Christentums in den ersten drei Jahrhunderten* (Wiesbaden: VMA-Verlag, 1924), 578–580. During the third century, the number of Christian soldiers increased rapidly.
37 Tertullian, *De corona militis* 1.2.
38 Tertullian, *De corona militis* 1.5.

they had to leave the army; if this proved impossible, he had to pay the "price" for it, according to Tertullian.³⁹

Another example of paying this price is Basilides, a soldier who had come to faith after the martyrdom of Potamiana (d. *c.* AD 205). He soon after refused to swear the oath of war. He admitted to being a Christian, was condemned and beheaded by the sword.⁴⁰ This, then, was the price Tertullian meant.

That Christians were opposed to violence and therefore could not go into military service, or did not want to remain in military service, must surely have been a widely shared view in the early church. Origen, who was popular among Christians, held this view as well.⁴¹

The apologists, the martyrs' writings and several documents paint the picture of a church that pursued non-violence in everything, because Christ asked this of his disciples. Being a Christian simply meant being against war and military service. After all, in the army, soldiers were trained to kill.⁴² The extent to which—even in the fourth century, yes even during the years of the sovereign reign of Emperor Constantine the Great (*r.* AD 306–337)—the idea that a dedicated Christian should not go into the army was still in evidence. This can be seen in the person of Martin of Tours (AD 316–397).

---

³⁹ Tertullianus, *De corona militis* 11.1–7. "Shall it be lawful to traffic with the sword, while the Lord declares that by the sword shall perish whosoever may have made use of the sword?" (2); H.U. Meyboom, *Oud-Christelijke Geschriften in Nederlandse Vertaling*, Vol. 46 (Leiden: Sijthoff, 1931), 208–209. See also Matthew 26:52.

⁴⁰ Potamiaena and Basilides were from the school of Origenes, see Eusebius, *Historia Ecclesiastica* 6:5.1–7. On the suffering of Potamiaena, see Henk Bakker, "Potamiaena: Some Observations About Martyrdom and Gender in Ancient Alexandria," in *The Wisdom of Egypt: Jewish, Early Christian and Gnostic Essays in Honour of Gerard P. Luttikhuizen*, Ancient Judaism and Early Christianity 59, ed. Anthony Hilhorst and George H. van Kooten (Leiden: Brill, 2005), 331–350.

⁴¹ Von Harnack, *Die Mission und Ausbreitung des Christentums*, 318: "Origenes stimmt mit Tertullian überein; an mehreren Stellen erklärt er, der Christ dürfte das ius gladii gegen Niemanden ausüben." See *Contra Celsum* VII.26.8–11. See also F. Ledegang, *Origenes, een experimenteel theoloog uit de derde eeuw* (Kampen: Kok, 1995), 58: "Christene dienen pacifistisch te zijn, vindt Origenes."

⁴² See especially Von Harnack, *Die Mission und Ausbreitung des Christentums*, 577–588 (577: "das Christentum verwarf prinzipiell Krieg und Blutvergießen").

Appendix 3: Martin of Tours

Sulpicius Severus (*c.* AD 363–425) wrote a *Vita* (biography) in AD 396 about the extraordinary figure of Martin of Tours. It is this writing that provides us with most of the information we know about Martin.

Martin of Tours was, after his death, widely venerated as a "saint" in what was then Gaul (France and surrounding areas). Sulpicius Severus had met him, and the monk had made such an impression on him that he interrupted his career and decided to live as a monk himself. Martin was also known to have supported Hilarius of Poitiers, a contemporary and bishop of Poitiers, in his fight against Arianism.[43]

Although the life of Martin is surrounded by legends, a number of facts are certain. It is certain he was the son of a soldier, and his father had the career of a soldier in mind for his son. It is also certain that Martin wanted to follow and serve Christ at an early age. Against his will, at the age of fifteen, he was enlisted in the army by his father and forced to take the oath of war. After taking the oath, Martin was bound to a full soldier life.

During his years of service, the young soldier remained a convinced Christian, although he had not yet been baptized. Sulpicius Severus writes:

> For about three years he remained under arms before he was baptized, but he remained unaffected by the sins in which this kind of man tends to be entangled. Great was his kindness to his brothers in arms, wonderful his charity, and superhuman were his patience and humility.[44]

Sulpicius Severus then tells the story which brought Martin worldwide fame.[45] One winter Martin, on horseback with only a soldier's garment draped around his shoulders, encountered a poor beggar at the gates of Amiens. No one cared about the man,

---

[43] On Hilarius of Poitiers, see Pierre Trouillez, *Bevrijd en Gebonden. De Kerk van Constantijn (4th–5th centuries AD)* (Leuven: Davidsfonds, 2006), 84–96.
[44] Sulpicius Severus, *Vita sancti Martini* 2.6–7.
[45] Sulpicius Severus, *Vita sancti Martini* 3.1–4.

and only Martin seemed to see his need. As a simple soldier, barely able to take care of himself, he took his sword and divided his cloak into two pieces. One half he gave away, the other he kept for himself.[46] The next night, Martin had a dream in which he saw Jesus dressed in the piece of cloak he had given the poor man. The Lord let the crowd of angels, who were watching in the dream, know that Martin, who was only a baptismal student, had covered Jesus himself with his garment.[47] This became increasingly legendary in the course of history and, partly because of the many other extraordinary deeds of Martin, led to a cult and veneration in Western Europe around the young soldier.[48]

At the age of eighteen, Martin was baptized (in AD 334) and wanted to leave the army. However, because of a close friendship with the tribune (an officer), he postponed his dismissal from the army. So, Martin remained a soldier, "albeit in name only," Sulpicius Severus adds.[49]

When the time did come to resign (AD 356), Julian was almost in power and Martin was by now about forty years old.[50] All in all, he had served in the army of the emperor for some twenty-five years, and we may assume that military action often involved violence. His heart may not have been in it, but they were still many years. They were the years when, under Constantine and his sons, the Christian church became a privileged church throughout the Roman Empire. Despite the privilege, the church had to deal with all kinds of internal issues, which soon resulted in serious schisms. For example, Hilarius, Martin's bishop and friend, was forced into exile for some time.

---

[46] As a soldier, Martinus could not give away more than half. Half of his cloak was his property, the other half belonged to the state. The state's portion he retained.
[47] See Matthew 25:40.
[48] In parts of the Netherlands, Saint Martin's Eve is on November 11. Children go around the doors with lanterns, sing a short song about Saint Martin and receive hands full of candy.
[49] Sulpicius Severus, *Vita sancti Martini* 3.6.
[50] Emperor Julian would go down in history as Julian the Apostate. He ruled from AD 361 to 363, and wanted to return the empire to the old familiar Roman idols. His meeting with Martinus at Worms took place earlier, in AD 356, when Julian was leading the army as a caesar with a special mission. Constantius II had promoted his nephew Julian to that office with the task of protecting Gaul from the advancing barbarians and restoring peace there.
See G.W. Bowersock, *Julian the Apostate* (Cambridge: Harvard University Press, 1978).

The moment when, after some years, Martinus requested the emperor to grant him dismissal from the army is of special interest to us. We adopt in its entirety the passage from the *Vita* by Sulpicius Severus, which reports on it:

> Meanwhile, the barbarians had invaded Gaul, and Emperor Julian, who had gathered his army near the city of Worms, began to pay out monetary rewards to the soldiers. And as was customary, they were called forward one by one, until it was Martin's turn. He now considered the right moment to ask for his resignation; for he felt that it would not be very sincere for him to receive the reward without remaining a soldier. "Up to now," he said to the emperor, "I have been a soldier for you; give me the freedom now to be a soldier for God. Whoever will fight may accept your reward; but I am a soldier of Christ: I must not fight." Nevertheless, to these words the tyrant responded growling, saying that Martin wanted to withdraw from army service not because of his religion, but for fear of the battle that would break out the next day.[51]

Martin was still of the opinion that a true soldier of Christ should not fight.[52] For years, his heart had not really been in the military service. Rather, when living as a monk, his heart was entirely in the service of God. Shortly after this confrontation with the emperor, Martin managed to leave military service behind him and devoted the rest of his life to spiritual battle, prayer and the proclamation of the Gospel. He laid down the iron sword for good and replaced it with the armour of God.

Appendix 4: A Constantinian turn of events?

Martin's position that "a soldier of Christ should not fight" could not have been an unusual position in the mid-fourth century. Many Christians were of the opinion that following Christ entailed a life of non-violence.

---

[51] Sulpicius Severus, *Vita sancti Martini* 4.1–4.
[52] *Christi ego miles sum: pugnare mihi non licet* (4.3).

However, after Constantine came to power, the prevailing view of the church on the question of whether Christians could be "under arms" had been shifting. In this regard, we can rightly speak of a "Constantinian turn." The emperor's conversion to Christianity influenced and changed the character of the church around the Mediterranean in many ways. Christianity was now privileged and experienced few obstacles. Indeed, all of a sudden the persecution of Christians was over.[53] From a marginalized and often oppressed minority, the church got full recognition and was allowed to gain status in society.

In February AD 313, an edict was issued in Milan that offered religious freedom and government protection to Christians.[54] With one stroke of the pen, the Christian faith was transformed from a so-called illegitimate religion (*religio illicita*) to a permitted faith (*religio licita*). Paganism was not yet completely done with, but now Christianity could at least legitimately engage in the spiritual and intellectual struggles in society.

A series of edicts quickly followed the Edict of Milan. In the years following AD 313, Christians were granted the same rights as other citizens. For example, they were allowed to hold government positions and their priests received the same tax benefits as other clergymen. However, Christianity also enjoyed the preference and direct support of the emperor himself. The church became, so to speak, hand in glove with the government and this had its advantages and conveniences. With government support, churches and cathedrals sprang up all over the empire.

Church leaders were now involved with social discussions and vice versa. The worldly authorities interfered in church politics and, where necessary, with the content of the Christian faith. In AD 325, at the initiative of the emperor, a council was convened at Nicea to settle the highly charged dispute over the nature of Christ (was he God or not?). We will not go into this council of

---

[53] The last persecution which the church had to endure in antiquity was under Emperor Dioclatian and was perhaps the most severe. In the East the persecution lasted longer (AD 303–311) and was also of a more gruesome nature. It was not until AD 324 that freedom was truly marked there. Diocletian had already abdicated the throne in AD 305. In the West, the persecution lasted from AD 303–305.

[54] See Trouillez, *Bevrijd en Gebonden*, 25–27.

bishops now, but it is certain the emperor had a decisive hand in the outcome.

The church was free from persecution, but it was no longer free to chart a spiritual course on her own. Its greatness fell in line—and possibly in the shadow—of the emperor's rule. Among historians of the fourth century, we regularly hear criticism of the mixing of ecclesiastical and imperial interests. For some, this cooperation meant the "fall" of the house of God. The church lost its character of grace, because it was no longer Christ but the emperor and all kinds of imperial powers who were in charge of the house of God.[55] At least, this is how most Anabaptists thought in the sixteenth and seventeenth centuries. This sentiment was later, and even more recently, confirmed.[56]

Nevertheless, the simple conclusion, "with Constantine the church went wrong," gives too one-sided a presentation of events. Those who carefully study the facts before and after Constantine, come to a more nuanced judgement.[57] We should by no means idealize Christianity of the first three centuries, nor did the dawn of the Constantinian era signify a complete calamity for the development of the church and Christian doctrine.[58]

The church in both the West and East of the empire rebounded after the coronation of Constantine. For the first time, Christianity could lift her head and show the world that it was a blessing to humanity, and she no longer had to hide. In the free West today, we have a hard time imagining what the Constantinian tolerance

---

[55] This is also called *caesaropapism*: interference of the secular ruler in the affairs of the church.

[56] See especially the now old but fascinating book by the Remonstrant theologian G.J. Heering, *De zondeval van het christendom. Een studie over christendom, staat en oorlog* (Arnhem: Van Loghum Slaterus, 1928), 48: "This radical change of Christendom with regard to such a far-reaching matter as war, we cannot but see...as a violent fall." See also François Roget, *Van Nicea tot Bonifatius. De kerk verbasterd in romeinse politiek en samenleving* (Kampen: Kok, 1981).

[57] See Henk Bakker, "Tangible Church. Challenging the Apparitions of Docetism (II): The Ghost of Christmas Present," in *Baptistic Theologies* 5/2 (2013): 18–35. See also Eginhard Meijering, *Geschiedenis van het vroege Christendom. Van de jood Jezus van Nazareth tot de Romeinse keizer Constantijn* (Amsterdam: Uitgeverij Balans, 2004), 385–386.

[58] For example, the Cappadocians (Basil the Great, Gregory of Nyssa and Gregory of Nazianzus) have largely determined the orthodoxy of the church in the East. The same is true of the so-called desert fathers (such as Antony the Great).

edicts meant for Christians. It is easy for us to say, "If only you had stayed in your prisons and dens, if only you had all run boldly to the funeral pyres, things would not have gone wrong for us!" Needless to say, Christendom recognized the hand of God in the changes initiated with the coming of Constantine.[59] We would have seen it exactly the same way, and of course it was a blessing when Constantine finally defeated Licinius, his last enemy, at the Bosphorus on September 18, AD 324, and new "humanitarian edicts" were issued in the East as well. This is how Eusebius (c. AD 260–339) describes the situation:

> All fear of the oppressors of old had now been completely removed from the people. People began to have wonderful holidays, full of joy. Everything was full of light; people who had previously turned a blind eye greeted each other with cheerful faces and shining eyes. In towns and villages, everywhere people praised God, dancing and praising with joy; they glorified Him as the almighty King; God in the very first place had to be acknowledged, so they were taught; then they also sang the praises of the pious emperor and with him his God-loved children.[60]

Eusebius spoke highly of Constantine, so of course we must read him critically, but the mood of this text is clear. The achievement of the sovereign rule of Emperor Constantine was a reason for Christians to glorify God. People sang the praises of God, and with that also the praises of the emperor. In the fame of the emperor, there was a sense of the greatness of God.

The Roman emperor was traditionally a sacred figure and was always involved in religious matters. In antiquity, there was no distinction between the profane and the sacred, the secular and the religious, and insofar as there was one here and there, these dimensions converged in the person of the emperor. In the emperor, heaven and earth touched.

---

[59] See Stefan Paas, *Vrede stichten. Politieke meditaties* (Zoetermeer: Boekencentrum, 2007), 231–233.
[60] Eusebius, *Historia ecclesiastica* 10.9.7; Fahner, *Eusebius' Kerkgeschiedenis*, 443.

When the emperor embraced Christianity, he represented both sides of life, especially in the Eastern Roman Empire.[61] Now autocrats there had the automatic right to meddle in kingdom affairs of two kinds: the kingdom of men and the kingdom of God. For Constantine, this meant the heavenly kingdom was superimposed on the earthly kingdom. The kingdom on earth had to be subjected to the kingdom of God. The order below had to begin to follow the order above. The order below became a reflection of the imperishable heavenly order.

It is interesting to read how Eusebius expressed this relationship between *above* and *below* when he delivered a eulogy in honour of the emperor during his thirty-year jubilee in AD 335. At this stately celebration, Eusebius said Emperor Constantine was the only one privileged to have received from God, as it were, a "blueprint" of divine supremacy. On the basis of this copy of the heavenly government, he could now attend to earthly affairs.[62] Imperial power was the realization of the words Jesus taught his disciples to pray: "your will be done, on earth as it is in heaven."[63] Thus, Constantine was the protector of God's flock on earth. As the Good Shepherd Jesus drove the wolves from the flock, so Constantine drove the Christian-haters before him, subduing them with the sword.[64] The question, of course, is whether this Eusebian equivalence is an unholy one, for if the imperial ground forces on earth were a reflection of God's heavenly powers, violence in the name of God was actually the most normal thing in the world.

It cannot be denied that since Constantine's reign, Christianity has thought and acted with more violence.[65] The ethics of the Sermon on the Mount was stripped of its sharpness with interpretive cleverness and came to serve a church that needed less to be guided through life by the protective hand of this teaching of

---

[61] H.I. Marrou, *Geschiedenis van de kerk*, Vol. 2: *Van de vervolging van Diocletianus tot de dood van Gregorius de Grote* (Hilversum-Antwerpen: Paul Brand, 1964), 28–31.
[62] Eusebius, *Laus Constantini* 1.6. See also Glanville Downey, *The Late Roman Empire* (Malabar: Robert E. Krieger, 1969), 30–31.
[63] Matthew 6:10.
[64] Eusebius, *Laus Constantini* 2.3.
[65] von Harnack, *Militia Christi*, 43–44: "'Holy war' in the real sense of the word was nevertheless never preached in the pre-Constantinian age."

Jesus.[66] The time of persecution was over, so why should Christians take these words of Jesus literally: "If anyone slaps you on the right cheek, turn to him the other also"?[67] The meaning of the Sermon on the Mount gradually began to change, and the idea of "holy war" was now considered acceptable by well-meaning Christians. After all, Scripture also spoke of Christian *soldiers*.[68] It actually spoke in terms of a "holy war," of *militia Christi* and *milites Christi* (warriors and soldiers of Christ). The rapid Christianization of the pagan empire took place first and foremost in the military, and it was from this widely dispersed military network that the acceptance of Christianity spread rapidly throughout the world.[69]

As early as AD 314, the Council of Arles promulgated the decree that "those who threw away their arms in (times of) peace would be excluded from communion."[70] In other words, if any Christian absconded from the army during a time of harmony, he was to be expelled from the church. By this, the church wanted to express how much it considered it necessary to loyally support Constantine's war policy. In addition, the emperor and the army made it clear how much they considered the imperial struggle to be a struggle of the Christian God. War between nations thus become a contest between the Christian God and pagan idols, and in this the support of the church was much needed.

---

[66] "In the post-Constantinian period a significant turn is apparent: The proponents of a literal interpretation of our text are now to be found in the circles of heretics, minority churches or groups: Waldensians, Francis of Assisi, Wiclifites, Erasmus, Schwenkfeld, the Anabaptists" and "The history of impact showed that with the Constantinian turn a fundamental change occurred which had to have its effects on the interpretation of our text," Ulrich Luz, *Das Evangelium nach Matthäus, Vol. 1: Mt 1–7*, 299, 302.

[67] Matthew 5:39.

[68] 2 Timothy 2:4.

[69] von Harnack, *Militia Christi*, 86–87.

[70] *De his, qui arma proiciunt in pace placuit abstinere eos a communione*, from *Concilium Arelatense I—Documenta Catholica Omnia* (the meaning of the words in pace is unclear, probably this "peace" refers to the peace between state and church), see http://www.documentacatholicaomnia.eu/01_20_0314-0314-_Concilium_Arelatense_I.html. See also von Harnack, *Militia Christi*, 87–89.

Appendix 5: Lactantius

How strongly this idea still ran counter to the culture and tradition of the ancient church even then is shown, for example, by the person and views of Lucius Cæcilius Lactantius (*c*. AD 250–325). Lactantius was a North African Christian and rhetor (teacher of rhetoric) and student of Arnobius. At the end of the third century, he was brought to Nicomedia by Emperor Diocletian (d. AD 316) as a teacher of Latin rhetoric. There, at the imperial court, he met the later emperor Constantine and experienced the beginning of the Diocletian persecution of Christians in AD 303. For Lactantius, the persecution meant a break from the court and from his work.

The teacher then turned to writing books on the Christian faith. Through these works, Lactantius grew into the well-known church father we know. After the toleration edict of AD 311, he returned to Nicomedia for several years. It is not inconceivable that the presence of Lactantius may have had some significance in the Christian course chosen by Constantine.

When Lactantius left Nicomedia and set about writing, one of the things he undertook was a comprehensive summary of Christian doctrine. The *Divinae institutiones* (*The Divine Institutes*), consisting of seven books, may with good reason be called the principal work of Lactantius.[71] It is the first ancient ecclesiastical systematic survey of Christian doctrine and was written between AD 304 and 313. Lactantius' intent was apologetic in nature. The church teacher wanted to shed light on the beliefs of Christians and at the same time set them against the ideas of paganism.[72]

In the sixth book of the *Divinae institutiones*, Lactantius discussed the seductiveness of the theatre, the circus and games, as well as God's commandment not to kill.[73] He explained that seeing dramatic events on stage or in the arena had a profound effect on people's emotional lives. During the games there was killing and murdering, and all the spectators sat meekly and breathlessly

---

[71] See Otto Bardenhewer, *Geschichte der altkirchlichen Literatur*, 2. Band (Darmstadt: Wissenschaftliche Buchgesellschaft, 1962), 531–536.
[72] Karl Suso Frank, *Lehrbuch der Geschichte der Alten Kirche* (Paderborn: Ferdinand Schöningh, 2002), 202.
[73] Lactantius, *Divinae institutiones* 6.20.1–35.

watching, without apparently realizing how fatally and negatively they were being affected by all these images and impressions.

Lactantius then questioned whether these people could be *pious* or *spiritual*, if they not only allowed victims who were begging for mercy to be slaughtered, but also wanted to see them suffer, tormented and tortured. The teacher emphatically declared that whoever wanted to be righteous could under no circumstances take part in this. A pious and righteous man would have no part in the killing of another, whether he be guilty or innocent. What might have been considered a "clean trial" and a fair execution, according to human law, was wrong in the eyes of God. According to Lactantius, God was against *any* form of killing, including the imposition of the death penalty after a measured legal process.

> When God forbids killing, He not only rejects murder, which is also not permissible under the law, but also advises us not to do certain things that are justified among men. For example, a righteous man cannot be a soldier, for his struggle is, after all, justice itself, nor can he condemn anyone to death. Whether you kill someone with the sword or with a condemnation makes no difference, the killing itself is reprehensible. No exceptions are made for this commandment of God. To kill a fellow man is always wrong, for God has willed that man should be an inviolable creature.[74]

At the beginning of the fourth century Lactantius—like Martin of Tours a few years later—was still fully immersed in the early Christian tradition where non-violence was the norm. Human life was so precious and valuable to God that no one, not even the worst person, should be put to death by another. Human life was profoundly sacred and inviolable. God attributed inviolability to human life, and it did not matter if people thought differently. After all, the value of the individual was anchored in God himself.

---

74 Lactantius, *Divinae institutiones* 6.20.15–17. See Anthony Bowen and Peter Garnsey, *Lactantius: Divine Institutes. Translated, with an Introduction and Notes* (Liverpool: Liverpool University Press, 2003), 375.

In summary, Lactantius' view was that killing was *always* wrong, in every case, as was reaching for weapons.[75]

Appendix 6: Chiliasm and the lack of royal ideology

Something else strikes us about the author Lactantius. The man was not only a non-violent Christian but also a convinced chiliast (chiliasm is the expectation of a coming 1,000-year peace). In the last book of his *Divinae institutiones*, Lactantius lifted a tip of the veil of the *eschaton*, as he understood it.[76] He declared, by analogy with the six days of creation and the day of rest, that world history would begin to take a turn after 6,000 years. All the evils of the world would be done away with and God, through his justice, would give peace to the earth for a thousand years.[77] This period would be a time of restoration and healing of the earth, and Lactantius believed it would not be long before that time would come, possibly within two centuries.[78] After this millennial kingdom, the final judgement would come upon the world and the eternal state of glory would dawn.

The way Lactantius outlined the kingdom of peace shows how strongly this expectation was stamped with Old Testament metaphors.[79] The eternal King of God would reign on earth among men. His kingdom would be a kingdom of law and justice.[80] People would reach high ages during those thousand years and produce a large offspring.[81] The earth would be extraordinarily fertile and blessed for a long time. Where before there were only bare rocks, honey would flow in abundance, like rivers filled with sweet milk. The heavy yoke of violence and wickedness would be benevolently lifted from the earth in those centuries of peace. Wild animals would no longer hunt and bait prey. They would no longer feed on the blood of other animals. The lion and the calf

---

[75] See Lactantius, *Epitome divinarum institutionum* 59.
[76] See Johannes Quasten, *Patrology*, Vol. 2 (London: Westminster, 1950), 408–410.
[77] Lactantius, *Divinae institutiones* 7.14.7–11. See also *The Epistle of Barnabas* 15.1–5; Irenaeus, *Adversus haereses* 5.28.3; Justin, *Dialogus cum Tryphone Iudaeo* 81.3.
[78] Lactantius, *Divinae institutiones* 7.25.5.
[79] Lactantius, *Divinae institutiones* 7.24.1–12.
[80] See Isaiah 42:1–4.
[81] Lactantius, *Divinae institutiones* 7.24.1–3. See Isaiah 65:20–22.

would stand together in one stall. The wolf would no longer go after the lamb and a child would play peacefully near the den of a snake.[82] The whole world would be adorned with holy peace and the holy city of God would stand in the midst of the earth. Nations would march up to the new Jerusalem to serve God there.[83]

It is remarkable that, for Lactantius, God's kingdom of peace contrasted with the Christian Roman Empire. Rome's dominance would come to an end, while God's kingdom would fill the earth.[84] Lactantius certainly did not expect the kingdom of peace to come "from below." Only God could give the world the peace it needed. Lactantius did not believe that in the dawning of the "Constantinian peace," the long-awaited kingdom of God had already begun—the teacher knew better. Most Christians in the first centuries AD expected that the blessing for the earth would come not from below but from *above*. Indeed, for the early church, chiliasm was a common Christian view of the future.[85]

The expectation of an imminent kingdom of God, which would restore the groaning earth,[86] had always kept early Christianity from being over-spiritualized, and from having lofty expectations of people and governments. Christian hope was not just an expectation of a coming static and supernatural timelessness. Early Christians generally thought in terms of concrete earthly peace, embellished and perfected with the colours and fragrances of below. The kingdom of God was coming to *this* earth, for no other earth existed. The peace of the kingdom of God did come

---

[82] Lactantius, *Divinae institutiones* 7.24.7–8 and 12–15. See Isaiah 2:4; 11:6–9; 65:25.

[83] Lactantius, *Divinae institutiones* 7.24.6. See Isaiah 11:10; Zechariah 8:22–23.

[84] Lactantius, *Divinae institutiones* 7.15.11–19.

[85] See Justin, *Dialogus cum Tryphone Iudaeo* 80.2–81.4 (a kingdom of peace and Jerusalem rebuilt, enlarged and adorned); Irenaeus, *Adversus haereses* 5.23 and 5.33.4; Tertullianus, *Adversus Marcionem* 3.24.3–6 (a kingdom on earth, built by God for 1,000 years in the city of Jerusalem). Chiliasm was a dominant form of expectation in the early church, see Jaroslav Pelikan, *The Christian Tradition: A History of the Development of Doctrine*, Vol. 1 (Chicago: University of Chicago Press, 1971), 123–125 (125: "It seems that very early in the post-apostolic era, millenarianism was regarded as a sign that belonged neither to orthodoxy nor to heresy"—that is, chiliasm did not belong in the corner of orthodoxy, but certainly not in the corner of heresy either). See J.N.D. Kelly, *Early Christian Doctrines*, rev. ed. (San Francisco: Harper & Row, 1978), 464–469, and Adolf von Harnack, *Lehrbuch der Dogmengeschichte*, 1. Band (Darmstadt: Wissenschaftliche Buchgesellschaft, 1964), 187–189, 614–620 (187: "Der sog. Chiliasmus…muss als ein Hauptstück der ältesten Verkündigung gelten").

[86] See Romans 8:19–23.

from above, but it had an effect on this world. We must never lose sight of the earth. The concrete and material expectation of God's kingdom on earth was both a correction to the overstrained expectations from above and those from below. The kingdom expectation could not be too heavenly, because after all it was about the earth, but it had to come from above, because it was impossible to build God's peace kingdom with human efforts. Ordinary kings did this; they built their empire with cunning, muscle power and military force. Kings, then, were but earthlings who could not do without martial power. And it was precisely this weakness of the kings that was widely reported in the Old Testament.

Indeed, there is no glowing and convincing ideology of kings in the Old Testament. Rather, the king of Israel was in God's zone of tolerance from the beginning. When the people of Israel asked for a king, the prophet Samuel was "not amused" to say the least. But God made it clear to the prophet that he himself, and not the prophet, was being rejected. God himself was no longer to be King of Israel. They now wanted a king "like all the other nations," not a vague and invisible Lord.[87] Just like all the other nations, they wanted a figure of authority they could look up to and put on a high horse. They could not count on Samuel's sons Joel and Abijah, judges in Israel, because they were corrupt. In addition, the need for a power figure was great because the Jewish people suffered from many conflicts and incidents with the Philistines.[88]

Although the request for a king disturbed the prophet Samuel, God nevertheless instructed him to fulfil the request of the representatives of Israel. But first Samuel described in detail what the king's behaviour would be like and what it would require—in terms of heavy taxes—from the people. A king needed a luxurious palace with a court, bakers, cooks, perfumers and guards. Not only that, he also had to have his own royal carriage with bearers, and an army with captains, horses and weapons. And this was only the beginning. All these servants and notables, and of course the many guests who constantly stayed in and around the royal

---

[87] 1 Samuel 8:5–7.
[88] H. Jagersma, *Geschiedenis van Israël in het oudtestamentische tijdvak* (Kampen: Kok, 1979), 128–130.

palace, also had to eat and drink. Therefore, the people would not only undertake to provide the necessary servants for the king, but also shares of their wheat, cattle, vineyard and so on.

The request for a king would cost Israel dearly. Samuel assured the elders of Israel that there would be times when they would mourn for their king. That time would soon come when, after Saul and David, King Solomon ascended the throne; it was then that things went awry.

Solomon was known not only for his wisdom, but also for his wealth and opulence.[89] Eventually the wealth, his many horses and many wives, demanded heavy taxes from the population, and his heart was led toward idols.[90] Solomon fell off his pedestal. After his death, his son Rehoboam was to become king over Israel, were it not for the fact that a delegation from the people asked the king for relief from the tax burdens, which was then peremptorily refused.[91] Indeed, Rehoboam planned to increase the burden and, if possible, rise in fame above his father. The consequences were serious, for the people of Israel subsequently broke up into two nations (932/931 BC). The king, who intended to centralize authority and rule with an iron fist against the surrounding peoples, was actually the cause of the break-up of the nation into two kingdoms (the ten tribe kingdom of Israel and the two-tribe kingdom of Judah).

Anyone who reads the Chronicles of the kings of Judah will notice the authors were critical of the kings. Their faults and sins were not concealed. In fact, they were sometimes widely reported. Part of the reason for this lay in the fact that the person of the king was nothing more than a tolerated figure before God and his prophets. He was allowed to be there but he was not to imagine anything great beyond that. Also, he had to adhere closely to the rules of God. The prophets and the priests, therefore, regularly

---

[89] 1 Kings 3:4–14, 16–28; 4:21–34; 10:1–29.
[90] Deuteronomy 17:14–20; 1 Kings 11:1–13. Solomon's many non-Jewish wives brought their gods with them. In order to be very wealthy, Solomon could not do otherwise, because "marriages" to women from all over the world also included favourable trade agreements.
[91] Solomon had introduced a system of gentlemanly services which resulted in a distressing division in the Jewish people. The so-called *dichotomy*, the gap between rich and poor, was large. See Jagersma, *Geschiedenis van Israël*, 171–176.

had to move heaven and earth to keep the king in line. The prophets in particular were often terrified to confront and advise the king in the name of God and thereby risk their own lives. This regularly went wrong. In Israel's history, too, there were only a few good kings.

Like a long thread, the disobedience of the kings runs as a theme through the story of God's people. One of the so-called "horror themes" was also the murder of the prophets. Repeatedly, obstinate prophets were arrested, gagged and killed in the king's name. This historical motif continued until the days of Jesus, and even after that.[92]

Kingship in Israel cannot be understood without the roles of the prophet and the priest, who flanked the king in the name of God to keep him in line with salvation history. The *royal* expectation of the Old Testament and also that of the New Testament must therefore always be filtered and interpreted *prophetically* and *priestly*. There is no royal expectation in Scripture without, at the same time, the face of God's priest and the face of God's prophet. Only in this way was the king not associated with the blunt pursuit of power, with violence and militarism, with purple and gold. Kings tended to be rulers who got in the way of God, with their craving for honour and power. For this reason, Gideon did not want to be king of Israel. When he was asked to rule over the Jewish people, Gideon said, "I will not rule over you, and my son will not rule over you; the Lord will rule over you."[93]

The glorification of the king also brought the glorification of violence. After all, a king needed an army, and an army needed weapons to boast of. Troops had to parade back and forth to the glory of the king, preferably with weapons in hand and many horses and chariots.

How different was—and is—Jesus, the King of kings and Lord of lords. When the apostle John in heaven heard the call, "Behold, the Lion," he looked and saw a Lamb.[94] The lion as the symbol of kingship was revealed by Scripture not with roaring and biting

---

[92] The murder of the prophet is also a theme in the book of Revelation, as well as in the Gospel of Matthew.
[93] Judges 8:23.
[94] Revelation 5:5–6.

and tearing, but with smallness and tenderness and innocence. The redemption Christ brought as the Lamb did not come through taking up arms.[95] Jesus was such a different king than people expected. He filled the messianic nature of the expected Saviour with the characteristics of a "suffering servant."[96] This was also understood in the early church. We already read of how Jesus was characterized as a totally different king in the *Letter to Diognetus*:

> Did He send Him…to oppress or to bring fear and dismay? Absolutely not, but in gentleness and humility He sent Him, like a king who sends a son who is king.[97]

Jesus came as a King in gentleness and humility. We can be thankful there have always been Christians who did not expect the realization of the kingdom on earth through any earthly king, no matter how rich and fantastic their power and majesty. In the ancient church, most Christians thought this way, and were therefore fundamentally opposed to any form of violence.[98]

There were also such Christians during the Reformation. Indeed, most Anabaptists thought this way, and they were almost all against the use of coercion and violence. The Anabaptists wanted to return the church of their day to the model of the ancient church. In this sense, the Anabaptist movement can be characterized as a *restoration* movement.

Anabaptists wanted to be a community like the early church and they considered themselves the *real* Catholic church.[99] The church of the Middle Ages was, in their eyes, an apostate church. Money, goods, power and violence made it corrupt and untrustworthy from within. Most of the Reformers also thought this way, yet they did not take the steps for thorough church reform that

---

[95] See Matthew 12:17–21 ("he shall not contend and shout, and no one shall hear his voice in the squares").
[96] Isaiah 53; John 19.
[97] *Ad Diognetum* 7.3–4.
[98] von Harnack, *Militia Christi*, 46: "das Christentum verwarf prinzipiell Krieg und Blutvergiessen."
[99] See David Wayne Layman, "The Inner Ground of Christian Theology: Church, Faith, and Sectarianism," *Journal of Ecumenical Studies* 27 (3, 1990): 480–503.

the Anabaptists did. We have seen how this led, among other things, to alienation between Zwingli and a number of radical students.

This fall of the church into the "compromise of the sword" obviously did not come out of nowhere. We have seen how in the second century the number of Christians who chose the life of a soldier was growing, and in the third century that number increased considerably. Although some church teachers spoke out against it, many continued to enlist. Constantine—during his reign—merely formalized what was already common among young Christians at the beginning of the fourth century: "If the duty of the Christian fatherland calls you, then go and uphold the honor of Christ."

Clearly, however, this position was not in keeping with Christ's teaching and the spirit of the Sermon on the Mount. Jesus' ethical rule regarding violence was different.[100] We can say, in general, over the centuries the church almost lost sight of its focus on this "forgotten side" of Christ. The kingship of Jesus was too often viewed as a kingship of triumph, submission and conquest, and the church believed it was sharing in this victory. Church and state together subjugated nations and cultures to the power and majesty of Christ. Crowns, thrones and sceptres, it was thought, were not out of place for the church. She could be rich and powerful without any sense of shame, and with kings and emperors, she could rule on earth.

---

[100] Richard B. Hays, *The Moral Vision of the New Testament: Community, Cross, New Creation. A Contemporary Introduction to New Testament Ethics* (New York: HarperCollins, 1996), 341–344.

Select bibliography

Augustijn, C., F.G.M. Broeyer, P. Visser and E.G.E. van der Wall, ed., *Reformatorica. Teksten uit de geschiedenis van het Nederlandse protestantisme* (Zoetermeer: Meinema, 1996).

Bakhuizen van den Brink, J.N., W.F. Dankbaar, W.J. Kooiman, D. Nauta and N. van der Zijpp, ed., *Documenta Reformatoria. Teksten uit de geschiedenis van Kerk en Theologie in de Nederlanden sedert de Hervorming*, deel 1 (Kampen: Kok, 1960).

Bakker, Henk, "Discerning Churches," in *Seeds of the Church: Towards an Ecumenical Baptist Ecclesiology*, FCCT, ed. Teun van der Leer, Henk Bakker, Steven R. Harmon and Elizabeth Newman (Eugene: Wipf and Stock, 2022), 44–54.

Bakker, Henk, "'We are all equal'" (*Omnes sumus aequales*): A Critical Assessment of Early Protestant Ministerial Thinking," *Perspectives in Religious Studies* 44/3 (2017): 353–376.

Belyea, Gordon L., "Origins of the Particular Baptists," *Themelios* 32 (3, 2007): 40-67.

Bender, Harold S., "The Anabaptist Vision," in *The Recovery of the Anabaptist Vision: A Sixteenth Anniversary Tribute To Harold S. Bender*, ed. F. Hershberger (Scottsdale: Herald Press, 1962), 29–54.

Bergsten, Torsten, *Balthasar Hubmaier: Seine Stellung zu Reformation und Täufertum, 1521–1528*, Acta Universitatis Upsaliensis: Studia historico-ecclesiastica Upsaliensia 3 (Kassel: J.G. Oncken Verlag, 1961).

Blok, Marjan, "'Discipleship in Menno Simons' *Dat Fundament*: An Exercise in Anabaptist Theology," in *Menno Simons: A Reappraisal*, ed. Gerald R. Brunk (Harrisonburg: Eastern Mennonite College, 1992), 105–129.

Brachlow, Stephen, "Puritan Theology and General Baptist Origins," *Baptist Quarterly* 31/4 (1985): 179–194.

Brachlow, Stephen, *The Communion of Saints: Radical Puritan and Separatist Ecclesiology, 1570–1625*, Oxford Theological Monographs (Oxford: Oxford University Press, 1988).

Briggs, John, "The Origins of the People Called Baptists" (2009), personally entrusted to the author [the article was to be translated into German, and to be published in *Zwischen Nonkonformismus und Quietismus – Geschichtliche Perspektiven zum 400 Jubiläum des europäischen und zum 175 Jubiläum des deutschen Baptismus*].

Bubenheimer, Ulrich, *Thomas Müntzer: Herkunft und Bildung*, Studies in Medieval and Reformation Thought 46 (Leiden: Brill, 1989).

Burrage, Champlin, *The Early English Dissenters in the Light of Recent Research (1550–1641)*, Vol. 1–2 (Cambridge: Cambridge University Press, 1912).

Clasen, Claus-Peter, *Anabaptism: A Social History, 1525–1618, Switzerland, Austria, Moravia, South and Central Germany* (Ithaca: Cornell University Press, 1972).

Coggins, James Robert, *John Smyth's Congregation: English Separatism, Mennonite Influence, and the Elect Nation*, Studies in Anabaptist and Mennonite History 32 (Waterloo: Herald Press, 1991).

Crosby, T., *The History of the English Baptists from the Reformation to the Beginning of the Reign of King George I*, Vol. 1 (London, 1738; repr. Lafayette, 1979).

Deursen, A. Th. van, *Bavianen en slijkgeuzen. Kerk en kerkvolk ten tijde van Maurits en Oldenbarnevelt* (Franeker: Van Wijnen, 1998).
De Vries, Olof H., *Leer en praxis van de vroege dopers uitgelegd als een theologie van de geschiedenis* (diss. Rijksuniversiteit Utrecht, 1982).
Durnbaugh, Donald F., *The Believers Church: The History and Character of Radical Protestantism* (1968; Eugene: Wipf & Stock, 2003).
Early, Joe, *The Life and Writings of Thomas Helwys*, Early English Baptist Texts (Macon: Mercer University Press, 2009).
Egli, Emil, et al, ed., *Huldreich Zwinglis sämtliche Werke, 4. Teil: Von der Taufe, von der Wiedertaufe und von der Kindertaufe*, Corpus reformatorum (Leipzig, 1927).
Estep, William R., ed., *Balthasar Hubmaier: Theologian of Anabaptism* (Valley Forge, PA: Judson Press, 1978)
Estep, William R., *The Anabaptist Story: An Introduction to Sixteenth-Century Anabaptism* (Grand Rapids: Eerdmans, 1996).
Garrett, James Leo, "The Nature of the Church According to the Radical Continental Reformation," *Mennonite Quarterly Review* 32 (2, 1958): 111–127.
Gunter, Stephen W., *Arminius and His Declaration of Sentiments: An Annotated Translation with Introduction and Theological Commentary* (Waco: Baylor University Press, 2012).
Haykin, Michael A.G., *Kiffin, Knollys and Keach: Rediscovering Our English Baptist Heritage* (Leeds: Reformation Today Trust, 1996).
Haymes, Brian, "On Religious Liberty: Re-Reading *A Short Declaration of the Mystery of Iniquity*," *Baptist Quarterly* 42 (2007): 197–217.
Hillerbrand, Hans J., "The Anabaptist View of the State," *Mennonite Quarterly Review* 32 (2, 1958).
Holmes, Stephen R., "When Did John Smith Embrace Arminianism – And Was the First Baptist Congregation 'Particular'?," *Baptist Quarterly* 52/4 (2021): 146–157.
Holmes, Stephen R., "The Church of Helwys, Murton, and Lambe: An Argument for Continuity," *Baptist Quarterly* 54: (2023).
Horsch, John, "An Historical Survey of the Position of the Mennonite Church on Nonresistance," *Mennonite Quarterly Review* 1 (1927): 5–22.

Hubmaier, Balthasar, *Ain Summ aintz gantzen Christlichen lebens. Durch Baldasaren Frydberger, Predicant yetz zu Waldßhütt, verzeichnet an die drey Kirchen Regensburg, Jngolstat und Frydberg, seinen lieben herren, briedern vnd schwestern in gott dem herren. Sonderlich ain bericht den kinder Touff vnd das Nachttmal belangent* (1525).

Janse, W., *Vrij of gedwongen? Erasmus, Luther en Augustinus over de vrije wilskeuze*, Willem de Zwijgerstichting, Reformatorische Stemmen (Amsterdam: Buijten & Schipperheijn, 2004).

Jardine, Lisa, *Gedeelde weelde. Hoe de zeventiende-eeuwse cultuur van de Lage Landen Engeland veroverde en veranderde* (Amsterdam: De Arbeiderspers, 2008).

Kardux, Joke and Eduard van de Bilt, *Newcomers in an Old City: The American Pilgrims In Leiden* (Leiden: Burgersdijk & Niermans, 2007).

Kerssenbrock, Hermann von, *Narrative of the Anabaptist Madness: The Overthrow of Münster, the Famous Metropolis of Westphalia*, Studies in the History of Christian Traditions 132 (Leiden: Brill, 2007).

Kirchhoff, Karl-Heinz, *Die Täufer in Münster 1534/35. Untersuchungen zum Umfang und zur Sozialstruktur der Bewegung*, Geschichtliche Arbeiten zur Westfälischen Landersforschung 12 (Münster: Aschendorffsche Verlagsbuchhandlung, 1973).

Klaassen, Walter, ed., *Anabaptism in Outline: Selected Primary Sources*, Classics of the Radical Reformation 3 (Waterloo: Herald Press, 1981).

Klötzer, Ralf, "The Melchiorites and Münster," in *A Companion to Anabaptism and Spiritualism, 1521–1700*, Brill's Companions to the Christian Tradition 6, ed. John D. Roth and James M. Stayer (Leiden: Brill, 2007), 217–256.

Krahn, Cornelius, "Anabaptism and the Culture of the Netherlands," in *The Recovery of the Anabaptist Vision: A Sixteenth Anniversary Tribute to Harold S. Bender*, ed. F. Hershberger (Scottdale: Herald Press, 1962), 219–236.

Lee, Jason K., *The Theology of John Smyth: Puritan, Separatist, Baptist, Mennonite* (Macon: Mercer University Press, 2003).

Liechty, Daniel, *Early Anabaptist Spirituality: Selected Writings* (New York: Paulist Press, 1994).

Little, Franklin H., *The Anabaptist View of the Church: A Study of Origins of Sectarian Protestantism*, The Dissent and Non-Conformity Series 11 (Boston: Starr King Press, 1958).

Lumpkin, William F., *Baptist Confessions of Faith*, rev. ed. (Valley Forge: Judson Press, 2011).

Lumpkin, William F., "The Nature and Authority of Baptist Confessions of Faith," *Review and Expositor* 56 (1, 1979): 17–28.

Mabry, Eddie Louis, *Balthasar Hubmaier's Doctrine of the Church* (Lanham: University Press of America, 1994).

Macculloch, Diarmaid, "Het Europese huis gedeeld. Religieuze tolerantie tijdens de Reformatie," in *Vrijheid in verdeeldheid. Geschiedenis en actualiteit van religieuze tolerantie*, ed. Stephan van Erp (Nijmegen: Valkhof Pers, 2008), 25–44.

Manley, Kenneth R., "Origins of the Baptists: The Case for Development from Puritanism-Separatism," in *Faith, Life and Witness: The Papers of the Study and Research Division of the Baptist World Alliance, 1986–1990*, ed. William H. Brackney and Ruby J. Burke (Birmingham: Samford University Press, 1990), 56–69.

Masters, Peter, *The Baptist Confession of Faith of 1689, with Scripture Proofs* (London: The Wakeman Trust, 1989).

Mellink, A.F., *De wederdopers in de noordelijke nederlanden (1531–1544)* (Leeuwarden: Gerben Dykstra, 1981).

Mellink, A.F., ed., *Documenta Anabaptistica Neerlandica*, deel 1: *Friensland en Groningen (1530–1550)*, Kerkhistorische Bijdragen VI/I (Leiden: Brill, 1975).

Muralt, Leonhard von, and Walter Smid, ed., *Quellen zur Geschichte der Täufer in der Schweiz*, I. Band: Zürich (Zürich: Theologischer Verlag, 1974).

Neufeld, Elmer, "Christian Responsibility in the Political Situation," *Mennonite Quarterly Review* 32 (2, 1958): 141–162.

Paas, S. Sr., *De gemeenschap der heiligen. Kerk en gezag bij Presbyteriaanse en Separatistische Engelse Puriteinen 1570–1593* (Zoetermeer: Boekencentrum, 1996).

Packull, Werner O., "Enkele aspecten van de hermeneutiek van Menno Simons," *Doopsgezinde bijdragen, Nieuwe Reeks* 22 (1996): 143–157.

Panhuysen, Luc, *De beloofde stad. Opkomst en ondergang van het koninkrijk der wederdopers* (Amsterdam: Atlas, 2000).

Payne, Earnest A., "Contacts between Mennonites and Baptists," *Foundations* 4/1 (1961): 39–55.

Rommé, Barbara, *Das Königreich der Täufer*, 1. Band: *Reformation und Herrschaft der Täufer in Münster*, 2. Band: *Das Königreich der Täufer. Die münsterischen Täufer im Spiegel der Nachwelt* (Münster: Stadtmuseum, 2000).

Rommé, Barbara, ed., *Das Königreich der Täufer in Münster – Neue Perspektiven*, Edition Kulturregiion Münsterland (Münster: Lit Verlag, 2003).

Rothmann, Bernard, "Eyne Restitution edder eine Wedderstellinge rechter unnde gesunder christliker Leer, Gelovens unde Levens uth Gades Genaden durch de Gemeinte Christi tho Munster an den Dach Gegevenn (eind 1534)," in *Reformatorica. Teksten uit de geschiedenis van het Nederlandse protestantisme*, ed. C. Augustijn, F.G.M. Broeyer, P. Visser and E.G.E. van der Wall (Zoetermeer: Meinema, 1996), 57–58.

Sellers, Ian, "Edwardians, Anabaptists and the Problem of Baptist Origins," *Baptist Quarterly* 29/3 (1981): 97–112.

Simons, Menno, *Opera omnia theologica, of alle de Godtgeleerde wercken van Menno Symons* (Amsterdam: Johannes van Veen, 1681).

Snyder, C. Arnold, *The Life and Thought of Michael Sattler*, Studies in Anabaptist and Mennonite History 27 (Scottsdale: Herald Press, 1984).

Snyder, C. Arnold, *Anabaptist History and Theology*, rev. student ed. (Kitchener: Pandora Press, 1997).

Snyder, C. Arnold, "Swiss Anabaptism: The Beginnings," in *A Companion to Anabaptism and Spiritualism, 1521–1700*, Brill's Companions to the Christian Tradition 6, ed. John D. Roth and James M. Stayer (Leiden: Brill, 2007), 45–81.

Snyder, C. Arnold and Linda A. Huebert Hecht, ed., *Profiles of Anabaptist Women: Sixteenth Century Reforming Pioneers*, Studies in Women and Religion 3 (Waterloo: WLU Press, 1996).

Sprunger, Mary, "Waterlanders and the Dutch Golden Age: A Case Study on Mennonite Involvement in Seventeenth-Century Trade and Industry as One of the Earliest Examples of Socio-Economic Assimilation," in *From Martyr to Muppy (Mennonite Urban Professionals): A Historical Introduction to Cultural Assimilation Processes of a Religious Minority in the Netherlands: the Mennonites*, ed. Alistair Hamilton, Sjouke

Voolstra and Piet Visser (Amsterdam: Amsterdam University Press, 1994), 133–148.

Stayer, James, *The German Peasants' War and Anabaptist Community of Goods* (Montreal: McGill-Queen's University Press, 1991).

Stayer, James, "Swiss-Southern German Anabaptism," in *A Companion to Anabaptism and Spiritualism, 1521–1700*, Brill's Companions to the Christian Tradition 6, ed. John D. Roth and James M. Stayer (Leiden: Brill, 2007), 83–117.

Steinmetz, David C., *Reformers in the Wings: From Geiler von Kaysersberg to Theodore Beza* (Oxford: Oxford University Press, 2001).

Timmer, Kirsten, "Revisiting the Chronology of Baptist Origins (1607–1610)," a paper presented at the opening of the John Smyth Research Library, IBTSC, Baptist House Amsterdam, January 24, 2019.

Tolmie, Murray, *Triumph of the Saints: Separate Churches of London, 1616–1649* (Cambridge: Cambridge University Press, 1977).

Visser, Piet, "Mennonites and Doopsgezinden in the Netherlands, 1535–1700," in *A Companion to Anabaptism and Spiritualism, 1521–1700*, Brill's Companions to the Christian Tradition 6, ed. John D. Roth and James M. Stayer (Leiden: Brill, 2007), 299–345.

Voolstra, Sjouke, *Het Woord is vlees geworden. De Melchioritisch-menniste incarnatieleer*, Dissertationes Neerlandicae, Series Theologica 8 (Kampen: Kok, 1982).

Voolstra, Sjouke, "Themes in the Early Theology of Menno Simons," in *Menno Simons: A Reappraisal*, ed. Gerald R. Brunk (Harrisonburg: Eastern Mennonite College, 1992), 37–55.

Voolstra, Sjouke, *Menno Simons: His Image and His Message* (North Newton: Bethel College, 1997).

Walton, Robert C., "Was There a Turning Point of the Zwinglian Reformation?" *Mennonite Quarterly Review* 42 (1, 1968): 45–56.

Westin, Gunnar, and Torsten Bergsten, ed., *Balthasar Hubmaier: Schriften*, Quellen und Forschungen zur Reformationsgeschichte 29, Quellen zur Geschichte der Täufer 9 (Gütersloh: Gerd Mohn, 1962).

White, B.R., *The English Separatist Tradition: from the Marian Martyrs to the Pilgrim Fathers*, Oxford Theological Monographs (Oxford: Oxford University Press, 1971).

Whitley, W.T., ed., *The Works of John Smyth: Fellow of Christ's College, 1594-8*, Vols. 1–2 (1915; repr. Cambridge: Cambridge University Press, 2009).

Whitley, W.T. and A.J.D. Farrer, "Continental Anabaptists and Early English Baptists," *Baptist Quarterly* 2/1 (1925): 24–36.

Wickman, Erik, "General Baptist Origins and Original Sin," *Baptist Quarterly* 51/2 (2020): 47–55.

Williams, George H. and Angel M. Mergal, ed., *Spiritual and Anabaptist Writers*, Library of Christian Classics (Philadelphia: Westminster John Knox Press, 1957).

Williams, George Hunsten, *The Radical Reformation*, Sixteenth Century Essays & Studies 15 (Kirksville: Sixteenth Century Journal Publishers, 1992).

Wright, Stephen, "Leonard Busher: Life and Ideas," *Baptist Quarterly* 39/4 (2001): 175–192.

Wright, Stephen, "Leonard Busher: An Additional Note," *Baptist Quarterly* 39/7 (2002): 360.

Wright, Stephen, *The Early English Baptists, 1603–1649* (Woodbridge: The Boydell Press, 2006).

Zijlstra, Samme, *Om de ware gemeente en oude gronden. Geschiedenis van de dopersen in de Nederlanden 1531–1675* (Hilversum: Uitg. Verloren, 2000).

Zijpp, N. van der, "Early Dutch Anabaptism," in *The Recovery of the Anabaptist Vision: A Sixteenth Anniversary Tribute to Harold S. Bender*, ed. F. Hershberger (Scottsdale: Herald Press, 1962), 69–82.

Discover other titles from Heritage Seminary Press

A Theologian in Service of the Church: The Collected Writings of Stanley K. Fowler
Edited by Michael A.G. Haykin & Jonathan N. Cleland
Volume 1 & Volume 2

For over fifty years, the writings of Stanley K. Fowler, long-time professor of theological studies at Central Baptist Seminary, Toronto, Ont., and then Heritage College & Seminary, Cambridge, Ont., have informed and clarified theological issues for Baptists in Ontario, Canada and beyond.

Using careful biblical exegesis to address issues facing the church—such as baptism, local church autonomy, public ethics, divine sovereignty and human freedom and divorce and remarriage—Dr. Fowler has sought to equip Christians to serve the Lord well.

In this two-volume collection of his works, the editors hope the church can continue to learn from his insightful handling of the Word of God and enter deeper into relationship with the Word made flesh, Jesus Christ.

Volume 1
ISBN 978-1-77484-160-0 (Hdcvr)
ISBN 978-1-77484-157-0 (Pbk)
ISBN 978-1-77484-158-7 (Ebook)
276 pages; 5.5 x 8.5"
Published January 2025

Volume 2
ISBN 978-1-77484-163-1 (Hdcvr)
ISBN 978-1-77484-161-7 (Pbk)
ISBN 978-1-77484-162-4 (Ebook)
296 pages; 5.5 x 8.5"
Published May 2025

An imprint of H&E Publishing
heritageseminarypress.com

Discover other titles from Heritage Seminary Press

A "phoenix of women" Puritan spirituality in the letters of Brilliana Harley
Introduced and edited by Michael A.G. Azad Haykin

The life of Lady Brilliana Harley was marked by a deep and living relationship with God. A Puritan Presbyterian by conviction, Brilliana was shunned by her neighbours during the tumultuous English Civil Wars and is remembered as valiantly resisting the siege of her home by the forces of Charles I.

Brilliana's letters reveal the heart of her spirituality. While concerned about her son Edward (Ned)'s studies at Oxford, his diet and exercise, she especially encourages him about the value of a vital relationship with God. Her letters also expose the breadth of her reading and her theological acumen. As the troubles around her increased, she took increasing solace in the truths of election, the sufficiency of Christ's work and the sovereignty of God. The soil of her heart was truly warmed by "the sweet waters of God's Word."

ISBN 978-1-77484-152-5 (Pbk)
ISBN 978-1-77484-153-2 (Ebook)
172 pages; 5.5 x 8.5"
Heritage Classics
Published September 2024

An imprint of H&E Publishing
heritageseminarypress.com

Discover other titles from Heritage Seminary Press

The oversight of souls: Essays on pastoral ministry
By Ray Van Neste

How do you understand pastoral ministry? What is the centre of your calling as a pastor? Is it difficult for your people to speak directly with you? Do you know your sheep? Do they know you?

In this book, Ray Van Neste looks to God's Word and church history to show that the oversight of souls is to be the very *heart* of pastoral ministry. The author of Hebrews writes that congregants are to: "Obey your leaders and submit to them, for they are keeping watch over your souls, as those who will have to give an account" (Hebrews 13:17). This guarding, shepherding and watching over souls requires knowledge of and meaningful engagement with the sheep and seeing them as "very dear to us" (1 Thessalonians 2:8), with the goal to "present everyone mature in Christ" (Colossians 1:28).

ISBN 978-1-77484-154-9 (Pbk)
ISBN 978-1-77484-155-6 (Ebook)
130 pages; 5.5 x 8.5"
Published October 2024

 HERITAGE SEMINARY PRESS

An imprint of H&E Publishing
heritageseminarypress.com

Discover other titles from Heritage Seminary Press

Losing Your Luggage: Finding Freedom from Sinful Baggage
By Rick Reed

Losing Your Luggage takes you on a journey through Romans 6–8, helping you find freedom from the sinful baggage that weighs you down. Your guide for this trip is Rick Reed, who brings out practical, down-to-earth wisdom from Paul's letter as he walks alongside you on this journey. He is one who speaks from experience and is a helpful guide to show you the main sights and lessons of these important chapters. Journey toward greater joy and freedom in Christ—and lose some sinful baggage along the route!

ISBN 978-1-77484-120-4 (Pbk)
ISBN 978-1-77484-121-1 (Ebook)
104 pages; 6 x 9"
Published June 2023

HERITAGE SEMINARY PRESS

An imprint of H&E Publishing
heritageseminarypress.com

Discover other titles from Heritage Seminary Press

Life is Worship: A *festschrift* in honour of Douglas A. Thomson

Editors: David G. Barker & Michael A.G. Haykin

These essays honour the life and ministry of Dr. Doug Thomson who, as a teacher, pastor, colleague and music leader, has influenced countless lives and congregations in Ontario, Canada, and beyond. The subjects of these chapters cover themes that are precious in the life of the church—revealing how all of life is worship.

Topics include expositions of psalms and hymns, the theology of worship, spirituals, hallmarks of a worship leader, friendship in the composition of hymns, lament, etc.—even some sermons for Easter weekend. It is hoped that these essays will encourage discussion, promote the development of an understanding of the theology around worship, challenge readers to think deeply about this crucial area and, most of all, bring glory and praise to our great God.

ISBN 978-1-77484-128-0 (Pbk)
ISBN 978-1-77484-129-7 (Ebook)
364 pages; 6 x 9"
Published September 2023

HERITAGE SEMINARY PRESS

An imprint of H&E Publishing
heritageseminarypress.com

Discover other titles from Heritage Seminary Press

Paul and His Christian Mission
By Michael Azad A.G. Haykin
Includes Study Guide

The mission of the apostle Paul is central to the New Testament, where it was vital in the establishment of the early church and spreading the gospel throughout the world of his day. This study provides a concise but rich view of Paul the man and Paul the missionary. At his conversion to Christ, Paul was given a clear mandate to bring the gospel to the Gentiles. Paul loved the church, and he was zealous to win the lost to Christ. He appreciated and cultivated co-labourers in the work of the gospel, as he depended on the power of the Holy Spirit.

Paul's experience challenges the reader. Study guide questions are provided to help reflect on and apply the things that are learned in this short, focused study of Paul's life.

ISBN 978-1-77484-106-8 (Pbk)
ISBN 978-1-77484-107-5 (Ebook)
88 pages; 5.5 x 8.5"
Published December 2022

HERITAGE SEMINARY PRESS

An imprint of H&E Publishing
heritageseminarypress.com

Discover other titles from Heritage Seminary Press

This Poor Man Called: Stories and Songs of David
Volume 1 & Volume 2
By David G. Barker

David Barker takes a unique approach in this exploration of the psalms of David. Each chapter begins with a creative retelling of the biblical narrative, setting the scene for the psalm arising out of that experience. Having grounded the psalm in the "story," Barker then goes into a verse-by-verse exposition of the psalm, and provides some explanatory notes and a statement of the key message of the psalm.

At the end of each psalm exposition, Barker asks three basic questions: What do we learn about God? What do we learn about ourselves as the people of God? and What do we learn about the world? Answering these questions helps us to understand how David's experience shaped his theocentric and biblical worldview.

Volume 1
ISBN 978-1-77484-063-4 (Pbk)
ISBN 978-1-77484-064-1 (Ebook)
122 pages; 5.5 x 8.5"
Published Spring 2022

Volume 2
ISBN 978-1-77484-110-5 (Pbk)
ISBN 978-1-77484-111-2 (Ebook)
192 pages; 5.5 x 8.5"
Published February 2023

An imprint of H&E Publishing
heritageseminarypress.com

Dominus Deus fortitudo mea | The sovereign LORD is my strength

www.ingramcontent.com/pod-product-compliance
Lightning Source LLC
Chambersburg PA
CBHW020518080526
44583CB00013B/644